Computerization and Work

A Reader on Social Aspects
of Computerization

A Collection of Articles
by Members of IFIP WG 9.1

Edited by
Ulrich Briefs   John Kjaer   Jean-Louis Rigal

Springer-Verlag
Berlin Heidelberg New York Tokyo

303,4834
C738

Dr. Ulrich Briefs
WSI/DGB, Hans-Böckler-Strasse 39
D-4000 Düsseldorf

cc.

John Kjaer
Royal Chartered Fire Ins. Co., Høbro Plads 10
DK-1248 Kopenhagen

Jean-Louis Rigal
17 Rue de l'Yser
F-92330 Sceaux

ISBN 3-540-15367-5 Springer-Verlag Berlin Heidelberg New York Tokyo
ISBN 0-387-15367-5 Springer-Verlag New York Heidelberg Berlin Tokyo

Library of Congress Cataloging in Publication Data. Main entry under title:
Computerization and work. 1. Labor supply–Effect of technological innovations on–Addresses, essays, lectures. 2. Man-machine systems–Addresses,
essays, lectures. 3. Computers–Social aspects–Addresses, essays, lectures.
I. Briefs, Ulrich. II. Kjaer, John. III. Rigal, Jean-Louis. HD6331.C674 1985
303.4'834 85-2858 ISBN 0-387-15367-5.

Printing and bookbinding: Beltz Offsetdruck, Hemsbach/Bergstrasse
2145/3140-543210

Preface

This reader contains contributions referring to one of the most
urgent problems in systems design: the effects of computerization on
human work and approaches to ameliorate systems design in order to
create better conditions for living human work in a computerized
world.

Of course the choice of papers has been operated somewhat arbitrarily.
It primarily reflects the work of IFIP's Working Group 9.1. "Computers and Work" and of some of its members.

The papers were compiled aiming at focussing on very material problems in the field of "Computers and Work". They substantively reflect in several points the discussions and the concern of the Working Group.

Some conclusions from a series of workshops held from 1980 onward by
the Working Group are likewise contained and directed to the IFIP
community and to other parties concerned.

The reader inserts itself into a rather extended line of activities
of the Working Group: in addition to contributions to the two IFIP
Working Conferences on Human Choice and Computers held in 1974 and
in 1979 (proceedings published by North Holland) a recent IFIP Working Conference on Systems Design For, With and By the Users (held
in September 82, proceedings published in March 83 by North Holland)
and a joint TC3/TC9 Working Conference on Education for Systems De-
signer/User Co-operation (proceedings to be published by end 84).

The Working Group will continue its work according to this tradition
hoping to contribute to some progress in one of the most sensitive
fields in computerization: Computers and Work.

As always, part of this work - especially technical work - had to be
done by persons outside the group:

- May Briefs-Thevessen (FRG)
- Carol Kanda (DK)
- Roswitha Zonne (FRG)
- Ingrid Krippes (FRG)

We are particularly grateful to these very material contributors of this volume.

Ulrich Briefs   John Kjaer   Jean-Louis Rigal

Chairman of the
Editorial Board

Chairman of
IFIP's Working Group
"Computers and Work"

Table of Contents

Section I

Information Technology and Work in the Present Society

To tell that Computers are a gift of fire also means that they can burn.

Burn - and destroy - workers, through unemployment, lack of interest in working process, also through material control. Burn - and destroy - citizens and users, through cultural control, through imposition of artificial needs - only gratifying for their producers - acting like those technocrats who know better than others what they need. Burn - and destroy - any culture alternative to the culture of scientists and of managers; and especially the culture of developping countries.

Are we going at increasing speed toward Dostoiewsky's "Great Inquisitor" who gave people everything they need, if only they agree to loose their liberty and their right to be different?

To summarize: is the growth of Gross National Product and Productivity which are in question now - not to be paid by a frightening impoverishment of human communication and by a growth of standardization, the last avatar of the taylorist myth of the "one best way", in the straight file of Plato's rationalism, elaborated when social division of citizens was installed in the Greek cities.

And the growing importance of microprocessors, compared to the big centralizing ones, does not seem to change the matter significally; probably in the contrary it worsened it, being more discrete and seemingly more convivial, thus better assumed.

Will the pessimistic prospects stressed here and elsewhere be sure to be fully realized? Must we kill ourselves or kill the computers?

We can first stress that it proved not to be so easy to build the "wired city", as seems to indicate the fact that the change is far slower than told by mass media and by people interested to tell the contrary; and also the limited success of experiments like Prestel or Teletex - both of social (no real need for them) and for technical reasons.

All the authors in this section also stress the contradiction and the challenges which are more and more difficult to meet, if we refuse to change the kind of organization, of computerization and of working process.

But, at the end of this section is stressed the possibility of alternative system designs, which may prove to be very positive for workers, for the citizens, for the users and even - last not least - for the managers and the companies themselves. And it is clear that nowadays - and even more tomorrow - the very progress of electronic technology will render possible a lot of solutions if every people wants them and assumes the right to be different (the exact contrary of the taylorian paradigm). And if society and organizations assume the risk that social partners speak different languages - instead of accepting lazily to be trapped by the dominant rationality (which is also the rationality of dominants) and dominant paradigms: a danger we called "semiocracy"-

Being clear that those alternative roads need a huge cultural and educational effort, which means it will take a rather long time to establish them, and we can't wait one or two generations to do it. Happily install more "industrial democracy", more decentralization, the possibility for every partner to participate in the technologi-cal choices (which are always structural, political and cultural choices) at the very beginning of the process, decrease the working hours and also install a collective reflection (with developping countries) on the real needs and challenges to meet will prove in-dispensable and decisive steps on this road. The following sections will develop a number of paths to explore and a number of researches or actions to undertake towards the direction from the present state of art and of society, taking into account the huge possibili-ties of men and of computers.

Thus the article of Gotlieb showing the potential dangers of an uncontrolled computerization (and the risk of it to meet no real social need), the article of Steinmüller rightly stressing the rela-tionship between information and power (and the underlying rationa-lities) and the article of Ulrich Briefs - through the rude affirma-tion that more computerization means more unemployment, erasing and reshaping of the skills of workers and steal their know-how and enhance control - are a necessary basis for a more optimistic idea that future can be better if we really want it and do what is neces-sary to try to promote a human process of informatization.

Computers - A Gift of Fire

Clavin C. Gotlieb

Department of Computer Science, University of Toronto, CDN-Toronto, Ontario, Canada

As the computer technology spreads globally, it begins to
behave like other modern technologies in that undesirable
side effects appear. Much more serious than computer
effects on privacy are the impacts of microprocessors on
industrial employment. Another issue arises out of
evidence presented by managers and social scientists that
using computers in decision making can lead to systems
which are too rigid and, especially in government, to
procedures which fail to meet human needs. In addition,
many countries see growing computer imports as threats to
their balance of payments and technological sovereignty.
Inevitably, the use of computers will become more
controversial.

Fire is a technology whose beginning is lost in antiquity, but you will recall the
legend of Prometheus who stole it from the gods to give it to man. Although it
has costs and benefits, only rarely and locally do the costs exceed the benefits.
From mankind's view it is a great gift but a terrible penalty was paid by
Prometheus for having brought it to man. Today's technologies have costs and
benefits with a much more complicated accounting of the debits and credits.
Those who bring the technologies to society are having to make decisions on the
merits, and in some sense a judgment is being or will be rendered, on their
actions. In the last decade the traditional suspicions that the people have of
new technologies have intensified. Nuclear power, terrifying as a weapon, causes
different concerns when it is harnessed for peaceful ends, because there is as yet
no satisfactory disposal of poisonous waste; pesticides spread widely and find
their way into the food chain; automobiles need highways that strangle cities;
television is a hypnotic.

Many third world countries reject these technologies altogether or seek to limit
their influences on their societies. Yet so far computers have escaped being
included among new technologies with doubtful benefits. Recent surveys of public
attitude to computers taken in different countries show that the favourable
opinion held ten years ago continues in the main to prevail.[1] In spite of serious
reservations about the erosion of privacy, the public as a whole still feels that
computers bring economies and efficiency, new ways to do useful things, and good
career possibilities.

Yet other voices are beginning to be heard. The most insistent voices speak of
jobs, of how robots controlled by microcomputers are threatening the industrial
work force, or how word processors will halve the number of secretaries, of how
the jobs that are left will demand less skills, and become more mindless, except
for the precious few held by those who know about computers and work with them.
There are other doubts--questions about the role computers play in business
administration and government.

Do computers inherently promote centralization? Centralization is sometimes necessary in business and government, but it is generally regarded as a process by which people ultimately come to have less control over their lives. Others worry whether computers result in diminishing concern for human values—the privacy issue.

Some focus on the growing vulnerability of soceity due to its increasing dependence on computers. And still others see computers as instruments of national policy. If they are not exactly weapons for waging economic warfare, they are still means by which the already rich and technologically advanced countries maintain their advantage over those which are poor and less developed. And even in the developed countries there are doubts about the benefits of, or the real need for the pervasive computerized systems about to be implemented—the electronic fund systems and the techniques to access gigantic data bases from computer terminals in the home.

You may feel that there is nothing new about this, that every important sociological change has its visionaries and its prophets of doom. That the most important thing for us who are involved in bringing about the change is to get on with the job, with goodwill, common sense, and competency. Judgments on whether the consequences are good or bad must be made later when there is more time to see and measure the effects and by society as a whole, rather than by the few who are involved in bringing about the change. But the essential thesis of this paper is that time for judgment is now come. We have at hand results of many scholarly, and credible studies of the social effects of computers. This is not to suggest that the data is all in. In fact a very great deal of work remains to be done. But we have results we can begin to trust, and the effects have reached a scale which does not allow us to delay in making plans on how to promote those consequences of computers we want to see come about—and how to inhibit the side effects which are socially destructive. So let us look at the evidence in support of this thesis.

COMPUTERS AND WORK

In discussing this I shall draw heavily, but not exclusively, on a recently published study in Canada, the Impacts of Computer/Communications on Employment in Canada: An Overview of Current OECD Debates [2]. The report has, in its bibliography, 87 papers from 12 countries and from international organizations, and it quotes in extensive detail from 42 of these publications which it regards as particularly important. These quotations are presented in a sequence from the most alarming to the most reassuring, or, to use the phraseology of the report, from those which see "massive unemployment" to those which see "business as usual." To appreciate the position from which the debate starts Table 1 shows figures for three industries in three different countries, illustrating how the introduction of microelectronic technology has brought about very large decreases in employment, while at the same time the productivity and total production has dramatically increased. In the various sources cited, there are similar but less precise figures given for employment and productivity changes in other industries and in other countries: the watch making industry in Switzerland, the automotive industry in the United States, the electronic industry in Holland, office work, banking and other service industries. While the reductions in employment and gains in productivity are not usually as dramatic as those shown, the overall trend is unmistakable. Almost everywhere the number of jobs decreases but output increases. From statistics, which are admittedly inadequate but must be regarded as significant, it is easy to prophesy massive unemployment. Take the figures for industries where data is available, and project them to other industries over longer periods. The result is unprecedented employment in almost every country. The trap is obvious. It is not legitimate to extrapolate the figures from a few specialized industries to the whole industrial scene. There are many social and economic barriers which always slow down change, and it is simply not credible to produce the overall job reductions which lead to such titles as "The Collapse of

(a) USA - Western Electric Switching Division*

Year	No. of Employees	Reduction	Productivity Increase
1970	39,200		"more than doubled"
1976	19,000	50%	
1980 (projected)	17,400		

*Source: Freeman [3]

(b) Federal Republic of Germany - Minining and Manufacturing

Year	Millions of persons employed	Reduction Persons employed	Persons × hours	Production volume increase	Office and data processing sector Year	Reduction persons employed	Productivity index
1970					1976	-	100
1975	1.246	14.5%	21.3%	13.5%	1976	18,300	116.7
					1977	20,600(25.8%)	148.9**

**Microelectronics were widely introduced in 1977

*Source: Friedrichs [4]

(c) Japan - Color TV Factories*

Company	1972	1976
Hitachi	9,051	4,299
Mitsuashuta Panasonic	9,875	3,900
Sony	4,498	2,778
Other 4 large firms	24,462	14,700

Production volume raised by 25% from 8.4 million sets in 1972 to 10.5 million in 1976.

*Source: Sherman [5]

Table 1
Job Reductions and Productivity Increases

Work" [6], or "Running Wild" [7]. The more careful analysts of employment statistics recognize the time needed for diffusion of new technologies, and adjust their projections accordingly. (See for example [8, 9].) But, and it is a very big but, it is necessary to say that even many conservative reports come out with some startling figures. In France the Nora-Minc report [8] suggests that within ten years 30% of the worker and service industries will become redundant, a figure of some four million people compared to the present number of 1.4 million. In the United Kingdom a survey of the University of Warwick in 1978 predicts 10% unemployment by 1982 and Barron and Curnow [11] predict 16% unemployment by 1990. This is supposed to be comforting compared to the Jenkins and Sherman [6] forecast of 25% unemployment by 1990 and Stonier's [12] prediction that in 30 years no more than 10% of the population will be employed in the United Kingdom, using employed in the present sense of the word. A widely cited report, "Buero 1990" produced in 1975-76 by A.G. Siemens [13] suggests that technological change could eliminate 40% of office work. On the other hand studies in Sweden, still incomplete, suggest that so far the total number of persons employed in the office sector has not diminished. Norway, however, no longer has the full employment it has experienced until now, with the result that unions are paying much more attention to automation and unemployment. In the United States and Canada, the debate on the effects of microprocessors on jobs is just beginning. It lags behind that of Europe for several reasons. For one, the North American unions are less powerful, and usually have had to concentrate on the fundamentals of job security, safety, and pay increases. They have had less opportunity to devote themselves to longer range problems. Also, the report, published in 1966 by the National Commission on Technology, Automation and Economic Progress, entitled "The Outlook for Technological Change and Unemployment" continues to play an important role in American thinking. That commission, in which representatives of government, business, and labour participated, came to the conclusion that technological change was not decisive in causing unemployment, nor in itself harmful, as long as a high rate of demand for work and services could be maintained. That supposition has to be looked at critically in the light of today's shortages of resouces and energy. Today, as data is still being gathered, the jury is still out on the question of how much computer and microprocessor technology will change employment figures by the year 2000. And it would be presumptious to attempt to come to specific conclusions. Nevertheless, there is good cause for concern. At least three observations can be made.

1. Because the predicted job reductions have failed to materialize in some countries or industries, does not mean that they will not come. The rates of reductions are not as great as some feared, but the direction, and the continuity are relentless. The pessimists see unacceptable unemployment in five years; the optimists think this will not happen until a decade later; a few believe it will not happen at all. But there is clear evidence that the extra jobs created by the computer industry itself do not begin to make up for the jobs which are lost. In my personal view, computers are job killers and the sooner we accept this, the sooner we will start to deal with the implications effectively.

2. With the exception of Japan, every country that is studying the problem is worried. Japan feels that it has profited from the transistor revolution, it is profiting from the growth of sales in computer hardware, and is drawing up a comprehensive plan to profit from the marketing of computer software. It looks forward to the continued growth of computer technology [14]. Other countries, notably Britain, France, and Germany, feel that they must use computers increasingly at home to make their industries more competitive, and carve out their share of the international computer and information market. It is for this reason that we have seen, for example, the widespread circulation of the film "The Chips are Down" [15] in the United Kingdom, and the beautifully orchested program, Semaine Informatique et Société, held in Paris, September 1979, which had as one of its principle purposes the education of the French public about the forthcoming changes. Still, if these countries succeed in taking advantage of the microelectronic and microprocessor revolution by becoming international distributors, or even by deflecting some of the more harmful consequences from their own people, one wonders what will happen in those countries which are their customers.

3. The responses of the trade unions to the introduction of computers are hardening and will continue to do so. In Great Britain the Trade Union Congress has adopted two principal points for future action. The first is that no new

technology which has major effects on the work force should be introduced unila-
terally. Full agreement on the range of negotiating issues must be a pre-condition
to the change, along with full job security for the existing work force. The
second point is the recognition of the need to search for opportunities of linking
technological change to a reduction in the working week, working year, working
lifetime. Simply put, this means job-sharing. Unions elsewhere in Europe are
taking similar stands. Wassily Leontieff, the Nobel laureate economist makes the
same point as do the unions about the need to share work [16]. In Scandinavia
many of the principles sought have already been won. There is intense union
activity in Austria, in Germany, and in Australia. Much of the activity is being
conducted in concert, principally through internationally based unions such as the
International Confederation of Free Trade Union (ICFTU) and the International
Trade Secretary of IGS [17]. In certain industries, notably typesetting, computers came in under strike and protest, but come in they did. In future the
resistance will be better organized and more successful. Those of us who work
with hardware and software can no longer expect to see the products regarded as
unmitigated blessings by the rest of society.

COMPUTER EFFECTS ON THE WORKING, ADMINISTRATIVE, AND POLITICAL ENVIRONMENTS

Many of the views I have to put forward on these subjects are based on papers
presented at the Second IFIP Conference on Computers and Human Choice which took
place in Baden, Austria, June 1979 [18]. So far attention has been focussed on
how computers affect the level of employment and the number of jobs. There are
almost as many reservations about how computers affect the kind of jobs, or as
this topic has come to be known, the "quality of working life." The problems of
automation in the factory are all too familiar and we only have to think of
Charlie Chaplin's "Modern Times" to recall what they are. We in the computer
industry have come to believe that computers are answers to the problem of dangerous working environments, monotony and strenuous work. But this does not
correspond with the experience of factory workers or union leaders. Their view is
that the arrival of process control machines and robots has left them with jobs
which are more routine, less interesting and less skilled. Requiring less skills
has sometimes, in turn, led management to declare the job is worth less pay. As
an example, in Canada there is a bitter struggle arising out of the introduction
of automation in the Post Office. In the view of management, attaching postal
codes to mail which enables it to be sorted automatically, means that the job of
the postal workers is less skilled, and therefore should be paid for at a lower
rate. The Post Office Union denies that less skill is needed, and in addition
makes a strong case that the jobs are more strenuous and are badly designed. In
recognition of such factors there have been attempts in many countries, particularly in Scandinavia, to redesign jobs so that they are subject to control by the
workers themselves. A historic example is in the Volvo factory in Sweden where
the plant was designed to have a number of work stations, each is manned by an
autonomous group of workers who make the main decisions regarding production
scheduling, rate of work, and authority on the shop floor. This arrangement is
intended to overcome the fragmentation of the work process or Taylorization, as it
is known, so that workers can have a much better feeling about how the job they do
contributes to the product as a whole, and be much less subject to routines
imposed by distant managers and demanding assembly lines. The reports on such
experiments in redesigning the work place are to be found in the extensive literature published by the International Labour Organization (ILO), and in such publications as the International Journal on the Quality of Working Life, and the
reports of the IFAC Committee on Social Automation. This work has been going on
for a decade and more. The ideas sound plausible and the hopes have been high.
But looking at the scene in 1980, one cannot see that there has been widespread
extension of the experiments into industry as a whole. This can only be because
the experiments have had a limited success. The accounts have been sympathetic,
and the claims of success, definite, but much of the advantage has to be attributed to the interest which invariably accompanies a novel situation. From the

point of view of management the results have been costly, and not sufficiently attractive to merit large scale replication. Now with the advent of microprocessors there is a completely new situation. The experience gained in redesigning plants which produce parts for which a great deal of human labour is needed is simply not applicable to the new kind of plants based on microprocessors. Volvo has indicated that they can now design an automatic plant in which twelve people could produce the output of 1200. The implications are enormous.

From one point of view the attempts to redesign the work place can be regarded as efforts to better integrate management with labour. In this vein a great deal of attention has been paid to the management process, and of this work the results of Bjoern-Andersen and his colleagues at the Copenhagen Institute of Management, and those of Mumford at the Manchester School of Business are particularly interesting. Bjoern-Andersen's recent report of studies on how computers have affected middle management describes three applications where small to medium sized computers were installed to carry out functions normally done by middle managers [19]. The first was for inventory and marketing analysis in a plant in the United Kingdom, the second for scheduling production in a radio factory in The Netherlands, and the third for patient scheduling in a British hospital. In all three cases the results were unsatisfactory, and the hospital system was abandoned because it failed to respond to the basic needs of doctors and patients. Difficulties arose because the systems were too inflexible to meet new demands. A bad weather spell accompanied by unexpectedly heavy snow-falls led to transportation problems which disrupted the inventory planning; changes in the taxation system resulting from new regulations in the European Common Market made the radio marketing program obsolete. Human managers have no difficulty in dealing with such emergencies. The limitations of the computer are those one hears about repeatedly in the artificial intelligence literature--an inability to deal with a problem when the context changes. The lesson is that management systems should not be designed so as to leave out human beings.

Of course there is something that makes us hesitant to accept such a caveat. Is it not a conclusion based on isolated instances? We all know that there are thousands of cases of successful computer applications and the result is a more efficient process that eventually runs smoothly, with economy and satisfaction. But it is important to realize that in almost all cases where there are undisputed successes, the program addresses itself principally to data collection, data processing, and report generation. These operations, carried out by clerks, are coverted into automatic procedures. Bjoern-Andersen talks about computers in the managerial process, and it is well known that there is a long history of unsuccessful sttempts to implement management information systems.

In the last few years we have begun to see results of extensive, longitudinal studies on using computers in government administration and planning, particularly at the lower levels of municipal and state government. Important contributions have come from Professor Westin of Columbia University [20], from Professors Kenneth Kraemer, Rob Kling and their colleagues at the University of California, Irvine [21] and from K. Laudon, City College, N.Y. [22]. In this area studies of Francoise Gallouédec-Genuys in France are also useful, as are those of Professor Klaus Lenk at the University of Oldenburg, Germany [23]. The results are too diverse to show a clear pattern. But there is enough agreement to make it clear that we cannot afford to take the view that widespread use of computers in public administration, leaving aside those situations where the processes are mainly those of data gathering and report preparation, necessarily lead to better government, fairer processes, and more responsible systems.

The conclusions of Klaus Lenk are particularly disconcerting. His examination of the use of computers in the Federal Republic of Germany leads him to say there has been systematic and callous disregard of the needs of the people who are supposed to be served. He points to such practices as making those who are seeking service fill out repetitious, long questionnaires and forms, and to systematic searches for those who might have been overpaid by receiving too much welfare or unemployment payments, but never to a search for those who may have been entitled to benefits, but failed to receive them because of the lack of understanding of how the system works. Generally computers make things more formal, more routine, more bureaucratic, inevitably leading to a less humane treatment of peoples. As a final insult, one of the states of the Federal Republic has actually a law on its books, which does not allow people to challenge a decision when it has been rendered by a computer; presumably this would imply an unacceptable lack of faith in the computerized system. Even more serious is the way in which automated and hence formalized operations reinforce the trend to bureaucratization and to fragmentation already present so strongly in many government agencies. It is this trend which Lenk regards as posing the greatest danger, even given that present shortcomings of automated systems, which so often result in decreased acceptance of responsibilities, decisions based on incomplete and incorrect information, and in unequal access of services, can be corrected.

Some studies of Francoise Gallouédec-Genuys carried out for the International Institute of Administrative Sciences centred in Brussels, and as part of the Informatisation de la Société reports which follow up the Nora-Minc report in France, are not so pessimistic [24, 25, 26]. She suggests that computers can be used either to aid the centralization of administrative decisions, or to promote a greater decentralization, placing more authority in the hands of local officials. Which is favoured depends on the tempermanent of those who are planning the systems. In other words, she suggests, the technology itself is neutral and the way it comes out depends on the intentions of the planners. However, in her studies of local governments in France she is not able to point to instances where use of computerized systems have promoted more decentralization. And one cannot help but get the feeling in reading her work that it is easier for the technocrats to control the system their way than it is for those who are devoted to making the system serve individual needs.

Collectively, the work of the Americans, Westin, Laudon, Kraemer, Kling, etc., cover a much greater span of time and a larger range of issues relating to computers and government than has been mentioned here. They examine hundreds of cases of computers brought into municipal and other government organizations for administration policy-making and planning. The observations are detailed, the cases are complex, and I would do them serious injustice if I attempted to summarize the conclusions here. I would like, however, to mention a few points on which there seems to be general agreement.

1. The arrival of computers has not brought about a shift of power from traditional politicians to information technocrats.

2. Computers and those who use them have not played vital roles in the important municipal and state government issues such as those centering around transportation, welfare distribution, justice administration, and so on. Although computers were often installed with the promise of helping to manage the government, and of helping to bring rationality and systematic control over these important and expensive social programs, in fact the computerized approach has been too quantitative, and computer programs have not been able to deal with the complex and dynamic social factors which are invariably present.

3. This disappointment in management information system has not meant that the computer departments have vanished. It has meant rather that the computer functions have been limited to those of data collection, data analysis, report preparation, dissemination of documents, and so on. The department that controls the computer does have influence.

4. There is no argument made that computers will never be of aid in planning complex social systems. However, experience and maturity have taught that the promises must be much more modest and that pace of automation must be much slower.

The real point I wish to make is that we now have the reports of sociologists, political scientists, and economists, in the form of substantive, documented evidence on how computers are really working in our social and administrative systems. The results do not contradict the usefulness of computers for data processing. But they very much question the possibility and the desirability of having computers make decisions about the sensitive questions that come up all the time when people have to deal with those in charge of governmental decisions affecting their daily lives. It is too reassuring to think that the computer technology has been neutral. So far the weight of evidence is that use of computers to make decisions results in bureaucracy which is even more heavy handed than one based solely on people, even though it is easy enough to point to extremes that can be present in a bureaucracy run by people alone.

Perhaps the best way to conclude this section is to turn briefly to the views of Joseph Weizenbaum. I am sure that many of you are familiar with these, especially as set forth in his widely read book "Computer Power and Human Reason" [27]. Weizenbaum's essential thesis is that computer programs are necessarily based on what he calls "instrumental reasoning," something which inevitably leaves out human emotions, concepts, and needs. For this reason computerized systems that purport to address themselves to real social needs can never be trusted. Weizenbaum presents his case with many ad hominem and irrelevant arguments, but nevertheless forcefully and intensely. He has a band of devoted followers, most of them not in the computer field, and also a scornful opposition which believes that he has betrayed his origin as a computer scientist and has gone soft and emotional. If one goes to the core of what Weizenbaum is saying one can see that it is not at all inconsistent with the reports of Bjoern-Andersen, Lenk, and Kraemer, just discussed. They have noted that so far a computerized program has not been able to make decisions on human needs by itself. Weizenbaum feels that it will never be able to make such decisions, and indeed, it should never be allowed to make the decisions. Little wonder the computer community finds it so hard to accept this. If I may be permitted to return to Greek mythology, 1 am coming to see Weizenbaum as a Cassandra-like figure who is making predictions about computers. I leave it for you to decide for yourself whether you believe in the predictions, but I will remind you that Cassandra's predictions were fated never to be accepted--and they were always right![2]

COMPUTERS AND THE INFORMATION ECONOMY

I have already referred to the importance that some countries, e.g., Great Britain, France, and Japan, attach to having their share of the Information Economy. This term was first used by Porat [30] and it is developed further in a recent publication of Rada prepared for the ILO [31]. In fact the growing importance of computers and communications in the economy as a whole has been the focus of attention in many countries for over a decade now, as witnessed, for example, by the OECD Informatic Studies, coming out from the OECD department directed by Han Gassmann [32, 33], and by the many national studies originating from Canada, United States, Sweden, etc., in addition to the ones already referred to by France and the UK [10]. It is not only the developed countries which see the writing on the wall, or should I say the text on the screen. Brazil and India have recently taken strong action to ensure that they gain the capability to deal with computers in their respective countries, and other countries are working through the Inter-government Bureau of Informatics (IBI) and recently through UNESCO and IFIP, to see how they can maintain national sovereignty over computer/communications-related matters. Although the range of issues is complex, governed as they are by both national and international considerations, the goals can be summed up simply. Every country wants to assure itself that, as far as new developments in computer/communications are involved, it will be able to maintain control over its national sovereignty, and can protect its national economy and culture. This is viewed as essential because of the vital role computers play in so many other industries. More than this the countries want to protect their position by seeing to it that

some important share of computer/communication jobs stay at home, and that imports
of hardware and software relating to those technologies do not add to the balance
of payment problems so may experience already.

In all the computerized computer/communication systems now moving out of the
laboratory into the market place we can see the potential for serious social and
economic consequences and in fact almost predict with certainty, the emergence of
such problems. I will not be able, in the remainder of this paper, to deal with
these in any adequate way, but let me cite a few, and give some references where
more detailed studies have been reported. Electronic Fund Transfer Systems (EFTS),
based on automatic transfers between banks, point-of-sale terminals, and electronic checkout systems are rapidly coming into being. The implications on consumer
credit, on the competitive positions of national and international banks, and on
privacy are large. Events have gone well beyond the discussion state and in many
countries legislation regarding EFTS has been or is at the point of being enacted.
Incidentally, you will have noticed that I have not said very much about the
subject of privacy, with regrad to computers. This is not because I regard the
subject as an unimportant one, but rather that it has moved beyond the stage of
discussion, and has provoked legislation in most European countries. Also,
although surveys show that people generally believe that computers have led to a
reduction of privacy, I am prepared to take a somewhat more optimistic position.
Most writers on privacy deplore the proliferation of data bases and terminals, and
are convinced that computers have led to serious erosion in spite of all the
public concern and debate. But there is strong evidence to show that in most
countries there was little protection of individual privacy even before the era of
computers. It is true that computerised data banks have made the possibilities
for invasion of privacy even greater. But what also has happened is that computers made us aware of the importance of privacy, and in country after country
legislation has been enacted to assure privacy rights. The protection may be only
partial, and the issue is by no means settled. Governments are now grappling with
what should be done with records in specialized fields, such as health, employment,
and law enforcement. But the battle is being waged. Moreover, the recognition
that individuals should have access to their own personal records has been broadened to asserting that individuals should have the right to see government
records in general. The result is a recent strengthening of the freedom of information laws in the United States, and such laws have been spreading to other
countries. Thus the effect of computers in the privacy debate has been a heigh-
tened interest in the rights of citizens and to a more vigorous assertion of these
rights even if they have not been won generally.

Most of you will know that Great Britain is the first country in the world to have
introduced Prestel, a commercial videotext system, and that many countries are
experimenting with similar systems, including France, Germany, Holland, Sweden,
Finland, Canada, and the United States of America. Although the concept of a
wired city, bringing computer-based services into the home through telecommunications and the public broadcast system was introduced some ten years ago, the
possibility of achieving such systems has only now become real with the decrease
in costs of computer hardware, and the spread of telecommunications systems. Such
systems allow subscribers, using the telephone and television services already
coming into their homes, and a simple keypad, to gain access to an enormous set of
data bases stored on computers, these data bases being connected in a national and
international network. The Prestel system which went into service in September
1979 in London, already provides a very large body of information including
classified advertisements, products for sale, weather data, entertainment, games,
educational lessons, employment opportunities, and stock market quotations.
Besides these messages there are protection and alerting services of the type
required for detecting fire, burglary, and medical emergencies. Developments are
also under way which could lead to having electronic mail initiated from, and
delivered to, the home. The market applications of all these services are poten-
tially enormous, but the long-term social implications are even greater. It is
conceivable that many people will be able to do an appreciable fraction of their

work at home, and this would lead to great changes in the pattern of transportation requirements in urban and suburban communities. Another result of widespread
text systems in the home is that the universal practice of concentrating schooling
into a few years ending about the age of twenty, could be changed because of widespread adoption of computer-assisted instruction. Education might become a normal
component of the working environment. One can only begin to imagine what this
might mean to the school system as a whole.

Coming back to the possibility of electronic mail, it is estimated that well over
half of the first class mail relates to the transfer of payment system. The
economics of electronic mail are already such that it will certainly soon be less
expensive to send a short message by electronic mail than by ordinary post, if it
is not already cheaper to do so now. The consequences of the reduction of employment in the postal system are obvious. In some countries, like Canada, there has
recently been an enormous capital investment in installing equipment to handle
postal codes; there will probably never be an economic return on this investment.

No one can say to what extent the development of videotext systems will be determined by the fact that the technology is present and therefore will be used, by
pure market forces, or by social needs. Few would like to see the market force as
the only one which prevails. Some see the industry built around software and data
bases as the dominant issue. Just as important, if not more so, are the regulations and agreements, both national and international, which govern broadcast and
satellite transmissions since these will govern how the services are delivered
into the home.[3]

I would like to give two or three illustrations of how these national concerns
spill over into international ones. India, in order to ensure that its indigenous
industry plays a real role in the development of computer technology, has insisted
that any multi-national computer company operating in that country, do so with a
company for which the majority control stays in the hands of nationals of India.
IBM has been unwilling to have its subsidiaries operate under such regulations
and, as a consequence, no longer operates in India. Brazil also has regulations
concerning multi-national computer companies, intended to ensure that it exercises
control over its own computer destiny. Companies which market minicomputers in
Brazil have to form partnerships with Brazilian companies, and to set up mechanisms which will guarantee that there will be a real transfer of technology to the
Brazilian company, including design capability. The regulations have been applied
selectively; they are different for minicomputers than for large main frames, and
similar ones are being brought into play for software; but the intentions are
clear and there is good reason to believe that they will be realized. Many other
countries are seeking to formulate national policies which will guarantee that
they not be subject to domination by those countries which are already major
exporters of computer hardware and software, principally the United States and
Japan.

Another example of an international computer issue is that of transborder data
flows, one which currently places high on the agenda of several international
organizations. OECD has put forward a set of recommendations to its member
countries,[4] and the Economic Council of Europe is formulating proposed legislation
which would have somewhat stronger force than recommendations. In part the problem arises because of the need to reconcile the different legislation concerning
privacy in different countries. One particular aspect of the privacy issue is
whether the concept of privacy applies to companies as well as to individuals, the
so-called question of "privacy of legal (as well as natural) persons." There are
different views as to whether the concept of privacy should be so broadened.
Another concern is that so-called data havens might be set up in countries where
privacy laws are weak, that is, places where information of a type that could not
be collected about the nationals of one country is nevertheless stored in the
haven country, and privacy laws are thereby circumvented. But some, and the
Canadian position is strong here [36], feel that the main issues which underlie

transborder data flows are economic, and not those of privacy. The problem is that data originating from one country could flow across the border to the other, be processed there, and come back in the form of information, that is, reports and decisions. One result would be to weaken the service bureau industry in the data-originating country, and the consequence of this in turn would be loss of jobs and contributions to the imbalance of foreign exchange. GATT agreements covering international trade recently completed after very long negotiations do not apply to information and data. In the discussions on transborder data flows now taking place, we can see the beginnings of the generalized GATT agreements which one day might come into being to cover information. But to appreciate how difficult such negotiations are and how long it takes to come to agreement, one only has to look at the work of the World Intellectual Property Organization (WIPO) in trying to negotiate agreements on copyright and patents. It is not likely that problems of dealing with information in general will be any simpler.

It is only in the last five years or so that these economy information problems have appeared in the agendas of international organizations. I have already mentioned OECD, ECE and WIPO. The Office of Science and Technology of the United Nations and the Intergovernmental Bureau of Informatics (IBI) in the past have been mainly concerned with education about computers in developing countries, but recently they are beginning to turn their attention to those other issues as well. IBI with the help of UNESCO held a SPIN conference in Madrid in which the main point on the agenda was how developing countries might deal with multi-national computer companies, and with planning, gain control over their computer capabilities [38]. Another international organization which is beginning to show some effective results in helping developing countries plan their computer activities is Data for Development (DFD), based in Marseille. DFD held a well organized conference in Chamrousse, France, in June 1979, in which there was substantial participation by knowledgeable people from developing countries [39]. The focus was on how developing countries might implement applications important to national goals. And at long last IFIP seems to be ready, with UNESCO, to undertake some serious work on the application of computer technology to development.

CONCLUSION

Let me now remind you of my thesis and indicate the connection with the title in case this has escaped you so far. The time for judgment, individually and collectively, is here. We are at the point when we have to make judgments on how we use computers, on whether to defer their application in some cases and, perhaps sometimes, whether to use them at all. The reason for the need to make judgments is that what to some appear as opportunities and markets, to others appear as costs and exploitations. The difficulties arise because we do not have, either at national or international levels, the mechanisms by which to negotiate the trade-offs involved in making the decisions. And the slogans one regularly hears to justify unfettered application of computer technology are not the right answers. The computer technology cannot be regarded as neutral, if experience shows that in reality, whatever the potentialities, the effect of introducing it is to almost always favour large centralized systems and inhibit local autonomy. Distributed data processing does not necessarily imply distributed control. High explosives can be used to make bombs or blast for tunnels. But the technology is not neutral. Moreover, it is too simple to say that we cannot stop progress by returning to the pre-computer, pre-communication age and prevent computer systems from coming into effect. We can nevertheless regulate the speed, so that we have a controlled dissemination of the technology - that is, control it in such a way that we do not have massive unemployment and job dislocations, or subject to our-selves to undesirable side effects. And the often-heard argument that if we fail to exploit some particularly exciting new computer application in our own country, we will end up by seeing it done elsewhere, and eventually turn out to be customers for it, does not necessarily hold. It is not always true, as we can see in the case of supersonic commercial air transport services, that an expensive new technology becomes widespread. Finally, the fact that so many judgments and decisions have to be made at the national and international levels does not absolve us of the personal and individual responsibility for making decisions ourselves. I hope I have convinced you that the employment implications of microprocessors are major. It may well be that we will have, in some countries, before a computer application is implemented, an employment impact, just as we have an environmental impact before a plant is built, or a pipe-line approved. It is not uncommon for physicists to refuse to work on certain nuclear problems for reasons of conscience. We may not be far from the day when computer scientists and engineers will have to consult their conscience in the same way before working on an application which will undoubtedly cause labour disruptions. This is not to suggest that I regard the computer technology on the whole as being dangerous and undesirable. I personally continue to believe that most of the applications are beneficial, and we must continue to apply computers in the many places where the overall cost/benefit ratio is favourable. But it is clear that there are cases where one does not have to look far beyond the immediate situation to see costs which are unacceptably painful. Computer applications like our stolen fire must be controlled. How well we do so will determine whether they come to be regarded as the useful fires of stone and forge, or the ravages of the volcano.

REFERENCES

[1] C.C. Gotlieb and A. Borodin, Social Issues in Computing, Academic Press, Inc., New York, 1973, 284 pp.

[2] Zavis, P. Zeman, Project Leader, the Impacts of Computer/Communications on Employment in Canada: An Overview of Current OECD Debates, Institute for Research in Public Policy report to the Department of Communications, Canada, Montreal, Que., November 1979.

[3] C. Freeman, Technical Change and Unemployment, Proceedings of the Conference on Science, Technology and Public Policy: An International Prospective, University of New South Wales, December 1977.

[4] G. Friedrichs, Microelectronics - A New Dimension of Technological Change and Automation, Club of Rome Conference, Berlin, October 1979.

[5] B. Sherman et al., Technological Change, Employment and the Need for Collective Bargaining, ASTM, London, 1979.

[6] Olive Jenkins and B. Sherman, The Collapse of Work, Eyre Methuen Ltd., London, 1979.

[7] A. Osborne, Running Wild - The Next Industrial Revolution, Osborne/McGraw-Hill Publications, 1979.

[8] John M. Bennett, Computers and Unemployment, Automation and Unemployment, Proceedings of an ANZAAS (The Australian and New Zealand Association for the Advancement of Science) Symposium, The Law Book Co.,Ltd., Sydney 1979, 15-25.

[9] Stephen G. Peitchinis, The Effect of Technological Changes on Educational and Skill Requirements of Industry, Technological Innocation Studies Program, Technology Branch, Ministry of Industry, Trade and Commerce, Research Report, Ottawa, April 1978, 272 pp.

[10] Simon Nora and A. Minc, L'Informatisation de la Société, La Documentation Francaise, Paris, January 1978 (four volumes).

[11] Iann Barron and Ray C. Curnow, The Future with Microelectronics: Forecasting the Effects of Information Technology, France Pinter (Publishers) Ltd.,

London, 1979, 234 pp.

[12] T. Stonier, Technological Change and the Future, British Association for the Advancement of Science Annual Meeting, Edinburgh, September 1979, Section F, no.119.

[13] A.G. Siemens, Buero 1990, New York Times, July 5, 1978, p.D1, Die Zeit (Hamburg) September 29, 1978, Spiegel (Hamburg), no.16, 1978.

[14] Y. Masuda et al. (JACUDI), Social and Economic Effects of Information-Oriented Investment, 1974.

[15] Colin Hines, The 'Chips' are Down: The Future Impact of Microprocessors and Computers on Employment in Britain, Earth Resources Research Ltd., London, April 1978.

[16] W. Leontieff, Employment Policies in the Age of Automation, USA, 1978.

[17] R. Malik, The International Arena of Technological Projects, Computing Europe, December 13, 1979.

[18] The Proceedings of the Second IFIP Conference on Human Choice and Computers, Baden, Austria, North-Holland Publishing Co., Amsterdam, 1980.

[19] Niels Bjoern-Andersen, Myths and Realities of Information Systems Contributing to Organizational Rationality, Proceedings of the IFIP 2nd HCC Conference, Baden, Austria, North-Holland Publishing Co., Amsterdam, 1980.

[20] Alan F. Westin ed., Information Technology in a Democracy, Harvard Studies in Technology and Society, Harvard University Press, Cambridge, MA, 1971, 499 00.

[21] Kenneth Kraemer, Computers, Information and Power in Local Governments, Proceedings of the IFIP 2nd HCC Conference, North-Holland Publishing Co., Amsterdam, 1980.

[22] Kenneth C. Laudon, Information Technology and Participation in the Political Process, Proceedings of the IFIP 2nd HCC Conference, Baden, Austria, North-Holland Publishing Co., Amsterdam, 1980.

[23] Klaus Lenk, Computer Use in Public Administration: Implications for the Citizen, Proceedings of the IFIP 2nd HCC Conference, Baden, Austria, North-Holland Publishing Co., Amsterdam, 1980.

[24] Francoise Gallouédec-Genuys, De l'Influence l'Informatique sur la Centralisation/Decentralisation de l"Administration, Informatique et Administration, Groupe de Travail Informatique et Administration, Institut International des Science Administratives, Edition Cujas, Paris, 1977, 91-112.

[25] Francoise Gallouédec-Genuys, The Effects of Computerization on the Relationship between Public Administration and the Community, Impact of Science on Society, vol.28, no.3, 1978, 219-225.

[26] Francoise Gallouédec-Genuys ed., Informatique et Développement Regional, Informatisation et Société 3, La Documentation Francaise, Paris, 1978, 324 pp.

[27] J. Weizehbaum, Computer Power and Human Reason: From Judgment to Calculation, W.H. Freeman, San Francisco, 1976, 300 pp.

[28] Don B. Parker, Ethical Conflicts in Computer Science and Technology, AFIPS Press, Arlington, VA, 1978, 201 pp.

[29] A. Mowshowitz, Information Systems and Ethical Judgment, <u>Proceedings of the IFIP 2nd HCC Conference</u>, Baden, Austria, North-Holland Publishing Co., Amsterdam, 1980.

[30] M.U. Porat, The Information Economy, Stanford Center for Interdisciplinary Research, Palo Alto, CA, 1976.

[31] Juan F. Rada, Microelectronics: A Tentative Appraisal of the Impact of Information Technology, ILO Unpublished draft, Geneva, 1979, 202 pp.

[32] U. Thomas, <u>Computerized Data Banks in Public Administration</u>, Informatics Studies 1. OECD, Paris 1971, 69 pp.

[33] Organisation for Economic Co-operation and Development (OECD), <u>Towards Central Government Computer Policies - Data Base Developments and International Dimensions</u>, Informatics Studies 5, OECD, Paris 1973, 216 pp.

[34] C.C. Gotlieb, <u>Computers in the Home - What They Can Do for Us - And to Us</u>, Institute for Research on Public Policy Occasional Paper no.4, Montreal, Que., October 1978, 54 pp.

[35] Consultative Committee on the Implications of Telecommunications for Canada Sovereignty, <u>Telecommunications and Canada</u>, Canadian Government Publishing Centre, Supply and Services Canada, Hull, Que., 1979, 98 pp.

[36] W.E. Cundiff, Issues in Canadian/U.S. Transborder Computer Data Flows, <u>Proceedings of the Conference on op. cit.</u>, Montreal, Que., September 1978, Institute for Research on Public Policy, Montreal 1979, Chapter One, 11-31.

[37] Rein Turner ed., Transborder Data Flows, AFIPS Panel on Transborder Data Flow Report, AFIPS, Arlington, VA, 1979.

[38] Intergovernmental Bureau of Informatics, Recommendations Approved by the SPIN Conference, <u>IBI Newsletter</u>, no.27, Fourth Quarter 1978, 9-20.

[39] National Policies and the Development of Automatic Data Processing, Data for Development (DFD) synthesis of reports, Marseille, March 1979, 79 pp. Six Pays Face à l'Informatisation, Informatisation et Société 5, l'Association Internationale Données pour Développement, La Documentation Francaise, Paris, 1979, 392 pp.

FOOTNOTES

[1] For a summary of public attitude to computers, see [1], Chapter 6.

[2] Weizenbaum's work is really about the ethics of computer use. Don Parker also writes on the ethics of computer use [28], but he concerns himself in the main with problems relating to professional issues; e.g., the protection of programs, computer fraud, and privacy. Abbe Mowshowitz has recently turned his attention to the ethics of computer use, and is attempting to provide a theoretically-based foundation to the very difficult problem of where one should or should not use computers in a particular situation [29].

[3] For further exploration of social issues and economic issues relating to computer and communications, especially as they concern Canada, see Gotlieb [34], and the Clyne Commission Report [35].

[4] At a meeting held in September 1979, several OECD member countries voted to defer accepting the recommendations.

Information Technologies and Social Power

On the Necessity of an Information Technology Policy Conception

Wilhelm Steinmüller

Dept. of Mathematics and Informatics, University of Bremen, D-2800 Bremen, FRG

Contents:

1. Relationship between "information" and "power".

The motto of early modern times: "Knowledge is power", was coined by the English philosopher Bacon. Vy doing so, he has given expression to man's objective to dominating nature and man. However, this phrase may be particularized bringing it thus closer to the essence of what is implied by information and their technologies.

Supposing, A was collecting information about B (bein immaterial whether A was acting in his capacity as an entrepreneur, medical doctor, police chief, or an authority; or whether B was an employee, a trade union, or a citizen), in each case, A would obtain an incorporeal image of B, namely a "model" in the shape of data, which we may call B'. The more complete the material of data obtained by A, the more easily he will be in a position to direct his activities towards B; he may (though by no means has to!) "control" him.

In other words: the possession of information implies possible control or power over another person.

Frequently it is not even of any consequence of whether or not B' actually exists: it suffices if B opines that A is in the possession of data about him (thus it is immaterial whether video cameras in a factory building are actually switched on or whether a workman merely conjectures them to be so).

Entire systems of information, that is to say, organized sets of information, do have the same effects though on a larger scale, depending on the reproductive ('modeling') quality of the data material - be it some antiquated archives or a filing system of a doctor, or a personnel information system of a multinational enterprise.

In case an information system is technology-supported, the same holds true as in the case of 'simple' information systems, though reinforced by the technical arrangements: in this way, possibilities of exercising power are being technically produced (by computerized information systems), multiplied or distributed (by the reproduction systems and communication networks). In the process, significant changes are taking place which though easily intelligible to the expert may at first appear alien if not estranging to an outsider until its simple causes are intuited.

What is happening in such a case is that qualities inherent in human labour are combined with the essentially wellknown laws governing systems of information technology:

Man, compared to a machine
- tends to be slow,
- imprecise and prone to psychophysical disorders,
- capable of encompassing but a few relational contexts,
- proves bound locally and temporally within close limits,
- but, unlike machines, is endowed with creative abilities, feelings, associative thinking, critical judgement, etc.

By contrast, a computer may
- function at a speed a million, even a milliard times faster than man (thus admitting, e.g., of complicated productive processes being regulated even in crucial situations);

- by the same token process proportionately bigger quantities of data and software (e.g., the Social Security Information System of the Federal Republic of Germany comprises 1oo % of all persons employed; the Police Information Systems at least 2o % of the population);

- run at a precision, dependability and constancy which must appear inhuman (allowing the operator only time for leisure if the computer is specifically programmed) for that matter: "Machines do not strike nor criticize" (nor are they in need of medical care) - making it a perfect rationalization instrument;

- operate, to boot, without being subject to any spatial bounds; wherever their connections may go, the entire stock of data and programmes (and that is to say, the entire controlling capacity) of the system is on hand, and, if need be, on a global scale - as, e.g., in the case of the commercial data bases (encompassing our planet - by means of telecommunication devices, such as satellites or cables), or in the case of aviation information systems or bank accounting systems; however, these data products are accessible only to those admitted for use.

Thus for the first time ever a combination of total decentralization (distribution of technology) and complete centralization (of power) has become feasible.

Due to their speed-of-light processing velocity
- they will before long outrun in part even the time barrier (they (they react in "real time");

- information once stored will remain so forever until it is going to be erased specifically; thus there is no humanizing "benefit of oblivion" - as has been discovered recently in the German Police Information System "INPOL";

- information systems even may react synchronously upon social changes: as it appears, there will be management information systems monitoring social discontent of the employees to the employer well ahead of the moment the employees themselves become aware that they will go on strike one day.

These developmental trends are particularly furthered by advanced communication technologies being integrated (such as "broadband communication" and digital networks), such as the DISPOL network which is used exclusively for the telecommunication of the three German secret services, the thirteen German police information systems along with the Federal Frontier Guards, finance departments and military organizations as well as some other special authorities.

In this way, even technological macro systems may communicate with each other - if necessary, to the exclusion of human beings as has been the case in the Vietnam war, or, in part so, with the U.S. military early warning systems.

On employing such macro information systems, two tendencies conflict with each other:
- Properly speaking, ADP (automatic data processing, that is to say the use of computers and micro-processors) represents the most adaptable and flexible instrument ever thought of by man. Contrary to frequent assertions there will be, at least in the medium run, hardly any "impasses on substantial grounds": You only need to change a programme to bring a new "machine" into being. The same holds true of the flexible integration of ADP in existing labour processes and organizational structures: Being a "thinking machinery", this new type of machinery comprises the greatest humanitarian potential ever attributed to a machine.

- In common practice, however, the inflexible macrosystem is still prevailing:
  - with quantities of data well beyond human scope,
  - with mammoth programmes comprising many tenthousands of commands of unknown, since poorly documented, structure,
  - with confusing hardware and system architecture,
  - with innumerable - and hence, for the citizen, uncontrollable data exchanges.

This implies, as has been pointed out by Joseph Weizenbaum years ago, a renewed social immobilism as well as conservatism brought about by technology.

Since such macro machine systems compare to "manual" information like multinationals to individual hobbyists, a novel stage of social division of labour may be said to have reached: the 'factories' of information have come to produce their commodities now on an industrial scale; they then distribute their product called "information" wherever it is required, that is to say, to those who can afford it, again on an industrial level: Information has become an industrial goods, far beyond the scope of the old mass media.

The "product information" takes on two shapes (and accordingly there are two forms of technology-supported information systems):

- as stored "knowledge" (= information-about-something-for-a-purpose): in documentary systems and data bases (e.g., the European patent documentation; data banks of industrial establishments),

- as processed "decision pro or contra", as instanced management information systems providing the bases of planning and decision-making with regard to measures of rationalizing the enterprise or selecting personnel for dismissal.

Either type of information systems (big ones often combine both of them) may be organized in two ways:
- as auxiliary systems integrated into existing decision-making processes (e.g., wage accounting systems);

- as external stand-alone producers of data (e.g. detective agencies; social research institutes); of software (e.g. 'software firms'); of hardware capacity (independent computer centres); of entire information systems including business reorganisation (frequently offered by producers of computers).

Hence there is a twofold economico-political function of information systems:

- Auxiliary systems reinforce managerial or official decision-making
  by providing additional technologically supported knowledge and/or
  decision-making, thus intensifying the managerial, respectively
  governmental, functions of guidance and control. They are only in
  a mediate sense relevant to the final decision and its material
  consequences.

They are merely mediate production means.

- Information systems operating independently are immediate means of
  production; that is to say, they produce a new type of 'commodity'
  (taken in a broad sense): of the commodity information. Information is being produced by these - by contrast to the traditional
  way - no longer by an individual (office clerk, journalist, scientist, civil servant; though it may be mechanically distributed
  via mass media) but is being produced (and distributed) for the
  first time ever industrially. However, as things are, the profits
  reaped from this collectively produced commodity remain in private hands.

To speak indifferentiatedly of an "information market" or of a "productive factor information" is hence misleading: Both functions of
information must be distinguished (and accordingly termed), since
they have different social consequences. These terms apply only to
stand-alone producers.

2. Impacts of the social system on information systems.

The account given would be incomplete if the social context into
which the various information systems are being integrated were
disregarded: each information system results from the machinizing
of one (or several) social functions.[1]

The major problems, to be sure, center on this aspect of the matter:
since they are of a relatively well-known structure, the following
brief observation may suffice.

The basic idea is that one and the same system may serve to fulfill,
depending on how it is interpreted and to which contextual use it
is put, very different, even opposite, social functions - a fact
vindicating once more that information is power-dependent:

- the same medical data bank (such as on ill persons) may serve medical, scientific, economic or police functions;

- a chemical data base may help the military-industrial complex as
  well as associations of citizens fighting against environmental
  pollution;

- a personnel information system may fulfill functions both of management and/or of employees;

- above all, the very same system may be constructed from the start
  to serve many different interests ("multifunctional systems":
  such as hospital residents', but also police information systems).
  This type has been called, not without good cause, "risky system",[2] since it proves particularly difficult to be controlled.

In any case, a novel organisational structure emerges, alongside
with and within the traditional (managerial or public) administration, namely the so-called "information administration".

It consists in particular of the computing centres, the miscella-
neous hard- and softwares, the staff (system analysts, organizers,
programmers and operators), the coordinating committees (charged
to facilitate a smooth cooperation with the traditional branch of

administration), finally also legally independent information structures (such as commercial data banks, or data processing agencies).

More important than any enumeration of information systems' elements
involved are the manifold effects brought about by the information
administration on their users and those affected by it:

- with regard to the "lord of the system" being in control of the
  system's capacity, the aggregate amount of information output –
  comprising those of the traditional and the information administrations – is being increased considerably; by the same token he increases his information advantage as regards his employees, compe-
  titors, clients as well as third persons; in return for this advantage he is burdened with (occasionally considerable) capital
  investments as well as with the necessity of reorganizing his office or enterprise;

- with regard to those affected, the information system is, depending on the kind of organisation concerned, more or less invisible
  in character; it appears to be a hidden – though efficacious –
  servo-system "behind" the facade of the enterprise, respectively
  authority, which must not necessarily get in touch with the client;
  and it may also be organized in a "distributed" manner so that its
  sole "central agency" may be reduced to a simple organisation manual.

3. Effects on society.

It would be premature to attempt already at this stage of discussion
a systematic treatment of the effects brought about by information
technologies on society.[3]) As it appears, most of the inventions to
be made in this area are still to come: the second industrial revolution (of mechanizing intellectual labour) is still at its first
beginnings.

However, what may be stated right now is a tendency towards a general control of society by means of "data", that is to say, a process
of increasing interlocking and "networking" of until now separared
nformation systems. It is worthwhile to attend more closely to this
phenomenon.

To facilitate a better understanding, a brief rehearsal of the background seems appropriate. There are several machine-based productive
and transport systems in society:
- the distribution of material goods (commodities) by rail and lorry,
- the water and energy channels of public utilities,
- the circulation of money effected by banks and insurance companies.

Add to this now one more social nervous system, the informational
network, run by different types of (novel or well-established) information authorities and firms, coming into existence in this decade.
There are, of course, "institutional" precursors to this: the libra-
ries with their inter-library loan service; the postal and telephone
networks of the postal and telecommunication offices; the mass media,
publishing houses and book and news agencies; the stations for radio
and television; and, last but not least, the universities and other
research and education centres as traditional 'information-producing'
and 'information-distributing' systems.

At the present stage, computer systems combine telecommunication
technologies as well as other information collecting, storing, and
multiplying technologies, creating a densely-knit 'communication'
network, comprising – more or less - all information technologies
hitherto known. They multiply their efficacy and combine their effects, too, to high levels of complexity.

Besides the systemic integration you find an increasing number of information-technical combinations: dozens of novel information-technical combinations spring up (such as data telephone, Prestel, cable text, office automation, "communication working place", and so forth) which themselves are joined to the emerging data network if deemed advantageous by their users.

Both forms of interlocking in the last analysis come to bring about an ever more densely-knit network system consisting of mutually interrelating informational systems.

It is worth noting at this juncture that such a data communication may be organized in most diverse (technical, legal, even "manual") forms - a most illustrative case in point is the cooperation practised by the (secret) German authority for the Protection of the Constitution and the Police system over many years, - which cannot be detected by the person affected except by its results perhaps many years later, when he (or she) seeks to obtain an employment-.

This situation does not imply, of course, that each system participant exchanges all data with all other participants. Rather the data exchange is effected in such a variety of ways that it is even for specialists hardly discernible.

There are impressive examples of the development already today in the areas of business and government headed again by the West German INPOL-DISPOL-system with its various lateral links.[4]

But there are numerous further national and international governmental, supragovernmental or commercial data networks about to be established, some of them being already in an operative stage.

However, it need be repeated that the actual "networking" (= the interlocking process taking place on the systemic level assisted by telecommunication technologies) is still at its initial stage; it is progressing though, rapidly bringing about profound social changes in its wake.[5] This situation implies for the individual, be it an employee or a citizen, a massive change of his situation: Wherever he is faced with a commercial or official agency he is no longer confined to the partner (or opponent) perceived; nor does he merely face the representatives or agents of the economic or governmental power he is dealing with. He is rather confronted, in addition, with a novel phenomenon of a worrying dimension: his partner disposes of the concentrated power of additional information systems to support his own which is not available to him.

This "servo assistance" is so perplexing since it is normally rather invisible and of unknown extent as well as of unknown content:
- He who, in future, is dealing with a policeman aided by a pocket terminal (a system at present at its trial stage) cannot know what information his opponent disposes of (on account of the bar of disclosure laid down by the Law on Protection of Personal Data (!)) by using the secret DISPOL telecommunication network to obtain the - equally secret - INPOL data on him.

- He who, in future, considers to take on an employment, or wishes to obtain a credit or an insurance policy, will not only see himself exposed to comprehensive questioning (something practised already hitherto), but will see himself in a position to be prodded to give his permission as to the passing on of the data collected by his medical doctors, by the various health organizations, by former employers if he prefers to seek the position/the credit/the policy. By choosing so, he will see himself exposed to a network of data for the rest of his life, partly extracted from him, partly stemming from other sources. To resist this development will prove very difficult: legally, - and above all, financially. As a result, nobody will be in a position to know for certain who has stored what on whom for whom and for which purpose, and which information has been passed on to other authorities. There are, of course, directories of data collections and similar things, furnished by data protection boards etc.; but they fall far short of being a remedy, due to high disclosure fees and an estimated 1oo,ooo (!) data storing authorities and firms in the FRG alone.

As a consequence, anyone being aware of this situation will be motivated to exhibit "good behaviour" and refrain from using too extensively his civil rights: well knowing that any well-established public or commercial personnel information system may contain sufficient data on him to have in ready supply sufficient reasons for dismissal in case of measures of "rationalization" - not taking into account the additional data flows produced by the workman/employee himself operating a microprocessor- and telecommunication-controlled working place of the near future.

Besides these rather specific effects, there are structural changes, when it comes to the struggle for information markets and information power,[6] and this on all social levels:
- within business enterprises and political authorities
- between enterprises and authorities ("division of information power")
- between business and government (phenomena of informational inter-locking and its reversal processes)
- finally even between multinationals and nations (international exchange of data; "sovereignty of information"; "war of information" between the E.C. and the USA).

Summing up we may put forward therefore the following theses on the social effects of informational technologies[7]:

(1) In general:

- Generally speaking, there are no socially neutral effects of the new information technologies. In most cases it can be shown that there are simultaneously in part positive, in part negative, in part ambivalent or neutral effects on different subsystems of society, complicated by the subjective element depending on the person evaluating and his range of value adopted;

- virtually all undesirable effects could be avoided, given the extremely adaptable character of information technology, were it not for the established and, for the time being, little flexible politico-economic interests. These effects thus represent mere tendencies, but no factual compulsion, based on the social status quo;

- looking at the technical side, there are two opposing developmental tendencies to be recognized: on the one hand there are very specialized systems emerging ("dedicated systems").- On the other hand, there is a rapid combination and integration of the different informational technologies, accompanied by side effects defying any specific prognostication. Along with this, however, goes a possibility for the first time to reverse in part the process of the division of labour. This applies, in the first place, to special machines doing 'manual' and 'intellectual' work at the same time ("intelligent tools" as the next generation of robots), but holds true, in principle, also in the case of man - though mediated technically (via a servo support of human functions (e.g.

office automation as a possible reintegration of secretary's and
clerk's work by several or multipurpose technologies).

(2) As regards the <u>individual</u>, information systems whether privately
or publicly owned will effect

- structural (technology-induced) unemployment for employees, in particular for clerks, on all levels. As to the remainder this will
result in part in an upgrading, in part in a down-grading of their
qualification; in most cases, however, to conditions of increased
stress. This phenomenon is due to the introduction of taylorization (i.e. the introduction of the production line principles) into intellectual labour. Viewed overall, these systems will subject,
at least in part, man to the (now informational) machine;

- in all persons affected a loss of the traditional "private sphere"
and in particular to a reinforced governmental (or employers')
control of public activities ("social sphere", consequent upon the
subjection of all social areas to "data technology");

- in all persons affected a fundamental deterioration of their "information position" as against any private and public agencies
monopolizing data: the individual will thus become transparent,
and this to an extent unimaginable and well beyond any anticipa-
tion on this part of the consequences entailed.

- The effect of gravest consequence and the one theoretically and
practically least researched consists of the mutual strengthening
and acceleration of the pressures of technological rationalization
and redundancy, on the one hand, and the potential of guiding and
controlling those affected by means of the information technologies, on the other; thus the dehumanizing effect upon labour by
technology is increasing in addition by the informational component.

- This feedback is further intensified by the increasing interlocking of business and government in terms of information, to the extent that governmental data collections (e.g. in the case of
appointments) will result in an added curtailing of the sphere of
operation left to the individual affected; vice versa private information systems (say of political parties) may trigger remote
effects for civil servants.

(3) As regards social <u>groups</u> of inferior power standing (minorities,
citizen associations, work forces, shop stewards and other representatives of employees), the above said holds true as well:

- information technologies are frequently introduced in order to en-
force interests not realizable by other means:

  - with a view to circumventing business or civil participation,
  obviating criticism or undesired initiatives;

  - with a view to increasing the opportunities for rationalizing
  human labour as well as the creation of factual compulsion
  thereof;

  - overall with a view to consolidating existing power positions
  and to weakening those of inferior standing.

- The supposed primary purpose of these systems (i.e., the improvement of information) represents, by contrast, very often a mere
side-effect if at all, as may be gathered easily from the operating costs of information systems showing frequently no decline
compared to the situation before.

- The activities of such groups will become increasingly transparent
  - and open to manipulation - for economic as well as political
  owners of information systems.
- It proves relatively easy to undercut legal rights of co-determination or participation by using appropriate information systems:
  In the struggle of social and political interests a principally
  novel weapon has been introduced which may not be obviated by con-
  ventional means: as against the machine gun a halbert proves in-
  effectual.

(4) On the level of the <u>organization</u>:

- Information systems underrun established frontiers of systems: be
  it frontiers between competing firms; be it frontiers of legal division of powers, not only in a horizontal direction (local self-
  government; departmental principle) but also in a vertical respect
  (between parliamant, administration, and courts). In particular
  this is achieved by an additional installing of independent
  "transborder" information systems. These impose on the powers conflicting the necessity of cooperation in order to use the valuable
  "ressource information" more efficiently. - The same applies to
  the interaction between nations, and between international markets; e.g., by establishing 'data havens' subject to slight control, or of)information holdings' and other novel forms of enterprises, or by fighting 'information wars' to gain informational
  dominance.

This situation gives rise to concentrations of power of a novel
(namely informational) type, with (occasionally) the previous orga-
nizational/legal entities being left in (nominal) existence.

By the same token, a progression towards a concentration of international and national capital power is implied.

(5) On the level of <u>social subsystems</u> (business enterprises, political parties, associations, executive, legislativem and judicial
  powers), the so-called "equilibrium of information" is being
  altered: those disposing of no or of less efficient information
  systems are being put at a distinctive informational disadvan-
  tage; this applies in principle to:
  - small and middle-sized firms, as against big business,
  - parliaments and courts, as against the executive.
  - By the same token there is an expansion of the "technological-
    ly supported" part of the economy and public administration,
    while functions not automized will tend to generate or atro-
    phy.

In the aggregate: Information, formerly a result processed by an
individual, is being turned into a macro-technologically produced
industrial commodity; this applies to both its aggregate states,
namely "knowledge" and "decision making". ADP-systems (data banks
and documentary systems) are the new-type productive plants with
the telecommunication networks being its macro-organs of distribution.

It is perhaps not any longer besides the point to claim: Aided by
information technologies, information has turned into the most important instrument of social control:

- informational superiority substitutes increasingly immediate
  governmental power;

- informational interlocking increasingly substitutes established
  financial or legal mechanisms;

- information is being transformed into a power resource.

To repeat the above a very last time: the positive and negative effects set out are by no means inescapable. They represent merely certain tendencies which will spring into being given three additional assumptions

- that they strengthen given power structures
- that too few counter-measures will be taken
- that unscheduled events will intervene

To speculate on the latter assumption ist not worth-while, while the first two are rather probable. They would therefore deserve to be discussed more thoroughly.

4. Practical conclusions.

An information technology policy designed to serve the interests of the majority of the population will be operative on all those social levels affected by information technology:
(1) on the level of the individual employee/citizen,
(2) on the level of social groups or groupings,
(3) on the institutional level of the individual business firm and governmental authority,
(4) on the over-arching level of inter-business and inter-authority interlockings,
(5) on the societal level of national and international division of labour.

According to the complex nature of information systems several aspects have to be taken into consideration:

(a) economic and political strategies
(b) technical measures
(c) informational structures
(d) organizational changes
(e) legal norms and legal policy standards, and finally
(f) other aspects (pedagogical, sociological ones).

Focusing merely on a few central problems, only some very limited options for action can be circumscribed in this article. In accordance with the fact that the situation is still in a state of flux, the discussion may give rise to new questions rather than answer old ones. In particular an impression of "utopianism" may emerge. This utopia, however, is not based on future technological risks - these have already become a signature of our present life -, but are grounded in the sins of omission performed in the past.

(1) As regards the individual level of the citizen employed, there are essentially four effects of information technologies (respectively of their users) that coincide in the working place:
- the long-known problems of a "private sphere" or privacy
- the effects of unemployment and demotion
- the increase of the managerial controlling capacities,
- the overlapping effects of these factors.

In the meantime, in Germany it has become a well-discussed point that "data protection" is not about the individualistic protection of privacy of well-to-do people against press or government curiosity, but a necessary measure to preserve (or even improve) the freedom of these spheres of political, social and individual activities, being a prerequisite (of survival) for a viable democracy, against rapidly progressing data processing and data communicating, modeling all areas of life.

Within the economy, the situation of employees is bein aggravated
by information technologies in a variety of ways: The menace of
technology-induced unemployment arising out of novel information
technologies is counterbalanced only in part by the creation of new
opportunities of employment; the anxiety of losing the chances of
finding full personal satisfaction in one's working place is intensified by the added possibilities of monitoring and control supplied
by these information technologies to taylorized work processes.

The structure of management information systems about employees
(these need not bear the name of personnel information systems -
they may be organized along entirely different lines and more incon-
spicuously) portrays, over and above pursuing the purpose of regulating the work process, the person and characteristics of the employee for managerial purposes. In this way the old trade unions'
demand for "transparent pockets" is put into effect, if at all, only
as regards the pockets of the employees. - The same, of course,
holds true as regards public information systems.

The partial alliance of interests between government and business
tends to intensify this kind of pressure: Data stemming from governmental information systems, particularly of security authorities, relating to off-duty conduct often influence managerial decision-making (e.g. on the filling of working places); vice versa
there are comprehensive legal obligations imposed on firms to supply
data to authorities, not to speak of informal channels between private enterprises and public authorities' security agencies.

These changes to the detriment of the persons affected are balanced
merely by minor improvements that do not even reach all employees.
Add to this that the realizable positive possibilities are not
clearly recognized - even on the part of trade unions - such as automatic health controls (without the data providing an additional
reason for dismissal, if properly organized).

A strategy taking into account the interests of the employees will
naturally make use first of the possibilities as provided by the
interaction of old labour law and new data protection statutes:

- individual rights of inspection and disclosure of one's own data,
- support by the employees' council as the proper "commissioner for
  data protection" (data commissioner) in the enterprise,
- well-considered cooperation between employees' council and the
  employer's data commissioner according to Data Law,
- invocation of the superior data inspection board.

It stands to reason that any exercise of individual rights will
prove far more forceful if backed by collective support. It needs
particular stressing that an employee, in addition, requires a basic
education in information technology in order to be able to cooperate
effectively with transenterprise groupings (such as trade unions,
media, and political parties), let alone to assert his rights, given
the widely spread lack of didactic guidance in this area.

(2) As regards the level of "groups" (such as employees, councils,
shop stewards, basis initiatives, minorities of all sorts), in the
first place a growing awareness in required that the increasing control by means of data may prove at least as menacing to social
groups as to individual persons: Once, e.g., a trade union is labell-
ed as "left-wing" and all data about it are recorded (according to
well-known patterns of the Federal Criminal Investigation Agency),
then each member or "sympathizer" will be socially stigmatized even
though he may have a "clean data account" as a private person. The
only informational difference to the star of David of former times
is the higher quantity of data collected and available technically
at any terminal of the system.

Once this process of collecting group data is tolerated, be it from

shortsightedness or because members of one's own group are supposed
to be unaffected, then the possibility of collective support for asserting individual rights is enduringly endangered.

Due to the informational interdependence between the private and
public sectors the fact who is storing such group data, and where,
is of rapidly diminishing importance: Principiis obsta- resist the
beginnings.

Ample clarification is moreover required on organisational and legal
possibilities of cooperation between individuals and groups to obtain a "humanization of the data system" in the business and public
sectors. There cannot be an actual cooperation, however, unless there
is a clear grasp of the global strategy along with its aims: if, e.
g., the employer's data commissioner is granted better protection
against unlawful dismissal (a claim put forward by the German Metal
Workers' Union), then this may appear advantageous, neutral, or detrimental to the employees - according to the organisation of the
relative information system.

Whether, however, the formation of citizens' action groups may prove
successful against the growing subjection to data collection may be
doubted since the "intangible" data processing does neither arouse
any suspicion nor does it give rise to any perplexity; moreoever,
this function, at present, is safeguarded by similar institutions
(such as the Humanistic Union). The situation may, however, change
rapidly in the case of non-ADP-technologies, as cabling and other
public "utilities". A greater success may be expected when the
people affected begin to organize themselves in trade unions; given
the tendency towards comprehensive automation of intellectual activities, this possibility is about to turn into an almost compulsory,
though by no means solely sufficient, option for those affected.

(3) As regards the institutional level of the individual enterprise
or the governmental agency (authority, court or parliament) it proves imperative in the first instance to the persons affected to get
to know as early as possible the technology plans.

For at a later stage that will prove too late: As a rule, uninform-
ed members of personnel committees and employees' councils tend to
give their consent to plannings of data processing, just as criti-
cally-meinded as well as conservative MPs do after having been hinted
at the consequences for working places or the necessities of com-
bating terrorism. -

Since major projects require a launching period of several years, an
appropriate participation of those affected is feasible in any case.
Hence result clear directives about the necessary steps how to exert
the right of co-determination - bearing in mind that even the powers
granted by law at present are hardly known, let alone made use of.

There are additional priorities to be noted for 'convivial' business
and public information systems, if we take into consideration that
intellectual work(ers) may be subjectto rationalisation in a widest
variety of humane or inhumane ways; that one cannot judge from outside which 'good' or 'bad' output an information system may actually
yield; that finally the interests of employees and citizens may only
be considered cost-saving unless these systems are co-designed and
con-sonstructed together with the persons affected straightaway from
the first planning stage. Such additional necessities are as follows:

- analysis and co-determination in the overall technology planning
  of the enterprise (respectively of the department) with a thorough
  view to the hazards but also chances involved;

- analysis and co-determination in the detailed technology planning as well;

- entering of company and collective technology agreements with a view to providing legal safeguards;

- especially, however, the co-determination in constructing and implementing such information systems as affect employees, respectively citizens.

This 'constructive' strategy (as compared to the still prevailing 'defensive' strategy of trade unions) proceeds however on the assumption that on a careful analysis of the overall situation the information systems to be introduced have proven or are thought likely to be conducive systems to the interests of both parties. If this is the case, nevertheless the interests of employees, respectively of citizens, normally will remain unconsidered unless the original plans are modified in their favour.

Supposing a right of storing data for the trade union's or the employees' council's purpose within the firm's information system has been conceded, such a concession will only be useful if there are safeguards to ensure that the employees' council is considered to be its sole legitimate user. If this is not the case, any cooperation, naturally, will have to be confined to preventing harm from those affected; apart from that consideration will have to be given to the idea of setting up information systems of their own - if need be on an external basis. (The novel micro-technologies even invite to do so.)

In both cases a clear overall technology conception is required for any meaningful action; moreover, the procuring of research and educational facilities (e.g. within the framework of employees' council /personnel eommittee) is instruction; not to forget the instruction given to special ADP shop stewards within major business establishments.

(4) As regards the inter-enterprise, respectively the inter-authority levels, what is foremost needed is an awareness of those affected that this level of information technology raises problems at all. No entrepreneur would dare to ignore the economic contexts into which his undertaking is embedded; he even proceeds from such a context as a base of his considerations (the same, of course, holds true in the public sector): the world-wide flow of commodities and money is accompanied by a flow of data. Hence business and public information systems and networks are from the start merely components of a wider context involving production and decision-making.

This, however, implies that any measure confined to a particular business establishment or to any particular authority may perhaps be meaningful though by no means sufficient, as has become plain to anyone, e.g. in the debate on automation in the publishing trade (within the context: news agencies).

This applies not only to the trivial observation that the necessary technical/organisational/legal expertise for technology assessment in favour of those affected will be available only in exceptional cases within the same firm or authority.

It applies moreover to the creation of computer facilities for employees.

In how far these necessities embrace the imperative of an inter-enterprise expert co-determination in matters of data technologies with a view to establishing an approximate equality of weapons, may only be posed as a question at this juncture.

In all these considerations due regard has to be given to the rather
divergent information interests involved; so, e.g., the possible
support provided by the governmental dada protection agencies in the
public and private sectors; the antagonistic coordinating committees
provided for the automation of the public sector; the Federal Documentation Centres (so far recognized as a possible power factor only
by industry); as well as the manifold individual interests pursued
by labour organizations. All these factors by no means agree at all
times, especially given due consideration to their different historical origin.

They have, however, to be considered when we try to obtain a global
conception as required in this context.

(5) On the societal level due regard has to be given to the implications of the information technology age:

that they represent a world-wide phenomenon affecting all highly
industrialized nations (in the West and East!) corresponding to the
present level of development of productive power: the world markets
for commodities and money are paralleled by a world market for information. As it appears, the increased global complexity (that is
to say: the increased proneness to crises of the western and the
eastern systems) may only be remedied in this way.

Hence international data exchange increases vigorously, supported
by a world-wide production, distribution, and application of the
novel technologies by transnational corporations.

We may observe this development, it is worth noting, not only in the
economic domain; the less well-known inter-statal exchange of information, too, is about to be fully established (e.g. between security
and social services), underpinned by international data and communication networks.

5. Towards a uniform information technology policy.

A shaping of information technologies along national lines alone is
feasible but to a limited degree, but - within this frame of reference - all the more urgent, in order to make use of any sphere of
action still left unoccupied.

Strangely enough, hardly any investigations on this matter have been
made; there only remain some unconnected considerations as regards

(1) communication technologies; in particular (for West Germany)
    - technocratical ones (of a parliamentary study commission)
    - selected communication aspects (of some political parties)

(2) data technologies (ADP; storage and reproduction technologies):
    - technocratical ones (1st to 3rd ADP promoting programmes;
      Information and Documentation Programmes)
    - microeletronics (employment consequences)
    - no informatio-political considerations;

(3) data collection technologies: no considerations

(4) on a different logical level the discussion of the trade unions
    on (1) to (3) is confined to
    - rationalisation (e.g., the "printers' strike", in part, how-
      ever, without having given due regard to the inter-enterprise
      context),
    - "humanization", however restricted to the common technological
      aspect of shaping the work process, without considering the

additional aspects specific to information technology, viz. of
regulating and controlling.8)

Since all lines of technology development, hitherto essentially
running separately from each other, at present have joined to form a
relatively uniform assembly of information technology (with relatively uniform effects going along with it), the only logical consequence we are left with is to thrash out a uniform political concept
of information technology development, and this for at least the
following four reasons:

- technological reason: Almost daily new combines of information
  technologies are introduced into the market that do not bother
  about the historical frontiers outlined above (data phone, video-
  tex, optical disc): A human choice has to be made between alternatives (e.g., television by way of satellite and/or cable); but
  which decision 'should' be made is unknown as regards its pre-
  suppositions and consequences.

  Moreover, information technology tends to become a rather uniform
  entity, with ADP being its key technology, which needs a corresponding uniform information technology policy;

- economic reason: almost all technologies are produced by the same
  firms. Thus a coordinated technology steering and promotion policy
  based on identical informatio-political inputs is required having
  due regard to the interests of the majority of the population (in
  particular of the employees);

- labour policy reason: The approach of the trade unions so far has
  been orientated rather at short term and requires to be integrated
  in a general conception on the entire range of information technologies including considerations on futurist perspectives ("intelligent tools" as ADP-supported intelligent robots);

- socio-political reason: There have been offered only partial re-
  cipes (e.g., 'data protection') so far on the social consequences
  as to how to subordinate the several information technologies to
  political aspects with higher priorities. Those remedies are
  lagging far behind the actual realities (e.g., of the world-wide
  data transfer in the informational, documentary, financial, and
  personnel areas).

All these lines of development are still in their infancy. This goes
to explain why numerous social effects such as the taylorization of
intellectual work are strongly reminiscent of the initial stages of
capitalism of the last century, although the general development,
owing to the general accelaration of social processes, is due to
proceed considerably more rapidly in the future.

Bearing in mind that such a conception is bound to take also technological alternatives into account (e.g., alternative solutions favourable to the idea of participation are hardly conceivable other
than by procuring micro data systems for wage-earning and social
groups aided by mini computers and similar items), then it becomes
plain that only organizations taking their bearings from society
as a whole will be in a position to provide the financial and intellectual capacities required to promote the considerations to that
extent.

This recognition, however, poses the more comprehensive question as
to the influence exerted by economic and political organizations on
the distribution of social power as a whole.

32

FOOTNOTES:

1) The non-German literature on the matter abounds; hence only some
references as to readily accessible publications - Cf. e.g.
Brunnstein, K. (Ed.): Gesellschaftliche Auswirkungen großer Informationssysteme aus der Sicht verschiedener Disziplinen (Institut
für Informatik Mitteilungen Nr. 46-46c), Hamburg 1977/1978 -
Danzin, A.M.: Die gesellschaftlichen Auswirkungen der Informationstechnologien (Report Nr. 118 of the Gesellschaft für Ma-
thematik und Datenverarbeitung), München/Wien 1978 - Engberg, O.:
Who will lead the way to the information society?. in: Impact of
science on society, 28. 1978, 3 pp. 283 ff. - Kalbhen, U. (Ed.):
Die Informatisierung der Gesellschaft. Der Bericht von Simon Nora
und Alain Minc an den französischen Staatspräsidenten, Frankfurt/
New York, 1979 - Steinmüller, W.: Informationsrechte, Informationstechnologien und der gesellschaftliche Arbeitsprozess, in:
id. (Ed.): Materialien zum Informationsrecht und zur Informations-
politik. Schlußbericht des Forschungsprojekts Informationsrecht,
Regensburg, 1978 - Steinmüller, W.: Legal problems of computer
networks. A methodological survey: Computer Networks 3 (1979),
pp. 187-198.

2) Steinmüller, W./ Ermer, L./Schimmer, W.: Datenschutz bei riskan-
ten Systemen. Berlin/Heidelberg/New York 1978.

3) Reference to those mentioned in footnote 1) is made again; furthermore to Dette, K./Kreibich, R./Steinmüller, W.: Zweiweg-Ka-
belfernsehen und Datenschutz (Werkstatthefte für Zukunftsfor-
schung, Heft 15), Berlin 1979. - Fölster, H.: Entwicklung und
Einsatz der elektronischen Datenverarbeitung (Informatik-Seminar
Bericht Nr. 15-2o), Berlin 1975 - Frederiksen, H./Björn-Ander-
sen (Eds.): The Copenhagen Conference on Computer Impact. Copenhagen 1978. - Heibey, H.W./Lutterbeck, B./Töpel, M.: Auswirkungen
der elektronischen Datenverarbeitung in Organisationen (BMFT Forschungsbericht DV 77-o1), Hamburg 1977 - Steinbuch, K.: Wenn Ma-
schinen denken lernen. Über zukünftige Probleme zwischen Computer
und Politik, in: FAZ, 23. Sept. 1978, p. 9 - In particular the
comprehensive material contained in both IFIP-Conferences Human
Choice and Computers. Wien 1974/1979: International Federation
of Information Processing (Ed.): IFIP-Conference Human Choice and
Computers, Vienna 1974 - Second IFIP-Conference Human Choice and
Computers, Vienna 1979.

4) On this point: Bölsche, J.: Das Stahlnetz stülpt sich über uns,
in: Der Spiegel 33. 1979, Nr. 18-24. 26 - Steinmüller, W.: Der
aufhaltsame Aufstieg des Geheimbereichs. Vom Verfassungsstaat
zum Sicherheitsstaat, in: Unser Rechtsstaat, Kursbuch 56. Berlin
1979, pp. 169. - Wiesel, G./Gerster, H.: Das Informationssystem
der Polizei INPOL (BKA-Schriftenreihe Bd. 46), Wiesbaden 1978.

5) In particular Briefs, U.: Technologie und Gewerkschaft, in: Die
neue Gesellschaft 1978, 7 pp. 526. as well as in this issue -
moreover: Projektgruppe Automation und Qualifikation (I-III):
Automation in der BRD; Entwicklung der Arbeitstätigkeiten und der
Methode ihrer Erfassung; Theorien über Automationsarbeit (Argu.
ment Sonderbände 7; 19; 31), Berlin 1975, 1978, 1978.

6) Steinmüller, W.: Automationsunterstützte Informationssysteme in
privaten und öffentlichen Verwaltungen. Bruchstücke einer alter-
nativen Theorie des Datenzeitalters, in: Leviathan 3.1975, 4.
pp. 5o8.

7) On this point, cf. Reese/J. et al.: ii Gefahren der informationstechnologischen Entwicklung. Perspektiven der Wirkungsforschung.

Frankfurt/New York 1979 - Steinmüller, W. (just like footnote no. 6).

8) Briefs, U.: Neue Technologien als Herausforderung für die Gewerk-schaften, in: Blätter für deutsche und internationale Politik 1978. 1o. Sonderdruck: Argumente zur Zeit 232.

The Impact of Information Processing on the Working Class

Ulrich Briefs
c/o WSI/DGB, Hans-Böckler-Str. 39, D-4000 Düsseldorf, FRG

1. Information Processing - a fundamental change of human work

2. The major consequences of information processing on workers

3. Capitalist crisis and the deformation of technology

4. The major target for the trade unions: an alternative system design

1. INFORMATION PROCESSING - A FUNDAMENTAL CHANGE OF HUMAN WORK

Information processing - and especially computerization, micro-electronics and new communication technologies as the basic tech-nologies of information processing - contribute increasingly to substantive changes of working processes, working structures, work contents.

A 1978 estimation of the Ministry of Research and Technology in West Germany forecast that by 1990 in the FRG 10 millions of jobs, i.e. approximately half of all jobs - and hence about half of all workers - would have come in substantial touch with these "new technologies" and would have been changed by information technology.

More and more information technology is used in organizations of all kinds to fundamentally "re-think" and re-organize the existing structures and processes in work.

No doubt, the industrialized parts of the world, and probably not only these, have entered a phase of deep change for human work and the workers.[1]

This can be seen clearly from the experience gained in this process
so far and it holds in spite of the fact that as a US study coined
it in 1975 "After 25 years of unparalleled technical progress, the
computer industry is ready to enter its infancy." Global estimations
in the US evaluate the state of the art in the field of information
processing as having exhausted up to now about 10 p.c. of its potential.

So we are in a phase of global change of the modes and ways in which
human work is deployed and have at a time to see that the major impacts and with them the major threats - and the major chances as
well - are still before us. The technical characteristics of information processing which promote and direct this process of global
change for human work are the universality and flexibility of these
technologies, its predominant character as a rationalization technology, its development in the form of networks and its technical and
economic dynamics.

Information technology - universal, flexible, embracing, efficiency
pushing and dynamic

Information technology is a universal and flexible technology unwitnessed before in human history. Large, medium and small-size plants,
firms in the industrial and in the services sectors, public and privately owned organizations, economic and non-economic activities -
they all resort to some degree already to information processing
technology and they will do this much more in the future.

At the same time information processing and its core technology -
computer technology - are highly flexible technologies which can be
adapted to very different working processes and structures.

With increasing maturity of information technology, however, more
and more complex systems arise and the typical and predominant form
of development becomes the development toward "networks".

These networks combine computer capacities and all sorts of peripherals, among them especially thousands and in some leading organizations already ten thousands of VDUs. These networks combine technologies like different information processing technologies - computers,
VDUs, communication systems like satellites, broad band facilities,
laser transmission - and more and more also material processing technologies like machine tools, industrial process equipment, transportation facilities a.s.o.[2)]

These networks increasingly put their tentacles into the different
departments and jobs run within a firm joining information and working processes across the traditional functional boundaries in a
complex man-machine-system.

In this system thousands or ten-thousands of "human components" of
these systems interact with their technological components. The
"human components" even have to interact increasingly via the system
with oneanother replacing traditional man-man-communication by
man-machine-communication.

The implementation of these networks, this has to be seen clearly,
is at a time a process of de-centralization and of centralization.

Networks, as a matter of fact, de-centralize computer power, they give the individual worker some share in the complex computer system and its facilities. But networks create for organizations at a time the opportunity to centralize human work to a degree never witnessed before in human history; more and more workers are becoming components of the emerging complex man-machine systems, are subject to the same operating rules, are made transparent in their performance and behaviour in work, are "aided", which means in reality: more and more directed and controlled, by computer systems and their software and "orgware".

Furthermore:

This capability of information technologies to facilitate networks is one of the main features which enables its use as a universal and omni-present rationalization technology.

Rationalization technology means that information technology is on one hand a technology which simply has to replace human work by the work of "systems". It is, as Simon Nora rightly put it in a public debate in Paris in June 1978: "the rationale of computer technology itself to destroy jobs".

Rationalization technology on the other hand means that information technologies offer very little in terms of new welfare to the existing societies. They only marginally produce new goods and ser- vices. Most of computer applications serve to replace work done hitherto by human agents by the "work" of computer systems. The few new products and "services" are mostly trivial like telegames or pocket calculators, are parasitarian, like the new accounting figures generated by management-information systems or are destruc- tive like warfare electronics.[3]

This character of being nearly exclusively a rationalization techno- logy, a technology which facilitates the more efficient production of already existing thing instead of creating new "use values" con- stitutes a marked difference to traditional technological break- throughs like railways, electricity a.s.o.[4]

This will contribute to making the "information society" a society of increased economic and social contradictions instead of an affluent society.

The fact that information technologies are powerful and universal rationalization technologies which permit within the existing forms of organization to centralize control of work substantially explains the technological and economic dynamics of the relevant sectors. In- formation processing is now nearly the only fast growing sector in the Western economies, the only other one is business consultancy increasingly orienting itself also towards dp consultancy. Computer systems are the only investment equipment which is now physically less expensive than in the beginning of the 70s. New technological breakthroughs emerge in nearly all sectors of technical development.[5]

One feature of this technological dynamics is particularly important: the increase of the share of the software cost in total dp cost from about 20 p.c. in the beginning 70s, to 40 - 60 p.c. actually and to 80 - 90 p.c. by the second half of the 80s. This certainly will likewise shift emphasis towards the part of the working class, who actively promote the production and application of these systems. It may give even chances for a better rôle of the working class in the process of change of human work coming along with information processing.[6)]

2. THE MAJOR CONSEQUENCES OF INFORMATION PROCESSING ON WORKERS.

The consequences of information processing for the workers in the western countries can be analysed under three headings[7)]

- the massive destruction of jobs
- the loss or degradation of many traditional skills, job contents and communication patterns
- new forms and intensities of control and supervision of workers in work and outside work

Computerization - a far reaching threat to employment

Information processing constitutes a far reaching threat to employment. Different and after all more or less reliable estimations point to a 25 to 30 p.c. reduction by 1990. But after 1990 the development will proceed even more "professional" and hence more dynamic. The number of jobs created in information processing is, in view of its capital intensity, low in the material production of information processing devices. If it is increasingly becoming more important in software production and application this has to destroy increasingly more jobs as well.

No doubt, it is illusionary to assume that EDP jobs will replace the jobs destroyed by information processing systems.

The job destroying character of information processing is most obvious for those who produce "systems". The programmer can minutiously and directly perceive, which jobs "his" products will destroy.

Nevertheless, there is one piece of experience which seems to contradict this fact: by the introduction of computer systems in an organization normally more work is made necessary than before its introduction.

This observation, however, points to another very important characteristic of the systems design process:

Organizations introducing information processing systems are not in a position to cope with this process. They have to "learn" and develop their ways and methods, they have to adapt systems and organizational components and to arrange for the conditions necessary to the functioning of computer systems.

The phase of massive job destruction is definitely reached when organizations have mastered the process more or less. In most cases this state of mastering the systems design and introduction process is reached much later than planned by systems management.[8)]

Information processing - erosion and re-structuring of skills

Computerization and information processing according to the
experience accumulated so far tends to degrade many human skills
and to create increasingly meaningless and boring jobs for many, if
not most workers.[9]

More than ever before clerical work, administrative work and
even engineering jobs are affected by Taylorization.

Taylor's logic which he expressed so cynically in his writings
is given new fields of application by computer systems:[10]

> "In my system the worker is told minutely what he is
> to do and how he is to do it, and any improvement
> he makes upon the instructions given to him is fatal
> to success."

And:

> "All possible brain work should be removed from the
> shop floor and centered in the planning or laying-
> out department."

Many, if not most, professional activities are changed into machine
operating activities relieving workers from insight into the nature
of working objects and operations, and into their logic within a
given organization.

The knowledge about working objects operation and organisational
structures is increasingly monopolized by small groups of experts:
Systems and communications-specialists, and some other small "eli-
tist" groups. These expert workers, most of them college trained,
many of them having knowledge of two or more disciplines (systems
and accounting, systems and material handling, systems and quality
control a.s.o.) will be on one hand privileged, on the other hand -
because of their strategic importance - a main target for manipu-
lative and controlling strategies of management.

Furthermore they will be put even under a certain pressure to enlarge and update their knowledge - in many, if not most, cases under
rather uncomfortable conditions.

What we are thus facing is an increasing polarization of those workers who remain employed into an un- and semiskilled workforce on
one hand and relatively small groups of highly qualified specialists
on the other hand.

But again the direct experience with computer systems development
appears to be rather contradictory:

Do firms not employ the best worker at the first visual display
unit and computerized numerical machine tools?

Here again we have to distinguish a transitory phase of learning and
mastering the process imposed to the organization: Firms follow this
strategy of choosing the best workers for their newly introduced
technologies because they need the knowledge of these workers for
the learning process of their specialists. They follow it, because

they need this knowledge to prevent imperfect and error-prone systems
- and in the beginning the systems are all errorprone - from spoiling
expensive working objects. They, finally, use this necessary feature
of the systems design process to signal to the other workers that
the new technology is something not to be afraid of.

The experience of workers' organizations in many countries tell this
story: In West Germany - the country in Western Europe where the
right to strike is most restricted - in 1978 trade unions in the
printing and in the metalworking industry had to resort to massive
strike movements to cope with these consequences of information processing.

Computer networks enhance control

The emerging computer networks systematically developed in firms
and especially international corporatons create new forms and intensities of control and supervision.

Management is given new powers to control and supervise the workforce and to screen and analyse worker's performance, behaviour
and even personality.

Outside the firms public networks are systematically developed and
used to control deviations of individuals and of social groups.
Workers and workers' representatives - increasingly forced to resort
to direct actions like strikes, protests, acts of resistance - are
"natural" targets of these activities.[11]

The bulk of the new possibilities is developed in business organizations. Four threats for workers have to be envisaged:

- Networks have to make the performance and the behaviour
  of their human component transparent in order to control
  the operation of the complex machine-systems
- personnel information systems as the direct application
  of information processing to workers' data enable mangement
  to sophisticated personnel evaluation and manpower planning,
  re-organization and rationalization measures.
- scientific systems of rationalization as e.g. operations
  research get new dimensions of applicability by mass data
  processing on the shop floor and by increased speed and
  capacity of computer systems.
- complex data banks, the "office of the future", management
  information systems remove working objects and the knowledge to be deployed in the corresponding transaction
  (paper documents, files, informal information processing
  a.s.o.) from the realm of workers, "objectivise", hence
  "de-subjectivise" work structures.

Computer networks for reasons of their internal technical control
and functioning must permanently store, process and evaluate data
on how the different components are operated. This means, that the
hundreds, thousand and soon ten thousands of human operators working
in complex network systems have to face the fact, that it is stored
and processed when they start their work, how often they iterate,
what functions they activate, what their deviations from standards
are a.s.o.

Basically, the control of human actors is necessary because of the necessity to control VDU operations, computer channel capacity, data transfer, time sharing computer operations a.s.o. It is made necessary by accounting procedures inherent to computer systems and it is made necessary by the need to optimise the performance of the complex and expensive network systems.

In some of the very complex systems for this reason up to ten times more information has to be processed for this internal control of computer network systems than is processed for "productive purposes".

Personnel Information Systems in development in the FRG now envisage to store up to 10.000 data items per worker including detailed information on health, skills, personal propensities a.s.o.

No doubt the target of these systems is to minutiously scrutinize workers' personality and to give management the possibility to re-compose work groups according to management's preferences.

O.R. methods and other scientific methods of work process control were said to be dead by the beginning 70s. Now they apparently are coming back to life again. The mass data seized and stored by complex computer network systems give firms a much better foothold for modelling work processes and departments in plants and offices. A Teller Management System developed in the U.S. e.g. - essentially a complex real-time simulation model - gives bank managers the possibility to continously re-schedule activities at the counters and in the background of a banking office - enabling them to make more work to be done by less clerks.

In one of the leading Insurance Companies in West Germany the "office without paper files" is in development: all the objects which tra-ditionally are processed, stored, maintained, updated a.s.o. by workers are now put into a giant data bank system and thus controlled by the business organization and its systems specialists - and with the objects the working procedures, the operational and organiza-tional knowledge, the communication patterns a.s.o.

Again, with regard to the emerging control potential which will give management (or part of management) a better control of workers we also have to make some relativising observations.

With regard to these control features we observe up to now only the peak of the peak of the iceberg. Organizations up to now are much too busy "learning" the sophisticated use of these systems and in many cases even mastering the technical and organizational structures and procedures so that they cannot yet fully exhaust the potential given to them. The full use of this potential will be emerging only after a time span of 3 to 5 years.

The same can be said with regard to the public control on workers enhanced by computerized mass data systems. The West German police and secret service authorities - institutionally, with their legal bases and even personally still seemingly somewhat rooted in the Third Reich - announce

- to develop systems to cover all the population in detail
- to use the systems for prophylactic purposes of screening entire subgroups of the population
- to give the police-forces possibilities to contribute to the shaping of the society of the future.[11]

We leave aside in this analysis that, of course, the effects on employment, skills and working conditions are not the only changes in workers' situation.

As a matter of fact in the context of the spreading of complex new communication technologies for public and private use not only the situation of the worker in this job but also his situation as citizen, consumer, as a person who is active in different social spheres is changed. However, the overwhelming impact on workers produced by information processing technolgies is produced in the sphere of work. It is the working class which is massively and with regard to its productive and creative activities attacked by these systems.

3. CAPITALIST CRISIS AND THE DEFORMATION OF TECHNOLOGY

The consequences mentioned before are of course linked to important changes in the economic and social development in the last decade.

As a matter of fact, the basic problem for the working class in the developed countries - and in a more long-term perspective also and also in an even aggravated way for the workers in the less developed countries - arises from the fact that the development and spreading of information technology coincides with a phase of marked decline of capitalism as an economic system.

The capitalist system has, as Ernest Mandel coined it, for now about ten years entered one of its phases with predominantly stagnative tendencies. For the FRG, for instance, this expresses itself in a tendential decline of the real growth rate of g.n.p.: it was about 8 p.c. annually in the 50s, it fell to 5 p.c. in the 60s and to 3.2 p.c. in the 70s. It has shown a further decline to nearly O p.c. in the beginning 80s. The estimations for further growth up to the 90s are at or below 2 p.c.

At a time the annual productivity increase remains on a high level, between 3 and 5 p.c. in the FRG. This productivity increase is, itself, increasingly due to the development and application of the "new technologies", especially of information processing technologies and especially in realms where productivity increases have been resticted up to now, like e.g. in clerical work. From the mid 60s until now in the FRG nearly 100 billion DM have been invested in computer systems, peripherals of all kind, communication devices, for soft- and orgware in these technologies a.s.o. The share of information processing in national outlay in investment equipment rose from about 3 p.c. in the beginning 60s to between 15 and 20 p.c. now. The value invested in computer systems (Western) worldwide is estimated to double from 1977 to 1983, the real increase of capacity being substantially higher in view of rapid tendencies towards further cheapening of edp equipment.

Clearly the character of these technologies prevents them from
massively stumulating growth: on the contrary tendentially - and
this holds particularly true when the first intensive learning phase
of the organizations has come to an end, - in Europe that will be
perhaps from about the mid 80s - the massive destruction of jobs,
the economic repercussions of deskilling, the increase of control
on workers a.s.o. have to further and massively depress economic
activity.

On the other hand the use of information processing technologies
increases fixed cost, thereby forcing organizations to reduce
variable costs and especially personnel costs, social benefits
a.s.o. But at a time increased fixed costs make organizations increasingly inflexible: the higher capital intensity and its costs
are, the more marked consequences of fluctuations in market demand
on the organizations.

The production of information processing equipment, on the other
hand, creates in view of its own high capital intensity and in view
of highly automated production processes necessary for the production of integrated circuits and other components relatively few
jobs: The increase of production in edp and office equipment and
micro-electronics components by 80 p.c. from 1975 to 1980/1 has
after all created 1000 (in words: one thousand) jobs. In the very
core industry of microelectronics components production in the
FRG the picture is the following: increase in value of production
(volume being higher even) from 3.4 to 4.4 billion DM annually from
1975 to 1980 and a decrease in jobs by 8 p.c.

Software production may create a certain additional number of jobs,
but the number of these jobs will by far not close the gap between
offer and demand in the labor market: in the FRG more than two
million jobs are actually missing, about 100.000 jobs (most extensive estimation available) have been created in about 15 years of
edp development in data processing centers, programming and organization departments of firms a.s.o. On the other hand: the more of
these jobs are created the more jobs in other lines of economic
activities are destroyed - at least with a certain time gap.

Therefore, no doubt, the "information society" will not be a
society full of wisdom (information) and harmony (rationality), but
a society of mass unemployment and economic contradictions, problems
and aggravations similar to the 20s/30s.[12])

This has to be stressed again and again: unemployment is and will
be increasingly the most important problem which the working class
in capitalist countries will have to face in the context of information processing technologies. In the countries of the European
community in 1972 about 2.5 million workers were unemployed, in
1976 about 6 million, 1982 unemployment is at about 13 million.
In the OECD countries actually about 50 million workers are unemployed. Studies for the end 80s forecast a 4 to 6 million unemployment in the FRG (in 1983 about 2,5 million, in 1976 about 1 million,
in 1972 no unemployment).[13]) With increasing "informatization of
society" and increasing maturation of the still immature technology
and organization of information processing this problem of unemployment will sharply be aggravated.

But unemployment is not the only economic problem for the working
class in the capitalist countries: at a time we have to observe:

- large scale non-utilization of productive capacities:
  in the FRG actually more than 100 billion DM of productive
  recources are idle, cannot be used by economic reasons,
  quite a bit of these recources being by the way very
  modern and fully competitive;

- giant idle capital masses, which apparently do not find
  productive outlets, have been accumulated and will be
  further accumulated: The Euro-Dollar market e.g. was
  estimated to be about 350 billion US $ in the beginning
  70s, it was estimated to be about 1000 billion US $ some
  four/five years ago, it is now estimated to be at more
  than 1500 billion US $. It is probably only a question of
  time until the international finance markets do collapse.
  Large national industrial corporations announce proudly
  that they have been earning more by financial than by
  productive operations.

These two facts and the massive unemployment mentioned before are,
of course, in contrast with the fact familiar to everyone: that
there are very reasonable and wide-spread needs of large segments
especially of the working population: The unemployed workers, the
unused productive facilities and some of the idle capital at least
could be used to satisfy these needs - if social organization of
the process of production would allow this: housing, education,
transportation, environmental protection, amelioration of working
conditions a.s.o. By the way, the introduction and the massive use
of computers, of econometric models, input-output-analyses a.s.o.
has not at all ameliorated the very bad and increasingly worsening
allocation of productive factors in capitalism.

The dream of the economic "sciences" to contribute to the "optimal
allocation of production factors" apparently is far from becoming
reality: the real use of human, natural, financial a.s.o. resources
is turning into a nightmare - in spite of the fact that computer
systems are sold as the universal means for better planning and
more economic rationality.

In the FRG the voluminous staffs of the state bureaucracies, as
e.g. the council of economic "experts", the economic research
institutes, the planning staff of big national and international corporations primarily produce erroneous prognoses, even the prognoses
on a short term basis (e.g. 6 months) and for very complex economic
aggregates like g.n.p. are stupendously wrong - on the basis of
computerized statistics, models, data and method bases a.s.o. If
workers, engineers, physicians a.s.o. would pursue their professional
activities in the same way in which "professional" economists and
policy-makers apparently pursue theirs we soon all would be living
in a state similar to the stoneage.

Apparently, the other great promise of the idelogists of the information society, a better use of resources by more efficient planning
and control, by better private and public management, by an affluance
of information and insight unwitnessed up to now was, is, and will
always be an illusion - under the conditions of the capitalist economic system.

Now, the poor (but very expensive!) state of our economic system has, under the conditions existing in a society, which is based on the exploitation and the domination of the working class by capital, to lead to the thorough deformation of information processing technologies, has to lead to its deliberate development against the working class: technologies and especially information processing technologies are developed and used as a new strategic means in class struggle. Basically these technologies give the opportunity to press out of the organizations and that means out of the workers the profits that can more and more not or not sufficiently be attained on stagnant and increasingly fought for and therefore uncertain markets, on a national as well as on an international basis. It is thus a strategy of "internalization" of profit production or as Karl Marx would have coined it, it is a universal strategy of increased relative surplus production which is put into operation by the development and use of these new technologies.

Workers in the developing countries will have to understand and I am confident that they will understand it very clearly that the "new technologies" are indeed new as physical systems comprising highly developed forms of capturing natural forces and natural properties of material substances but that the "mechanisms" ruling the socio-technical process in the field of information processing are the old "mechanism" of the capitalist society. Thus the "third industrial revolution" is perhaps more its contrary, i.e. the deliberate production and use of technology to maintain the capitalist system. The information society, therefore, is certainly not the society of and for the working class.

On the other hand even in the existing development and use of information processing we observe some developments which indicate solutions that can be fought for in the interest of the working class.

4. THE MAJOR TARGET FOR THE TRADE UNIONS: AN ALTERNATIVE SYSTEMS
   DESIGN

The question remains how the workers, the working class and its organization should face this development.

Before indicating essential directions in which solutions can be found three preliminary remarks are necessary:

- from the preceding analysis it follows that the problems
  of information processing technologies and their impact
  on the working class cannot be separated from the more
  basic problem of the nature of our economic system: if the
  ruling capitalist system is maintained information processing technologies will be increasingly used against the
  masses of workers - in a chaotic and more and more aggravated economic struggle; at a time the danger increases
  that - as in the 20s/30s - the ruling forces in the western
  countries will have to resort to neo-autoritarian or even
  fascistoid political solutions to cope with the aggrava-
  tion of economic and social conflicts.14)

- the existing mechanisms of the given state organization
  - that is certainly also the case with the "welfare state"
  of social-democrate origin - is apparently absolutely power-
  less vis-à-vis the forces and chaotic turbulences which

the giant capital masses accumulated generate to secure their further profits.

- one of the institutions most questioned in this process is the western management-system; in spite of the massive support by the new technologies of information processing it is less than ever before capable to secure stable and continuous conditions for capitalist development; on the contrary it is even systematically developing technical systems to make itself partially at least redundant.

So, the basic challenge for the working class is - and that can be done only by a permanent struggle against the process of further economic decline - to create its own institutions for a sound development of produciton which provides for rationality, continuity and truly human conditions and relations in production and in society at large.

With regard to information processing technologies that means to struggle for conditions which give workers a permanent control on the development and use of these technologies. The essential target for this fight is to secure a permanent human choice controlled by the workers, a deliberate and selective choice of systems of the new technologies according to the needs of workers in work and outside of work. Basically a process has to be pushed which allows to screen every system and system proposal in an organization in the light of four questions:

1. Is it a system which has to be prevented altogether from being developed? - An example for those systems are personnel information systems: the 1982 Federal Congress of the West German Trade Union Confederation (DGB, 8 million members) has demanded the interdiction of personnel information systems: in 1980 the Union of Public Services and Transportation in the FRG (1.1 million members) has demanded the destruction of existing personnel information systems.

2. Is it a system the development of which is to be stopped in order to screen it first for its social consequences and its alternatives? - This is the "Moratorium" which is for instance demanded by the Australian trade unions.

3. Is it a system which can be suffered to be developed? - Examples are quite a few systems for management information, which in some cases do not very much harm but which apparently are not always useful as well.

4. Is it a system, which could be replaced or transformed into a system useful for the workers? - Examples are systems which give clerks better overlook about materials or time schedules of orders a.s.o. A particularly rewarding realm would be systems providing for permanent and concise information provided to workers to save scarce and precious materials and energy in the production process.[15)]

Information processing technology offers itself basically for such
a permanent screening procedure by and in favour of the workers.
It offers itself by the very characteristics of its development
and application process:

- Information processing systems are substantively developed
  in the firm(s) and the department(s) in which they have
  to perform afterwards as complex man-machine-systems
  comprising hundreds, thousands and soon ten thousands
  of human agents in their networks

- The development of information processing systems presupposes the participation of workers, their development
  is based on the disclosure and use of workers knowledge
  and on their involvement in the design process.[16]

- The process of production of information processing
  systems is a permanent process of production of alternatives: the "producer" - programmer a.s.o. - of these
  systems is every few weeks or so forced to select one
  alternative out of quite a bunch of alternatives

- The process of systems development is particularly
  based on the loyal and conscious co-operation of workers;
  conditions of continuity, transparency, confidence are
  essential for a sound systems development in an organization.

These properties of the systems design process convey definitely
the idea to secure a full and autonomous participation and control
of workers in this process in order to fully deploy the positive
potential of information processing technologies. Multifold steps
towards - up to now very limited - forms of this control have been
done by the unions in many Western countries up to now:

- in Scandinavia e.g. in form of veto rights for workers
  representatives and in form of special institutions for
  edp development (e.g. the installation of specially
  trained data shop stewards in Norway)

- in France by the endeavours of the major unions CGT and
  CFDT to give workers autonomy and time to discuss on
  their proper conditions and alternatives in systems development

- in England (as well as in a few firms in the FRG) by the
  activities of workers to develop their own socially useful
  products using partially e.g. microprocessors to develop
  for instance portable and cheap kidney dialysis machines,
  rail-road-vehicles a.s.o.) and by new approaches to dis-
  close company information on technical developments.

- in Austria and West Germany by the endeavours to ameliorate
  the legal rights of worker's representatives to better and
  earlier information on systems design and to create more
  transparency of this process for the workers by campaigns
  and training

- in the socialist countries by a permanent debate among the
  workers about new forms and directions of use of new technologies to promote the productivity and by concepts like
  "work design to promote personality development".

This adds to multifold activities going on in scientific bodies like IFAC and IFIP to promote the involvement and participation of users activities - which have not prevented up to now most of the users from being more used in the systems design process.

The most general and practically political approaches, however, have to be seen in the demands raised throughout the international trade union movement to reduce working hours. The nature of information processing technology leads essentially to reducing the time considerably which is "socially necessary" for the intervention of human agents directly and indirectly into the process of production, administration, distribution a.s.o.

This gives chances - and these are the most important and urgent direct measures for solutions of the problems sketched in chapters 1 through 4 -

- to reduce weekly working hours even far below 35 hours and to make other forms of reducing working time like earlier retirement and longer schooling effective.

If e.g. we take the quantitative framework of studies like Siemens' "Office 1990" we can estimate now that by 1990 an average of about 28 to 30 weekly hours is necessary to maintain actual production, comprising the necessary administration a.s.o. This opens up new horizons for further steps to use working time, time made free from the necessity to intervene into the process of production, administration a.s.o., that means it gives possibilities for

- reductions of working time within working time

that means by a selective and conscious development of information processing technologies time can be gained for

- a thorough desintensification of working processes (e.g. having more pauses, increasing operating time of work cycles, more communication in work, lower productivity norms), a strategy followed by the West German trade unions in their practice for quite a time now

- a really life long learning process in work, meaning to give workers chances to acquire knowledge about systems, their internal functioning (e.g. the importance of software and software design), their technical alternatives and social consequences[17]; this strategy is e.g. very substantially followed by the 150 hours program of the Italian metal workers union, which gives every worker a right to 150 hours training per year the contents of which are subject to the workers' control

- most important of all: more participation, more democracy, more self-determination and collective control of operations in the different departments, in the factory, in the firms, in the corporation.

So the fomula for a solution in the interest of the working class and in full consciousness of the positive potential of information processing technologies might be

- less working time plus alternative forms of work
  plus a true workers control of production

Systems development should be absolutely made an appendix to
this production policy of the workers: system designers must never
be in a position to impose their systems to the workers.

And from this universal challenge imposed by the development and
spreading of information processing technologies it becomes clear
why these targets will only be attained by fighting against the
mechanisms of the capitalist society and why it is indispensable
to replace the capitalist logic of production and work by a logic
developed, imposed and controlled by the workers and the organizations of the working class themselves.

Footnotes and References:

(1) Briefs, U. Arbeiten ohne Sinn und Perspektive? - Gewerkschaften
     und "neue Technologien", Cologne: Pahl-Rugenstein-Verlag, 1980

(2) Significant of this technological development are concepts like
     "computer integrated manufacturing"; for the analysis of the
     social impacts cf. Doumeingts, Guy; Odin, Danielle (eds.);
     Les Aspects Socio-Economiques de l'Automatisation, Bordeaux:
     Université Bordeaux-Adetaa, 1982

(3) Briefs, U. Mit neuen Technolgien in eine neue Gesellschaft? -
     in: Blätter für deutsche und internationale Politik, Nov. 1979;
     translated into French in: Berleur, Jacques; Du tilleul, Roger;
     Poswick, Ferdinand; Rainotte, Guy; Van Bastelaer, Guy;
     Une Societé Informatisée - Pour qui? Pourquoi? Comment?, Namur:
     Presses Universitaires, 1982

(4) Railways created opportunities to move around in dimensions
     undreamt of in the pre-industrial era. Railway technology
     thereby compensated for the loss of million jobs in traditio-
     nal (horse powered) transporation. Can we expect in the same
     dimension to multiply the use of information?

(5) cf. Briefs, U. (1980)

(6) This will probably be particularly due to the increasing
     rationalization of dp. departments and software production
     itself

(7) Extensive references in Briefs (1980);
     cf. the SOTAC proceedings, esp. Briefs, U. Computerization
     and employment, in: Computers in Industry, vol. 2, No. 4,
     Dec. 81

(8) This fact is expressed by a German interpretation of the
     initials "IBM" as "Immer besser manuell" (always do it better
     manually)

(9) Mowshowitz, A. (ed.) Human Choice and Computers 2, Amsterdam,
     New York, Oxford: North Holland, 1980

(10) References given in Mowshowitz (1980) p. 80

(11) This, for instance, was publicly announced by the former head
     of the Federal Criminal Agency Herold, cf. the numerous criti-
     cal analyses of Wilhelm Steinmüller

(12) Briefs (1979)

(13) Information processing, so far and in spite of its relative
     immaturity, in the FRG has destroyed jobs as follows: - The
     lower boundary is judging from a modest payoff of investment
     in information technologies - about 500 000 jobs; - The upper
     boundary is judging from typical cases of substitution ex-
     perience up to 0.9 million jobs

(14) It is necessary to stress the differences and the parallels
     to the general crisis in the 20s/30s:
     unemployment and economic decline so far have only attained
     a relatively small volume in comparison to the 20s/30s.
     Productivity is now about seven times as high as in the
     beginning 30s.
     On the other hand - and that is the most important parallelism
     - capital accumulation has attained dimension far beyond the
     level of the 30s.
     We are probably now just entering a long period of further
     marked decline. Apparently this process is lasting much
     longer than in the 20s/30s.

(15) cf. Briefs, U., Informationstechnologien und Zukunft der Arbeit
     - ein politisches Handbuch zu Mikroelektronik und Computertech-
     nik, Cologne: Pahl-Rugenstein; 1984

(16) Briefs, U., Ciborra, C.; Schneider, L. (eds.), Systems design
     for, with and by the users; Proceedings of the IFIP Working
     Conference, Amterdam, New York, Oxford: North-Holland Publishing
     Co., 1983

(17) It is not sufficient to transfer the existing computer know-
     ledge to the workers. Instead a new - much more complex -
     knowledge about socially useful information systems has to
     be developed.

Section II

The Major Specific Impacts of Computerization on Work

Four major areas of impacts of computerization have been emerging with regard to human work and the workers: One positive and three largely negative ones with regard to human work. The first - the positive one - is the at least in the long run considerable gain in productivity respectively in the reduction of costs and especially of the outlays on human work.

This area will not be dealt with here for two reasons: first because this fact is known to everyone who is dealing with computer systems, secondly because productivity and productivity increases are of material importance to the workers as well as to their welfare and nevertheless productivity is at a time not (or only marginally) controlled by workers.

It is nevertheless important to stress that a full development and use of computer systems to serve workers' interests presupposes to install a full workers control on the ways in which productivity is organized and increased and hence on production.

So, under the conditions given, the analysis has to focus predominantly on three areas of overwhelming negative impacts on the workers: redundancy, erosion of skills and increasing polarization of workers due to the fundamental changes of work organization, induced in the context of computerization, and new forms and intensities of control and supervision, exerted by management.

The following Section II contains material papers with regard to these three classes of impacts:

The first paper, that of Rigal, examines the conditions under which the process of computerization, the direct task of which it is to reduce the amount of labour to be spent on the production of (a more and more stagnant) social welfare, has to lead to large-scale unemployment and concludes that only very basic changes of human culture - including the understanding of human work, of rationality and of organization - can provide for the necessary solution.

The second paper - the paper of Kubicek - discusses extensively the changes which are effected by computerization on human skills. This discussion examines several theoretical hypotheses, indicates a series of open questions and draws several conclusions of a practical (political) and scientific character.

The third paper - by Kilian on personnel information systems - deals with one major aspect of the new forms of control and supervision brought along by computerization in an empirical way reporting findings from a survey comprising more than 200 large industrial companies in West-Germany.

The article points to a series of basic problems for the workers and their unions which have emerged from this development.

Especially this class of impacts will have to be dealt with much more by technologists. It is interesting enough to note that these new forms up to now have been mainly treated by legally trained specialists, much less even by social scientists, nearly none at all by specialists in computer and computer networt technology. Solutions, however, are to be expected from these three scientific realms in the reversed order.

All three papers - as the papers in Section I - contain major indications to get to solutions. They hand the topic over to the papers in Section III which deal with specific directions to arrive at some solutions.

Computerization and Employment

A Short of Survey

Jean-Louis Rigal

Professeur à l'Université de Paris IX/Dauphine, French representive TC.9, F-75 Paris, France

Linking computerization and employment cannot seriously
be done, unless we say that both have a common origin :
the leading (mechanistic and taylorist) paradigm, including the conservative myth of the "one best way".If we
want to solve the dilemna "how not to be luddist ?". We
show -using the case of bank workers- that we need a radical change of organisational and cultural paradigms ;
and first a new definition of work, workers, jobs and
production.

Finally the article analyses the importance of mastering
data/models and stresses the necessity to be aware of their
meaning and the importance to promote the function of "data
(information) administration" (datawaring and industrial democracy versus semiocracy). It then explains (from two
french examples) what kind of educational effort is necessary to face new technologies and new working processes ; a
fascinating challenge to meet indeed !

I - THE QUESTION TO ANSWER

In business as well as in the whole society, the use of computers is steadily
increasing ; so are the unemployment rates. One should seek a possible relation
between "computerization and unemployment", analyse the possible consequences
of computerization on the employment market. We will restrict our study to
Western Europe, so as to avoid blurring our analysis with structurally different situations. Moreover, the crucial problem of qualification change will only be slightly dealt with, despite its essential importance.

II - CAN WE REALLY LINK COMPUTERIZATION AND UNEMPLOYMENT ?

Many difficulties arise :

1) Can one argue that computerization increases unemployment without comparing
with a non-computerized world ? Where do we find a world where computerization
has yet to induce a measurable change, but where other conditions are close
enough for a valid comparaison ?

2) Can the same type of analyses be used for robotics, bureautics, development
of decision-making techniques and telematics ?

3) Of course the development of E.D.P. (electronic data processing) is not an isolated phenomenon ; it is closely interrelated with development of modern technologies. Furthermore, notice that it can not even be separated from the deep modifications of society, its procedures for decision-making, leadership and manufacturing, though these modifications are far slower than usually described, as they are described by sociologists whose interest steer them toward the extreme cases. Clearly the process is just beginning and cannot be separated from the very nature of goods and services produced or to be produced to meet real challenges and "social needs". (cf 1)

4) It is becoming increasingly clear that computerization is mainly an organizational technique ; it therefore cannot be studied apart from the science and practice of management ; it is even deeply rooted in the whole development of our culture, our practices and our industriality, the kind of needs we value and privilege. (cf 2)

5) Yet another more serious difficulty for linking : the simultaneous increase of E.D.P. and unemployment in no way proves a causal relationship between the two evolutions. Saying so would be a serious methodological mistake, as well as a radical mean of denying an economical crisis. Though we do believe they are fundamentaly related by the schemes and paradigms of which they are both issued, the crisis does not appear as a direct consequence of the computerization development. We have shown that our "western civilization" - in fact a reading through Plato of the first chapter of Genesis - is based on the primacy of physical paradigms considered as the strongest weapon for mastering nature (if not ourselves) and for becoming masters of our own freedom and makers of history; the scientists of the last century were all aware of this concept, and Karl Marx himself relies heavily on it. The very foundation of our industry is mechanics (cf 3); what cannot be translated into mechanical concepts (eg space, time and mass) is not to be taken into account, the excuse being that such concepts are difficult to quantify and enter as data in the memory banks of a computer. (Notice the term "computer" used in the anglo-saxon world). Thus the climax of our society is mechanical science: industrial and classical managerial sciences, data processing, computers and organizational sciences appear as the essential tools needed to insure the "splendor" of our industrial age. Similarly, Weber (cf 4) showed long ago the importance of "protestantism" (a pessimistic view of life, emphasizing sin and damnation); Bjorn-Anderson and Weisenbaum (cf 5), myself and many others spoke in terms of rationalities.

This age clearly relies upon material industry and heavy manufactoring, combined with the idea that "work" (cf 6) must be enclosed in special places called "factories" and cannot be performed anywhere else (cf 7). These two pillars of the 19th century - industrial mecanism and emprisonment of work inside the factory - are threatened by telematics; this is probably the real reason why automation and especially telework develop at far slower rate than the literature would make us believe.

6) Thus appears an intimate relation between computerization, organizational theory and practice on one hand, and cultures on the other ; cultures differing from one type of organization to another, from country to country, continent to continent. Culture thus has an essential importance ; this calls for a more intricate and enriching analysis and tends to explain why authors like Gotlieb (cf 28), U. Briefs (cf 8) and Lorenzi-Pastré-Missika (cf 9) differ so widely in their conclusions, despite a rather coherent set of initial data. Our restriction to the case of Europe is also partly recommended by this particular problem.

7) Another difficulty : computerization is a rather recent process. Mass application started in the US in the mid 60 s, in Western Europe in the late 60 s. At that time the Western economies were in a booming phase of rapid growth and expansion. Such structural reasons for full employment made the influence of computers hard to measure and even detect.

This situation is now entirely different. The highly developed industrialized countries of the Western world presently seem in a deep economic crisis with the rather gloomy prospects of long-term stagnation. The conditions under which computerization is going on (and still gaining momentum) is an economic crisis and apparent long-term stagnation coinciding with high-level productivity increases. There is no apparent way out of such a solution within the existing logic. It become necessary to seek the satisfaction of new needs, which are currently disregarded because they are not expressed in the measurable fashion so convenient with consumer goods. In our economic and cultural system, there are no channels through which these needs can be expressed and taken into account (cf 1).

8) The development of E.D.P. is just beginning, and its very nature will evolve. Precise estimates are hard to ascertain, but a rough evaluation heavily relying on shopfloor experience could perhaps show that up to three or four years ago the positive and negative effects on employment were small and globally well balanced (at least in France, which seems to be quite different from other countries — compare for example 8 and 9).

This suggests a careful study of all the consequences of computerization; for instance, these can greatly differ for big computers or micro-processors, and depend on how the computer system and network are used. The balance must also be stated in dynamic terms for employment, and more especially in terms of strategy, wondering which one will induce globally positive effects on employment. Recall the example of the automobile industry, initially destroying employment, now providing 25% of the jobs. Of course, planification and participation of all social parties is an important factor, and so is time: abolishing 10.000 jobs in a particular branch bears a different economical and social meaning depending on whether it is spread over two or ten years, or on what is done to provide alternate employment to those laid off. The same is true for company and employment reconversion and variations of international contingencies.

Hence, in order to grasp the interconnections between short - and medium - term evolutions, we must reason in terms of flux rather than volume, even if static perception of available data is the starting-point of the analysis. And of course, evolutions, restrained by many human obstacles, are never as swift as specialists might imagine. Not so many wired cities will exist in any near future, as we can see illustrated by the "failures" of Trestel, Teletex, and the ambitious plans of Japan in the 70 s. Here again, historical realities may turn out quite different from mass media's description.

9) We must also take direct and indirect effects into account. Direct effects are the easiest to grasp: if the same employee can supervise two M.O.C.N.s simultaneously instead of running a single tool-machine, automation means a 50% employment cut-down. But the same operation may have other indirect effects, harder to calculate, and increasingly important as the integration of varied types of application grows more advanced. In our example, if a direct connection is made between the C.A.O. (Computer Assisted Conception) and M.O.C.N. (multi-functions permitted by an automatic tool changing device), a whole group of operations, formally depending on the methods department, can be disposed of with the help of the engineers in the study department. Then, what will the new work and labor organization be?

For instance, what will be the effects on employment of generalizing the Telefax system (telecopy making possible distance communication of documents through the telephone) ? This will bear little consequence on the mailing inside companies, but indirect effects on the mail are likely to be important, since the business mail makes up 60 % of current mailing, and a big part of that could be handled by Telefax.

10) We must also consider yet another important fact : there is no simple relation between canceling a particular work-post and reducing employment. Indeed,the disappearence of a particular work-post may well be compensated by the creation of another (possibly held by the same employee, which means only a transfer with a change in the nature of the job) or by the appearance of new needs (for instance, upkeep and maintainance of automatic machinery). On the other hand, automation often implies an increase in posted work ; the passage from 2 x 8 schedule to a 3 x 8 schedule increases by 50 % the number of jobs per post, and this increase might partialy compensate the decrease in the number of posts.

One last remark : most analysis, including ours, are based on Occident. As Western-built computers tend to become a universal norm, we tend to forget the third world, its ressources, its cultures. How will such an environment adapt to the Western tools of automation, and how can the tool be adapted, if at all, to very different cultures. Without going into this difficult problem, we only want to point out that the changes required by the development of automation need not be an asset for better harmony between different nations and different countries. If it turns out to be impossible to adapt automation to such different cultures (eg if the very concept of a computer is essentially Western), the practical effect could be the destruction of many cultures, consequence of their contact with Western culture that has so often shown a tendency towards cultural imperialism, little tolerance for cultural particularisms, and little interest for the right to difference.

Quite a few voices have made themselves heard to warn about the disastrous effects of computerization on the number of jobs (but, must we add, all other things remaining equal, ie if nothing changes in society to adapt to new conditions); let us sum up these voices, add the voices of workers themselves, those who were or are affected by computerization, let us believe the opinion of systems' planners and E.D.P. managers. We then have sufficient evidence to support the idea that the growing process of informatization is a job-destroying technology, probably one of the most powerful labour saving technologies ever invented. This very fact is indeed the main argument for the producers of these systems and technologies: if we analyse the very logic and structure of E.D.P. systems, we see that its main tendency is to replace human work. Nowadays, only a small fraction of E.D.P. applications really constitutes new activities (building of hardware and software,...).

This crisis induces capitalists to favor investments over salaried work. E.D.P. has rapidly become a field for major investments. On the other hand, it often constitutes no more than "rationalization investment", i.e. investments aiming at increasing productivity without necessarily expanding production. Indeed, it accounts partially but substantially for the fact that the share of rationalization investment in total annual investment has increased since the beginning of the 70s, especially if we include microprocessors and bureautics.

Should we then conclude that since computerization is by its primary aim a substitude to human work, it contributes and will increasingly contribute to gloomy perspectives for the mass of workers ? This has to be seen in very close connection with overall economic development, which is apparently condemned to a long period of stagnation and economic crisis. Must we agree for instance with the Nora-Minc report, which foresees that about 30 % of white collars will be unemployed in the next years ?

After summing up the different tendencies, opinions and impressions, must we conclude that current technologies constitute a far-reaching threat to employment and workers — this includes computerization, its basic structure and its underlying rationality (scientism, mechanism and taylorism) ? But if there are real massive negative effects of computerization on the labor market, must they be linked to the "essence" of computer systems or to the organization of social systems, in a context of adverse economic conditions ?

III - <u>CHANGING TASKS AND JOBS, THE CASE OF THE BANK</u>

We have summed up the arguments that come into mind when first approaching the problem. But these are abstract ideas, conceived and presented as the product of a purely intellectual process, without supporting evidence from actual situations. In fact, we wholly disagree with all these argumentations, and especially with the Nora-Minc report, who are all only supported by a technological approach (which supposes among other things that technology is neutral and that nothing is to be changed in the organisation of society and of working habits). Such an approach supposes a forecasting and not a prospective mind, and gives little weight to two facts:

1) Working hours need not remain constant : if there are less tasks to be performed, one can either diminish the number of workers, or decrease the number of work-hours. Indeed, most reports do not take into account the duration or intensity of work.

2) Neither the production nor the working process are invariable in nature.

Let us examine this second point. For that purpose let us consider how jobs will change and new jobs be created. Let us analyse the part played by the banking system before wondering how it can perform once it has been computerized (cf 10).

Banks have two different functions : (1) transferring funds and money (administrative function) ; (2) collecting deposits from many and granting loans to a few.

Much has been said on the first one, describing electronic message systems and different forms of cashless societies. Depending on the different possible schemes, we can deduce quite accurately the consequences in terms of number of jobs, quantify a mutation that will strongly increase the number of transactions and simultaneously reduce - even faster it seems - the cost in work hours of each transaction. One can also analyse (cf 11) changes in the work process and the way it is felt by white collars. One can wonder why they are more negative and more negatively felt in France than in Northern Europe.

In any case, this function, highly automatable, is less important than the loaning activity — especially from the viewpoint of employment. For this second function, modifications are far more fundamental.

Initially, moderate loans were granted to a household or a company by the head of each branch after a long discussion with the customer; the formalization of criteria seemed neither possible not desirable. The arrival of computers put an end to that era: in almost every case, the loan is now granted, refused or at least deeply influenced by a standard decision-making program after computing the mathematical function of certain "ratios" defined and often stored outside the banks (for instance, the "Centrale des Bilans" held by the Banque de France). The staff and even head of each branch office then have no more control over the decision. The collective human know-how of the organization (here the branch office or even head office) is made no use of, the only ability made use of is an ability defined statistically OUTSIDE THE BANK and almost without any contact with human, social or historical realities.

This example shows the reduction and eventually disappearance of the staff's function and obviously of the cashiers'; the dispossessment of the individual and collective abilities of the bankers; a considerable transfer of power "justified" by an equally important transfer of knowledge; complete alienation of the whole staff; and the appearance of a new dialogue between customers and bankers, a very artificial and complex one. The customer is more or less conscious of the machine's criteria and will doctor his data so as to provide the most convincing ratios, or at least those he believes to be the most convincing. Managing a company no longer means being efficient and productive but rather being skilled in the handling and manipulation of figures devoid of any kind of real meaning (cf 10).

Nowaday's practices (collecting standardised data, using them together with a well-established abstract algorithm to compute how risky the grant will be) lead to a drastic reduction in the number of employees and deprive the managers of their responsibility. It also means disconsidering the real banking function, which relies on the special nature of the relationship with the customers: the dialogue over the sharpest peculiarities of his company's or household's management is not taken into account - not that it really is negligible, but it cannot be quantified and is therefore of no help for a computer program. We see here the catastrophical pregnance of the mechanical model: there is no place for any original idea, original management, original organization, original production. In the long run, this spells stagnation and eventually disaster for any economy.

On the other hand, suppose the economical and mangerial ratios, once carefully computed and statistically analysed, are considered as mere tools, helping the decision but not overthrowing human, social and political considerations - this means examining the company's originality; then on the contrary there will be more need for "bankers". The result is need for more workers and thus less unemployment, and also a much better management of both the bank and the company asking for funds. This also means that there is no standard way to manage an organization - and, by comparison, a unique and universally dominant set of criteria for evaluating a productive unit and its production. To sum up, it means that the myth of the one best way is to be done away with; it can at best be used as a first approximation to an evaluation which must then be refined and analysed by taking into account the specificity of the organization, its management, its culture and its utilities.

The same holds for the health function: once a physician has analysed the results of his examination, his job is not merely to mechanically assign the right pills and drugs. More and more he must then take into account the whole medical history of his patient, and his environment. The same can be said of the teaching function: E.A.O. is of no use without a human help to the student.

MORE PRECISELY TAKING REAL ADVANTAGE OF COMPUTERIZATION TO ACHIEVE MORE AMBITIOUS
GOALS WILL REQUIRE MORE LABOR; BUT OF A DIFFERENT KIND. THE DECREASE IN WORK HOURS
HOLDS ONLY IN A FIXED ENVIRONMENT, WITH AN UNALTERABLE ORGANIZATIONAL PARADIGM,
AND THE RULING MYTH OF THE LAPLACIAN "ONE BEST WAY".

Thus it would seem that the most important and urgent task is the working out of
new organizational and managerial sciences. Such an elaboration must clearly originate from an exhaustive study, from a clinical and social point of view, of a
great many number of different cases. Such a task must be a joint work, with close
association of academics and workers. To sum ourselves up, the central problem is
the dual problematic of new needs and of new types of organizations.

To conclude this first analysis, it is a swindle to state that computerization
implies unemployment if one doesn't add: all other things remaining unchanged.
This means in the current state of society, and if we still trust the dominant
paradigm, and mainly if we leave uncriticized the very nature of goods and services and the working process. These are also related to the dominant rationality
(cf 5).

The two examples we have expanded as well as many others clearly illustrate how
computerization can be used to fulfill new ambitions and to create a many new
jobs, at the price of more qualification and responsibility among the workers. For
example, a bank employee could still make use of the classical ratios, which are
quite valuable if correctly interpreted, (which requires a sense of relativity
and a good dose of humor). He would then have to know to shape a complex judgement,
subjectively taking into account all human elements - a process similar to the
passage from a-priori to a-posteriori probabilities.

Finally, the prophecies of the Nora-Minc report can be contradicted; but for this
to happen, it is essential to undergo a radical change of aims and goals of our
society. More emphasis must be given to a social-oriented rather than matter-
oriented logic, to the right - even the duty - to difference, with equal status
and mutual respect. This will bring to notice a whole group of new needs, new services and goods currently neglected.

WE WOULD THEN HAVE A DIFFERENT ECONOMIC GROWTH, THUS A STRONG ONE.

IV - A NEW MANAGERIAL PARADIGM

Thus a new type of decisions requires a new managerial science and a new work organization. Apart from the computer's software and hardware, we would like to
stress the importance of dataware (collective memory's semantic and managerial
sciences). We will consider this huge field in the following paragraph. It is too
often overlooked by academics, workers and even computer manufacturers, whose main
goal is often merely to sell a certain type of goods, with little concern for software, let alone the complex interconnection between computers and organization,
information and power, management and work organization.

a) A lot of new tasks and new jobs.

Not only must there be changes in the current functions, but also new functions
need to be created, in order to better satisfy existing needs and to satisfy new
social needs. How than can one be so sure that unemployment will increase? It
would seem on the contrary that need will be for more work.

New tasks in hardware and software of course, and in manufacturing, program writing and maintainance. There are a great number of jobs that cannot be automated,
and therefore create a monnegligible number of jobs. This seems clear if one stri-
ves to create not universal packages, but rather individualized packages, designed
for a particular task and a particular client: technological advances in programming and micro-processors make precisely that quite feasible now.

b) Jobs, tasks and functions.

Before considering new tasks, let us point out that reasoning in terms of jobs is
a rather poor approach. We have seen the bank employee change profession with the
arrival of computers, he will now have to change again. The same holds for the
doctor: he first was a comforter before the existence of really useful therapies.
He then became a statistician when he searched the memory of medical science for the
case closest to the one in question, and the most adequate known treatment (providing almost automatic answers). Now he must also be a psychosomatist: once he has
listened to the patient, analysed the symptoms and given a short-term solution to
the preliminary problem of healing, he then must come back to a wholistic and humane
view of the problem for a deeper and more complete solution.

The problem is: what are the needs and how can all the citizens be trained for
the satisfaction of those needs. From this question comes the very rich concept
of "function", ie the set of all the effort collectively made in order to fulfill
such or such a need. For example the medical function is not restricted to the
sole specialists (doctors, nurses,...), but consists of all the efforts the people
collectively and more or less consciously make in order to improve the global state
of health. The same holds for other functions that could be similarly defined. The
information function will not remain the monopoly of professional informaticians,
but will increasingly become a data administration function, in other words concerned with datawaring.

c) How to reason: jobs versus functions.

Of course, reasoning in terms of functions denies too rigid a separation between
different fields, different skills, different jobs; it sets the stage for an enriching pluridisciplinary dialogue between different cultures and different workers. Job changes then become easier, and skills become more precise.

We now come back to the datawaring function, which here is more of our particular
concern, apart from being a typical example.

V - THE DATAWARING FUNCTION.

a) What are data?

We call data "anything which is sufficiently well defined, measured, codified,
"formated" so that it can be fed in a computer memory" (cf 12).

Notice that:
        . the fact that the reference is through a computer system is not neutral.
Furthermore, this definition supposes that data and computers are the high point
of our culture, the "ministers" of our "seriousness". Note that the important part
is not to actually encode say my weight or height, but simply that such an enco-
ding is possible without epistemological difficulty, and that the measuring instruments exist.

. our whole science is built in such a way so that can be highly or "nobly" considered only those branches which are essentially based on space, masse or time (this can be stretched to money, here considered as a standard of reference). Such an attitude is biased: our "seriousness", as well as our whole industry, is based on mechanistic paradigms.

. in fact, our real concern is "data/models". They are closely related: both can be manipulated by a computer (this similarity in the treatment of data and models is the basic discovery of Von Neumann); data cannot exist without a model sketching a view of the world, and models are useless without the corresponding data.

. data (from now on, every time we speak of data, we will be thinking of this concept of data/model) is a specific way to interpret nature corresponding to a specific point of view, a specific finality. There are no universal data, all data are subjective, they illustrate a restricted part of reality under the assumption of a given model, and rationalize a given type of decision-making.

More generally, creating new data is just another technological tool; we have shown (cf 14) how it is a specifically human trait to know how to build up in one or two generations special extensions of our senses that enable us to better understand an aspect of reality, better appreciate a potential danger, and better define our aims. Animals and other living creatures have a given set of sense organs, almost beyond bettering: how many generations did the bacteria require to define the message: "there is streptomicin in the air around here"?

b) Data nunquam data.

Its quite surprising to see that data are never actually given.

. No datum can be a simple answer to a simple question to nature. Physical tools and concepts always interfere. "What length is this table?" is not such a simple question. The number of unemployed, the G.N.P., the number of working hours, or the salary are even less "raw"; they suppose the interference of controversies and representations.

. no data is objective: the status of objectivity implies both observations which can be exactly reproduced and experienced without any influence on the phenomena. This is a double impossibility, especially in the field of decision, were we know that coherence rather than objectivity is the main goal (cf 3).

. other reasons prevent data from being given: they are almost never free to get, and are not easily transmitted, since they are loaded (or supposed to be loaded) with power, in their definition (which we call semiocracy) as well as in their reading.

Clearly the power lies not in the possibility of access (that would make telephone girls the top of the hierarchy), but in the possibility of reading, understanding, and especially defining data: whoever reasons only in terms of G.N.P. or financial ratios is prematurely trapped, his freedom of decisions is very small. We already noted how this leads to conservatism and to a social and human waste.

c) An ill-used ressource and a little-practiced function (cf 13).

The organization's semantics is a particularily interesting field of studies and a huge source of employment.

. Data/models and goals are closely related in an organization: (we called this metascience). The knowledge of data in an organization - the manner in which it has coded and mathematified its collective memory - illustrates its goals, those pursued and those which consciously or not it refused to acknowledge. This initial analysis already gives a lot of information on the organizations, their culture and the relations between power knots and information flows. The contraposite procedure may turn out even more interesting: the knowledge of the many goals and interests of an organization can hint at what data are relevant.

. Thus semantics and power are related; any study of data implies a study of the goals; it becomes a political study, if we take that word to mean thinking over the global social choices, defining means and priorities, and location of power.

. Without such a careful consideration of data, one cannot avoid the huge waste which we can currently note. On one hand certain crucial data are not available and prevent efficient decisions; on the other, too many incoherent data can be a disaster. From one organization to another, even one service to the other, concepts such as work hours, clients, market, housing are given different meanings, as the logical consequence of different point of views, cultures and goals. We find a dozen different definitions of a late train or of night work - each one illustrating a different balance of powers.

In no way do we mean that vocabulary should be limited, and a one-and-only definition of a late train, the G.N.P. or inflation rate should be agreed upon. On the contrary, there should be as many definitions as there are goals and constraints to consider, but clearly keeping track of data-gathering processes and meanings. Only at this condition can confusion be avoided.

. We have already noted (cf the examples of bankers) that the semantic choices are not made by the official power-holder (in our example, bank officials are dispossessed, decisions are now made by the central "Banque de France" and an administrative school which closely mirrors the dominant point of view of twenty years ago); not to mention, of course, workers and users (cf 10 & 21).

d) Datawaring and industrial democracy.

If we want to increase the information system efficiency (not just computer capacity) and establish better concertation between social partners (inside or outside the company), isn't the simplest way to act on the information system itself and on its data? Indeed, we have seen that working closely with the different parties concerned (capital holders, workers, consumers, sub-contractors, local and national collectivities, etc...) requires that one mode of expression - technically and ideologically related to a unique school of thought - cannot become dominant, leaves some space for other complementary points of view.

From this analysis springs the idea to collectively create a set of social indicators. We can already note an important potential for creativity created in those countries where concertation already exists (this includes industrial democracy for planification and data control, criteria for control and management, and eventually management itself). This process of generalizing concertation to semantics further extends the positive effects; this field seems more neutral, more easily understood and very efficient in the short run (this is no negligible asset); it also helps to render social debates less passionate by introducing a scientific character built together by management, staff and unions, more generally all the partners concerned inside or outside the company; NO ONE PARTY CAN AB INITIO BIAS THE DEBATE THROUGH THE SEMANTIC IT INTRODUCES. One cannot expect rapid results from such a relational policy. Note that here the staff has an essential part to play, by simplifying and demystifying its own language, the jargon

currently used by managers and computer scientists (now the sole protection of
their power). Many resistances will appear, a huge educational effort is needed
starting from the current state of habits, know-how, culture and managerial
technics at all levels of the company. We will shortly dwell on that problem.

e) What must absolutely be avoided.

In France, a lot of technocrats - never consulting trade unions - define a lot of
data to be legally included in what they call the social account, and every organization must publish the corresponding figures; no account is taken of the
company's originality. Needless to say, nobody is interested in such an artificial social balance, except some statisticians from the Secretary of Industry!
Our point is the exact opposite: the right to as many balances as there are organizations, whose data are to be determined - conflictually of course - by all
the social partners, taking into account their specificities, their habits, their
culture and their environment.

f) The risk of getting lost.

Of course, there are risks involved in this multiplication of data: a "babeli-
zation" may occur, even if this could be viewed as an needed counterpart for the
current tendency towards over-unifying languages. This can only be avoided through
an important effort toward transparency, clearness, awareness to others and
humility. We must learn to give rise to and to listen to the differences, instead
of hiding them off as is done only too often (for example by using one word or
one concept in a various number of circumstances, when background or even data
collecting processes give them widely different meanings).

      . Building a semantic is a long-term task. One or two generations are
needed to sharpen tools as precise as the accounting data currently used (cf 15,
16 & 17). Besides, definitions evolve because problems and methods are increasingly better known and because goals, needs and constraints evolve.

      . Such a work can only be collective, because it requires a thorough
understanding of different knowledges and knows-hows. It can only be the task of
educated citizens (cf 18), masters of their destiny, and provided with vast
amounts of time. These prerequisites, especially the last one, require an evolution of the whole educational system; we'll come back to that point after two
remarks.

      . As far as management is concerned, software, hardware and dataware
fit together inside an organization which they help to change. The computer industry in a country cannot merely build machinery; it must also think over new
types of architecture, new data and new types of relationships related to a new
kind of management. Beyond software we must get to the very logic of an organization, and analyse (with the help of the consumers) alternate systems, work organization, structure and data. Unfortunately, this field is almost unexplored;
we're thinking for instance about cooperation with the third world, with small
companies, with cooperative companies, more generally with any type of organization.

      . The dialogue with the consumers must also be led with clarity, not
the esoterism so common with computer scientists. For more on this idea, we send
the reader to all the TC.9 work session, and in particular the two congresses
"Human choice and computers" and the last Riva del Sol (nov. 82) who'se title
was precisely "System design for users, with users and by users" (cf 21 & 25).
This requires refusing the artificial separation between working hours and leisure hours, this old fordian notion. Currently each function (health, education,
work, baby-bearing,...) is attached to a specific emprisoning location (hospital,
school, factory, home,...) (cf 7).

VI - THE CORRESPONDING EDUCATIONAL EFFORT.

a) Its location and its goals.

It follows from above that all artificial separations (like the one between school, factory or manufacture, personal life and consuming time) are to be avoided in order to preserve the unity of man and of society in its whole. The education system is a whole; working habits must be considered as part of the educational system. We must also remember scientific vulgarisation, where experts should expose, for their own good as much as for the reader's, their working hypothesis, their conclusions, their scientific methods and the link between them. As of yet, certain aspects of managerial sciences (for example writing a complex algorithm for operational research) can only be performed by a small number of specialists. Such a program aims to optimize the goals under constraint; the definition of goals then becomes deeply imbedded in the program, not to be decided by those they currently concern. The first role of experts chosen by different parties (union experts for example) is not to check the good or bad faith of the computer scientist, but to question whether he might have unconsciously betrayed the complex aims he was to optimize.

The educational system here viewed as a whole must convey a spirit and a culture as well as precise skills. Such a spirit must be pluridisciplinary - the concept of function precisely emphasizes that very point - a spirit refusing the separation of contents of men and knowledge, favoring the possibility for every one to choose alternatives on the social, technological and organizational level, favoring trahsparency and the ability to listen to others; this we regrouped under humor, humility and honesty (our three "H"s). Such an educational system must be built in order to help every one to understand the organizations in which he lives: power and information knots, and freedom locations, basis of his development as well as his company's.

We must not forget that any organization is a goal-oriented set of resources, AND THUS A STRUGGLE AGAINST NATURE TO CREATE HISTORY. An organization has many optimization networks, but must also allow thinking over common goals; without that, local minimums can induce global disasters - of this we have only too many examples: the director of the Amoco-Cadiz, whose job was to cut down transportation costs, was right in doing what he did, but the lack of coordination and common reflection over global goals resulted in a disaster on the breton coasts, whose cost is far greater than the economy it was meant to realize.

In an organization, we thus find some goal-oriented systems, and some optimizing systems. The former can very well be taken in charge by all; the latter are more technical, a task for specialists who can be trusted insofar as they are transparent. In other words, the classical question of "HOW", must be preceded by the question of "WHAT FOR" of even of "WHY" or "FOR WHOM". The main positive result of the meeting of managerial sciences held in November 82 in Paris is precisely that: for the first time in France, the need-oriented questions where asked before the technological questions (cf 1). An organization is the product of, and then creates, a culture and a history; thus the desire to learn history and epistemology, and to take one's destiny in one's own hand (what in France is called "autogestion") are basic qualities for a citizen. On this particular point, note the following:

. any one who wants to more or less assume his own destiny will encounter many cultural difficulties, as we bear the stamp of almost two centuries of Taylorism and 25 centuries of Platonicism (cf 2). The problem is so much more difficult because trusting scientism is quite restful and an excellent way to accumulate material goods - the only risk being to lose one's originality. We need

only to accept the deal proposed by Dostoievski's Grand Inquisitor: give us all
power, renounce all freedom, we will give you strength and glory (cf 25).

. any scientistic paradigm refuses all difference. We have yet to build
a science tolerating differences, i.e. a science where internal coherence will
take the place of objectivity.

. we want to emphasize more particularly one last obstacle to the participation of every individual in the organization: the perception of time. Each
one of us has a different temporal horizon, this is one of the crucial sources of
social inequality. A basic factory worker is taught to reason on the short term
of his everyday acts, highly automated tasks. The overseer thinks on the level of
a day, the engineer on a month, the director on a couple of years, and the general manager is supposed to compute on a 20 years basis. This is the only clear
criteria that explains the hierarchical differences. This was proved especially in
France during the attempt to enrich tasks: the factory worker seemed hardly able
to think on the level of a whole day, and should he succeed, the overseers would
see his particular function already taken care of, and would become useless.

The main problem seems to be to enlarge personal temporal horizon, and to give to
the greatest possible number a prospective view of situations. Prevision is a
simple extrapolation of the past, but what we call a prospective view is more:
time is the time of history, not of physics; it is also volitional and based on
a political analysis of social evolution, basis of democratic planification. If
need was, this would confirm the necessity to develop creativity, thinking over
needs, the sense of time, and the essential quality of listening to others and
respecting other cultures.

b) Two French examples

Let us rapidly describe two French experiences, one five years old, the other attempted last year.

The Secretary of education had accepted that in certain voluntary high schools
four or five teachers of all origins would meet during three days on the theme:
"what is ...". They were asked to choose the subject (what is a student, what is an
inhabitant of the city, what is a healthy man, what is family revenue, what is an
unemployed, etc...). Little more was needed to initiate a fascinating discussion,
and people would rapidly realize the part played by data and the difficulty encountered in defining them (cf 19).

During a university program on the subject "computers applied to management", till
then a very technology-oriented course, a section was set up on the idea that a
computer scientist who only knows how to write programs or perform functional analysis will rapidly become useless, in a time when hardware and even software problems are relatively easy to solve, when consumers feel concerned, and when problems are more political, power-seeking, goal-defining rather than problem that
can be solved by the good usage of available material. In this section, the importance of culture and habits was heavily and successfully stressed, as well as the
relationship between paradigms of organizational techniques, of working habits,
the manner in which the consumer's wishes are or are not fulfilled, and the type
of production. Of course, we also covered the subject of evaluation: the
decision-making criteria, promotion criteria for each individual, and social criteria for the company. Here like elsewhere, the most important is to encourage
thinking over alternate models (cf 20).

c) The other functions

All we just described for the datawaring remains true for the other functions of any organization: for example the "communication" function, covering both the human and the more formalized data communication.

We now run into the very important problem or the relationship between communication system and technology, and there is evidence that a communication system which relies too heavily on a technological intermediary (micro-processors or cables) runs the risk of an uncontrolled blooming of communications which is in reality a deep improverishment. This probably explains partial failure of experiences like Prestel or Teletex which are less and less used, except as toys or certain special well-designed systems.

Anyhow, we are entering an age where the important people will be those who know how to listen, to pinpoint the needs and propose technico-organizational alternatives. This required creative, non-conformist minds, with an extended culture, a feel for history and a personal humility. The datawaring function is quite typical in that respect, but other fields also give a prospective glimpse of a future industrial democracy. The first task is to do away with expert secrecy, the myth of the one best way, and any form of esoterism.

VII - HOW NOT TO BE LUDIST

As we have seen, hanging into the current hierarchy of values (in particular scientism) and to current practices might well transform this "gift of fire" into a dangerous and deadly danger (cf introduction of that book). There has to be a third choice apart from destroying computers or committing suicide. Negative prophelies like the Nora-Minc report are ideological points of view, analysing realities which evolve much more slowly than is usually said: the wired city and telework are still far in the future. It is quite amusing to note that at least in France, a technology is so much more studied when it has little chance of becoming reality. The "damage" of progress (cf 24) also point out at the possible dangers of a brutal computerization of society, instead of socializing (ie giving back to man) computer technology.

Our stand is more optimistic, and we hope more realistic. We have striven to show that possible alternatives can be found, at the condition of changing in a rather radical way the educational system and the very concepts of work and of need which this system transmits.

Our demonstration is mainly based on examples chosen in the branch of services, but the same would hold for other activities: for example, we could have analysed the function and related skills of managing stock. The solutions require a general broadening of all human abilities, starting with his temporal horizon and his right or duty to difference - and by difference we do not mean that an individual need be excluded from power because he has a different system of ideas and opinions, but merely that one particularity gives him the possibility to judge from the very standpoint of his particularity. Tomorrow's world will require many varied skills, first of them all the art of listening. Of course experts will still be needed, but the main task will be the synthesis between different cultures, different practices, and different know-hows. We believe that the development of computer technology, which made this change unavoidable, will also make it possible; for instance, it will create a considerable amount of leisure time which can be used for educational purposes, at work or at home. It will make possible a brandnew hierarchisation necessary for a better unfolding of an electronic information system able to produce a much more varied array of goods and services. It will also enable a more decentralised structure of decision-making. Computer science is now a high point of the mecanistic tayloric though, but could be the high point of a paradigm based on the human being and his differences.

The main problem is the will to change.

VIII - FACING NEW TECHNOLOGIES AND NEW WORKING PROCESSES

We would like to conclude by stressing that computerization is a great mutation of our society (by computerization, we mean not only the use of computer systems, but also a rationality that appears as the achievement and the apex of an industrial paradigm). We can analyse neither this change nor its consequences in classical terms and classical criteria of evaluation (such criteria work for an evolution, but are useless in the case of such a radical and brutal change). It will take a rather long time to build the necessary institutional tools to analyse it, as the sociological work is slower than the technical evolution. But what a fascinating task! Perhaps the major task of our generation, to be done by workers, trade unions, researchers, consumers, and in last analysis, by all the citizens. One example will be enough here: the manner in which telework is evaluated clearly forces to think over the use of factories, the rigidity of work, the use of free time, and the various concepts of "time" (cf 6). Here we can wonder why so many studies on telework and so little practical applications.

What is the relation between technological mutations and the different types of needs and production, the way of thinking, putting forth the question "what to produce" rather than "how to produce" - a whole new set of questions. Let us assume that trying to solve progressively those questions will mobilize everyone's energies, create more work rather than unemployment - if of course that productive time is not separated from thinking time: both must grow together. Let us go on analysing the conditions for a cultural, educational, political, structural and technological change. A different meaning will be given to work and efficiency, a now educational system will be geared to freedom, industrial democracy will penetrate in the company and in the home.

Computers can be very helpful for all that: they are growing cheaper, at least as far as hardware is concerned, but one must keep in mind that alone, they are unable to solve human, social and political problems, especially with the data and models currently in use. Above all we need free citizens educated to assume their duty to be different, in the equalization of status - the exact contrary of the taylorien myth of the "one best way". Toppler (cf 27) has a point when he says that a third wave, based on the power of computerization, can use computers with memories so big they would be able to make use of a great number of information on every individual, thus taking in better account each one's personality, resulting in a more complex and human management than in the first over-simplifying machines. I don't share such an optimism, because though the computer's very power can be used to help human freedom, it is in no way a sufficient weapon. A blind and irrational trust in the dominant rationality is no good enough reason to believe that things automatically tend towards the best solution. On the contrary, tools now exist but cannot do the job alone: they must be complemented by a change of culture, of science, of paradigms, of data and or organization. We sum this in three points: duty to tolerate differences and even encourage it, taking in account all knowledge, not just quantifiable knowledge, and a new educational system and social ethic. Of course this task will be long and difficult, which is a good reason to get started right away, by building new paradigms and new data, and by using what we already have, however inadequate it may be, but using it with enough humility, humor and common sense to overcome the impoverishment of reality it supposes.

This article was concerned with employment. We have illustrated our belief that new kinds of organizations and cultures can help avoid the risk of a rising unemployment and will also lead to a more efficient society. The transition period, longer than is usually thought, is the only troublesome period.

INTRODUCTION GENERALE : LE CONCEPT DE "BESOIN" TOME 1.   pp2-6

(1) Les Assises des Sciences des Organisations (AFCET-CESTA
     Paris - Novembre 1982)

(2) J.L. RIGAL................... Faits et données de la conclusion occidentale
                                   (cahier 50 - Université Paris IX/Dauphine,
                                   no. 18. 1982)

(3) La Quantification en Sciences Sociales (Table ronde CNRS - Brive 1979)

(4) Max WEBER.................... Gesammelte Aufsätze zur Religion Soziologie

(5) TC.9 Human Choice and Computers 1 (Vienne 1975) 2 (Baden 1979)
                                   North Holland Publ.

(6) J.L. RIGAL................... Le temps du travail (publié Lesseps
                                   Université de Paris IX/Dauphine - 1982)

(7) Michel FOUCAULT.............. Surveiller et punir (Gallimard, Paris 1975)

(8) U. BRIEFS.................... Computerization and employment. The relation-
                                 ship between technology, productivity and em-
                                 ployment (Computers in Industry 2. 1981
                                 pp 259-266) TC. Publication (Conference in
                                 Budapest)

(9) MISSIKA..................... Informatisation et emploi : menace ou mutation
                                 (Inf. et Soc ; Documentation Française
                                 n° 11-1981

(10) Journée du Parti Socialiste Français "Informatique et Socialisme"
                                 (Paris C.S.L. 1980)

(11) KJAER...................... R.O.S.A.C.

(12) J.L. RIGAL................. Brave New Dataware (IFIP Tokyo 19) ou Publica-
                                 tion LESSEPS, 1973)

(13) J.L. RIGAL................. La fonction statistique (CEREQ. Paris 1972 ou
                                 Publication LESSEPS, 1973)

(14) J.L. RIGAL................. La régulation socioculturelle (Publication
                                 Collège de France, Paris, 1978)

(15) J.L. RIGAL................. Les mutations technologiques (in réf. 1 :
                                 tome 1, pp 165-172 et tome 3)

(16) M. LESCA................... Compétitivité, structure et système d'informa-
                                 tion de l'entreprise (thèse universitaire,
                                 Grenoble 1981)

(17) F. LEFEBVRE................ Du traitement à l'administration de l'informa-
                                 tion (Information et Gestion, Paris,
                                 avril 1982)

(18) J.L. RIGAL................. Towards Date Conscions Citizens (IFIP Nelbour-
                                 ne et Publication LESSEPS)

(19) J.L. RIGAL................. Initiation à la pensée statistique (Publica-
                                 tion LESSEPS, 1980)

(20) J.L. RIGAL................. Une option "administrateurs de données"
                                 (Publication LESSEPS, 1982)

(21) J.L. RIGAL................. Consultation with users : a new paradigm and a
                                 new culture (TC.9 Congress at Riva del Sole,
                                 September 1982)

(22) N. COOLEY.................... The architect and the bee : the hussman/
                                   technology relation (Services, Langley Techn.
                                   1980)

(23) C.F.D.T..................... Les dégâts du progrès (Editions du Seuil,
                                   Paris, 1974)

(24) U.C.C., C.F.D.T............. Journée U.C.C.-C.F.D.T. revue "Cadres" n° 297,
                                   février 1981

(25) ORWELL...................... 1984 (London, 1944)

(26) DOSTOIEWKY.................. Karamazov Brothers (1879-1880)

(27) TOPPLER..................... The third wave (London 1980)

(28) GOTLIEB..................... R.O.S.A.C. (introduction) A gift from fire

(29) B. CORIAT.................. Robots et automates dans les industries de sé-
                                  ries : esquisse d'une économie de robotique
                                  d'atelier (rencontre de ADEP)
                                  Chantilly les mutations technologiques,
                                  12-19 septembre 1980 C.R.S.G. (54, Bd Desgran-
                                  ges - 92330 SCEAUX - FRANCE)

Several of the articles can be ordered at Publication LESSEPS (Université de Paris IX/Dauphine - 75775 PARIS CEDEX WVI - FRANCE).

Information Technology and Skills: Problems in Research and Politics[+]

Herbert Kubicek

Department of Buisness Administration, Economics and Sociology, University of Trier, D-5500 Trier, FRG

In this paper the real life problems of technology induced
changes in skills are confronted with the scientific problems of
gaining clear cut empirical and theoretical insights. After a
review of the state of the art of empirical research polarization
theory will be presented as the dominant interpretation. Then
two lines of criticism of polarization theory and their practical
consequences are discussed. It will be shown that depending on
the theoretical assumptions different practical consequences are
derived but that the controversy over these assumptions from a
workers point of view is still open.

1. The Given Situation: Confusion and Conflicts in the Scientific and Political Debate

For some time now, it is generally accepted, that the computerization of information processing changes both job skill requirements and - in the longer view -
requisite occupational skills. A large number of empirical studies, which are mostly
based on the theoretical framework underlying organizational theory and only to a
lesser extent on that related to industrial sociology, analyze these changes. Politicians, trade unionists and employers have also been discussing this issue thereby
either citing one or the other research study or referring to personal experience
based on their individual theoretical considerations.

Social scientists primarily focused on identifying predominant upgrading or downgrading tendencies in skill levels.[1] Their research activities, however, have not yet
provided a clearcut description of and precise explanation for these changes. And a
closer examination of political statements also reveals a large amount of confusion
about present and future trends, about underlying assumptions, and, most of all,
about necessary measures for avoiding, or at least minimizing negative social
consequences and detrimental effects on workers.

There are apparently two basic reasons for this confusion: First, a lack of clarity
about the social implications of skills and skill changes, and second, a general
uncertainty about the appropriate political instruments for controlling the economic
and social development of a so-called developed industrial society facing several
crises at the same time. This general uncertainty obviously also influences the more
specific issues discussed in this paper. This uncertainty also makes most of the
completed research in this problem area rather doubtful. For the sake of empirical
operationalization and statistical analysis, the highly respected and scientifically
rigorous research approaches define their problem under investigation as an
examination of the relationship between the two variables information technology
and skills. In using this approach, they neglect the social implications of skills and

+)   This paper has been written in 1981. The author wishes to thank Dipl.-Kfm. B.
      Pool-Brosi for the translation of a German draft of this paper.

the potential for conflict inherent in technology induced skill changes. Thus, the gap between research and politics is growing larger and larger, but remains unnoticed by both sides.

Especially those researchers which base their investigations on an organizational theory framework, tend to neglect the social conflicts posed by the problem of technology induced skill changes. This conflict potential exists because, for the individual worker, occupational skills mean more than challenging jobs, opportunities for self actualization, job satisfaction, social status and other aspects related to organizational psychology. For the dependent wage-earner, occupational skills also reflect the achievable market value of work effort. For the individual worker, then, higher skills embody higher attainable wages, greater means of subsistence, and, most important, a better safeguard against unemployment. The employer in the profit-oriented enterprise system, on the other hand, must strive to pay the lowest possible price for whatever skills he requires. As technology induced skill changes inevitably change the relative prices for the factors of production, these price changes determine the firm's factor-utilization decisions which include those on technological innovation. This illustrates why the two sides of the labour market are so much in controversy on the issue of technology induced skill changes: in order to prevent demotions, unions firmly oppose downgrading skill levels.

The issue also addresses employment and educational policy. Recent years have shown substantial increases in the relative number of unemployed unskilled labourers. This census group is apparently unusually susceptible to unemployment. During the same observation period, however, the demand for selected higher-level skills has continuously exceeded their supply. This supports the hypothesis that today's downgraded skill levels embody tomorrow's hardcore unemployment. In sum, it can be argued that technology induced skill changes have destabilizing effects on the labour market. For the most part, arising frictions must be compensated by the individual worker. Inadequate labour market related forecasting tools and inappropriate control mechanisms inevitably generate frictions in educational areas.[2] Vocational training elements, for instance, can't be adjusted in time to the economy's changed skill demands if technological development and resulting changes in requisite skills can't be predicted with some degree of accuracy and sufficiently beforehand. Without this data, much of an individual's and society's investments in schooling could be wasted. The assumption of predominantly upgraded/downgraded skills furthermore raises questions about the economically justifiable relative numbers of high/low skilled workers and the relative value of the various levels of education.

The above statements indicate that conflicts in the interrelationships of technology, employment and education policy have increased, both in number and in scope.[3] The two sides of the labour market contribute still other conflicts.[4] The individual firm cannot evade the issue: political measures and industrial relations both provide the premises for respective decisions in industry and in individual firms which influence changes in skill levels in one of either ways.

The traditional approach to resolving society's problems related to employment and education policy via an aggregate of entrepreneurial profit-oriented decision-making no longer seems acceptable. Instead, demands for systematic personnel planning and for changes in job evaluation methods are gaining momentum; demands for a more forceful pursuance of employee concerns via a stronger enforcement of the participatory rights, both of shop stewards as defined in the Betriebsverfassungsgesetz ("Works Constitution Act") and of workers' representatives on the board as defined by the Mitbestimmungsgesetz ("Codetermination Act") plus realigned collective bargaining guidelines for technology agreements are growing louder.

On a societal level, policy makers responsible for resolving technology induced social frictions appear helpless. The Federal Ministry for Research and Technology has attempted to introduce new dimensions into technology policy, which formerly focused almost entirely on goals concerned with the "modernization of industry".

Proposed readjustments of research funding guidelines have promised to provide funds for research investigating the social consequences of information technology ("impact research").[5] Other developments, as for instance employment and education policy related problems, a fear of labour unrest, and the fear of new conflicts within the Social-Democratic-Party, have led the Minister to invite the labour market parties for a "Dialogue on Technology Policy".[6] Both measures, however, have not yet yielded practical consequences. The proposition for readjustments in research funding was repealed, the only result of the "Dialogue" was the joint request for further in-depth research.

All efforts aimed at resolving perceived shortcomings of control strategies are hampered not only by conflicting interests and by implementational constraints, but also by substantial information gaps in data and theory. These data and theory deficits, in fact, seem to be so enormous in scope that all attempts at designing an appropriate long-term problem-solving approach may fail for just this reason alone.

Policy makers and leaders in industry and unions have tried to overcome their helplessness by assigning a substantial number of projects to research institutes - as they have been doing for almost 25 years now. The few studies showing clearcut statements are rather speculative in their underlying approach, and more or less reflect an attempted conformity with the respective commissioner's position. In many cases, however, these studies conclude that empirical evidence prohibits consistent statements on future developments.[7]

This illustrates policy makers' and other decision-makers' helplessness in the true sense of the word. Social scientists are apparently not able to provide the appropriate theoretical and methodological tools for arriving at urgently needed consistent statements on pressing real-life problems, i.e. prevailing or menacing misery of demoted or redundant employees. The scientist who reprimands policy makers for their supposed lack of concepts, thus admonishes the - often unnoticed - lack of progress in research and admits failure in scientific analysis.

This critical statement may seem astonishing, especially as the social science school of thought does have an accepted theory describing the relationship between technology and work content, i.e. the so-called polarization theory. With the help of this theory, seemingly divergent empirical findings can be linked together. The theory's underlying conceptual framework seems well-evidenced and sound. From an empirical point of view, the approach is absolutely straightforward and correct. From a methodological point of view, however, this approach - as will be shown later - is not so sound, because its conclusions are directly determined by whatever interpretations have been assigned to the ill-defined basic assumptions. The approach does not solve methods-related difficulties and elegantly overgoes conceptual problems by referring to empirical evidence. The wording of the following typical research question illustrates the described shortcomings:

"What are the impacts of information technology
on requisite occupational skills?"

The employed terms are vague and could be interpreted in several different ways. Each of the interpretation alternatives listed below redefines the initial research problem, i.e. would lead to a different set of findings:

(1)   Information technology

-    in its original meaning of "knowledge about methods and tools for information processing", or in terms of technical equipment such as microprocessors, or in terms of specific forms of technology application (e.g. word processing, decision-support systems etc.);
-    in terms of given and/or expected, but not yet existing forms of applications for existing technology;

(2) skills

-   school education, task requirements, personal competence;

-   job/occupation related and/or general educational type;

-   static and/or dynamic perspectives (i.e. considerations related to potentials in personal development);

-   definition of standards for measuring skill changes: empirical-historical or normative-theoretical;

-   reference base for definition/description of change: individual-biographic and/or general, trend type changes in productive factors;

(3) impacts

-   nature of relationship under investigation:
    induced by "natural" laws or technological determinism, induced by socio-structural mechanisms or statements of empirical consistencies, e.g. in the form of statistical correlations;

-   duration of observation: past, present, short-term future, long-term future.

Most studies usually do not distinguish among these and other interpretation alternatives. In cases where one alternative was chosen, selection criteria were not elucidated. A conceptual basis for establishing selection criteria is apparently not yet available. But investigators are at least consistent in lamenting deficits in conceptual framework.

2. Stagnation of Empirical Research

The above mentioned dilemma of social science research is emphasized by the fact that empirical research in the area under discussion here, originated 25 years ago, and ever since has been - and still is - consistently producing divergent findings.[8] A pure empirical approach is obviously an inadequate tool. Whereas epistemology supports this statement, policy makers and other decision-makers have not yet learned their lesson. The (West German) Federal Ministries of Labour, of Economics and of Research and Technology jointly and separately assigned several research projects on "information technology induced impacts on employment" as late as two years ago. Many other official agencies, such as the European Trade Union Institute in Brussels, the EEC Commissioner, the West German Federal Bureau for Unemployment, and many Länder(=state) ministries independently sponsored still more research on this topic.

During the 1950's, political pressure resulting from a very detrimental labour market situation - first in the USA, soon afterwards in the FRG - led to the first series of research projects on the impacts of automation.[10] Sponsors, then and now, typically demanded results on a short-term basis. Time pressures hindered researchers, then and now, in accomplishing conceptual groundwork and forced them to concentrate on a small number of case studies in selected areas.

Comparisons of the many sets of empirical findings identify two basic categories, research with an "optimistic" and research with a "pessimistic" undercurrent.[11] The "optimistic" type research bases forecasts on the assumption that technology raises job skill levels. Technological progress is seen as a basically desirable development which, despite some (minor) frictions, will eliminate physical exertion and routine tasks, introduce more satisfying and challenging jobs, and create a new type of cooperative, mostly non-supervisory controlled work environment.

"Pessimistic" type research, on the other hand, evidences that progressing automation will not completely eliminate physical stress or monotonous work. Instead, the creation of highly simplified and physically more strenuous jobs can be observed as well. The underlying research philosophy views the worker's future responsibilities as stopgap or filler functions in a rigid and highly specialized work design. Any decreases in physical stress will be compensated by increases in nervous stress. A retrenchment of supervisory control mechanisms is not expected - the shift to more machine control, however, may make control less visible.

The classification of research findings described above is not only appropriate for research on the automation of industrial production via computerized process control (such as in the chemical and steel industries) and NC-machine tools. It also can be applied for research on the computerization of administrative and service jobs. The classification, like all synopses, rests on generalized categorization criteria. A synoptic classification of research findings on computer induced changes in clerical and administrative tasks and job skills, however, shows more detailed subcategories.[12]

A substantial amount of research effort focused on clerical jobs and first-line supervisory and/or middle management level responsibilities. New data processing jobs were also investigated. While studies of skill changes in production areas very often only define skills in terms of levels of formal education or wage levels, administrative and service area related research also includes statements on changes in work design, in skill requirements and in attitudes. The most commonly used methodological approach involved a small series of case studies compiled via surveys and job analyses.

For the most part, individual case studies evidence individual sets of findings. The majority of studies concerned with clerical jobs consistently states that computerization has eliminated a lot of the routine work. Statements on personnel placements and on new job designs for transferred employees, whose old jobs had been eliminated, are not consistent. Statements on personnel placements either evidence an accumulation of auxiliary tasks (stopgap or fill-in function) or decision-making enriched responsibilities. Supplementary attitude analyses indicate that employees perceived the computer induced devaluation of personal job experience and the subsequent upgrading of formalized abstract tasks as a downgrading of their job skills. Statements on new job designs, especially on new data processing jobs for transferred employees indicate both an upgrading of job skills (especially computer programming) and downgraded skills (especially data entry and compilation).

Statements on middle management level job skill changes show even less consistency. One group of investigators supposedly observed an extensive reduction of middle management jobs and a subsequent redistribution of respective responsibilities into the first-line supervisory level. Supporting evidence expounds that some of the former middle management decision-making authorities are being re-centralized to top management. Other competencies are being computerized or reallocated to staff department specialists.

Another group of investigators contrastingly observe an expansion and upgrading of middle management jobs. Supporting evidence here emphasizes that top management is increasingly prepared to delegate authority, and that much of the routine in middle management jobs is being eliminated to allow more time for supervisory responsibilities. The latter are rapidly gaining in importance because a satisfying work climate is considered to be vital for the smooth functioning of an automated work organization.

More recent research efforts have continued the "tradition" of presenting a large variety of divergent findings. Former areas of investigation, however, have been enlarged: Research on automated industrial production now also covers the printing industry and computer-aided design. Research in the administrative area is being rapidly enlarged with visual display jobs, information retrieval systems, computerized word processing and innovations in communication technology.[13]

In sum, however, case studies still give a rather confusing depiction of reality. Some findings indicate job promotions, others demotions; linking criteria for combining tasks into jobs are divergent; in industry, persons with divergent requisite training are assigned to one and the same kind of job. This illustrates the need for a conceptual classification scheme and a theoretical interpretational framework. With the help of these tools, prevailing incrementalistic and opinionated evidence should be eliminated, well supported forecasts and problem-solving strategies developed. Polarization theory represents one attempt at designing such an explanatory tool.

3. Polarization Theory

3.1. Polarization Theory as the Dominant School of Thought

Two recent inventories of existing research indicate that polarization theory has apparently been accepted as the dominant school of thought in German industrial sociology since 1970.

In 1978, a research group investigating automation induced job skill changes prepared a synoptic overview which classified the results from about 60 earlier studies on mechanization and automation induced changes in work design and job skills.[14] The studies included in this survey are concerned with forms of technology application in automated production and with mechanization and automation in administrative and service areas. The overview shows the following results for studies evidencing trends in skill changes:[15]

	$\uparrow$	$\downarrow$	$\updownarrow$	$\sim$	c	Σ
INDUSTRIAL PRODUCTION	14	5	7	3	—	29
ADMINISTRATIVE SERVICE AREAS	4	1	9	1	1	16

Legend: $\uparrow$ = upgraded skills, $\downarrow$ = downgraded skills, $\updownarrow$ = polarization, $\sim$ = no conclusive findings, c = unchanged skill level, Σ = number of studies

Polarization theory, in effect, states that a relative large number of jobs requiring medium-level skills are eliminated, that the majority of employees is reallocated in low-skilled jobs, and that a relative small number of new and higher skilled planning and monitoring type jobs is created. Polarization theory type findings are most prevalent in studies on administrative and service areas.[16] In production area related research, skill upgrading theory prevails but most of the respective studies had focused on highly specialized jobs. The more extensive and conceptually sophisticated studies, especially research by the Soziologisches Forschungsinstitut, Göttingen (SOFI), however, presented findings in support of polarization theory.[17]

In addition, an inventory of impact research concerned with information technology, which was compiled in 1978 with the participation of this author, identifies the polarization of changes in job skills as the dominant trend and discusses the social consequences of this development.[18]

3.2. Elucidation of Concepts in Polarization Theory

The above mentioned inventory of impact research on information technology carefully elucidates various concepts and assumptions connected with polarization theory. These explanatory efforts are discussed in the following paragraphs.

3.2.1. Information Technology, Technology Families, and Technology Applications

The first step in developing a conceptual framework involves the precise identification of whatever component of technological change is being investigated. Impact research focusing either on information technology in general, or on microelectronics, or on new input and communication equipment, or on computerized word processing in typing pools are obviously investigating non-identical problem areas. The classification criterium indicated here is the level of concretization.[19]

The term information technology describes the sum of know-how on data and information processing and communication. Those characteristics which most modern technologies do have in common (e.g. formalization, algorithmic sequential processing) are so general in nature that they do not yield sufficiently precise grounds for linking them with specific changes in jobs and job skills. A linkage would only indicate that tasks have been formalized - a "result" which is actually the necessary condition for computer application.[20]

The term microprocessor describes a basic hardware piece unit which is installed in numerous kinds of technological equipment. This, then is a too general term. This indicates that classifications deriving from a distinction of technology family functions might provide more appropriate criteria. The resulting classification would, e.g., distinguish among data and information input technology, storage unit technology, processing unit technology, output technology and transmitter technology, each of which comprises several technologically different hard- and software elements which perform the respective function on the basis of different physical processes and with different effects regarding capacity, accuracy, costs etc. Most applications of information technology employ at least one element out of each family.

A crucial aspect in analyzing "impacts" is represented in the fact that the combination of technical units and subsequent work redesign offers several options in technology application. The various alternatives have a level of concretization allowing diffentiated impact analyses, for instance

- office automation
- monitoring and control of industrial production
- computer aided design
- electronic mail - electronic funds transfer.

Technology application is also determined by organizational and personnel related provisions. Impact analyses, therefore, must investigate more than just the combination of technical units.

3.2.2. Dimensions of Technology Application

The several dimensions of technology application viewed as socio-technical systems can be compared with the layers of an onion:[21] The hardware, i.e. a universally employable programmed machine or set of machines is the technical core of the system. The first layer folding around this core is the software, i.e. programs specifying which functions the hardware should perform in which way. Communication devices and standard operating procedures which regulate the man-machine interface from the user's side also link the machine to the work procedures in the user department. The next layer represents the work organization of the user department. The non-machine tasks which are positioned before and after machine tasks and which can be arranged in a variety of ways are included here. The last and outer layer represents personnel related standards on placement procedure (e.g. job rotation, standards on duty hours, on compensation, etc.).

This distinction has a dual purpose. Firstly, the analogy illustrates that job skill requirements are jointly determined by technological, organizational, and personnel related provisions. Secondly, the analogy allows room for surmised options in each of the "layers".

3.2.3. Technology Potentials and Their Utilization

Information technology and its related technology families offer an undefinable number of options for redesigning work systems. The sum of options may be called potential. The basic features of information technology described above assign end points to this potential which can now be compared with a hallway connecting two buildings. The "hallway", of course, is not static, because time will change technology. However, an alternative information technology, in contrast to energy technology, is not foreseeable - and hasn't really been attempted.[22] Although the evolution of information technology - with its cultural roots going back to the Age of Enlightenment in the 18th century - has brought impressive progress in computing capacity and speeds and constantly changing equipment, the underlying philosophy has remained unchanged. But as long as this same philosophy determines the way of life in industrialized societies, heedless of differences in economic and societal systems, the development of an alternative information technology is unlikely.

Although it is disputed whether or not societal factors determine the development of basic technologies, the societal influence on the development and distribution of different forms of technology application available at a certain point in time is now undisputed.[23] The present level of technological development comprises a very large number of possible technology utilization options, of which only a selected few are carried out. This selection is neither random nor arbitrary.

In our socio-structural context, only relatively few groups have the authority to make technology related selection decisions and to assume technology utilization responsibilities. In doing so, indicated individuals generally base their decision-making on the same type of objectives which also govern all their other activities. The above mentioned inventory of impact research - motivated by this assumption - formulated a general hypothesis stating that the utilization of information technology tends to reinforce whatever conditions or trends prevail in affected areas, i.e. that information technology utilization - in terms of status-quo assumptions - basically reinforces given trends.

3.2.4. Polarization Resulting from Rationalization

In terms of a work related utilization of information technology, the above general trend-reinforcement hypothesis indicates a more specific version concerning the reinforcement of prevailing rationalization trends. Rationalization in terms of economizing work designs is, of course, a basically desirable objective. The type of rationalization indicated here, however, primarily rests on the onesided interests of capital, i.e. of employers, and so reflects existing entrepreneurial objectives of profit and domination.[24]

The traditional taylorian and bureaucratic forms of organization, now supplemented with corresponding forms of technology application, provide the means for achieving indicated ends. The utilization of formalized procedures involving information technology, in fact, presupposes a consistent pursuance of related principles. Planning efforts related to technology implementation reflect a tayloristic division of manual and mental tasks because programmable task elements are first separated from non-programmable ones, then recombined and programmed.[25] As soon as it is cheaper to process programmable task elements by machines, human-processing is substituted. Required returns on capital investments demand maximum machine capacity utilization and subsequently induce further centralization of routine activities. A total conversion to machine processing, however, is not feasible for reasons of technology related and/or economic restraints. As a result, low skilled jobs comprising residual programmable tasks are created. Other low skilled jobs (e.g. data compilation and assistant operator jobs in data processing) are created as fill-ins for non-computerizable gaps in the technological system.[26]

The emergence of new high skilled jobs is partly induced by the afore mentioned separation of executing, planning, and monitoring and control tasks, and partly by the disclosure of previously unfathomed complexities in control and monitoring functions. The indicated high skilled tasks, however, are concentrated in a relative smaller number of jobs. Other high skilled jobs are created in technology related research and development areas. Both developments taken together result in a polarization of job skills, whereby the relative number of emerging low skilled jobs by far exceeds the number of emerging high skilled jobs.

Typical target areas for advanced implementation stages in technology utilization involve non-automated, previously routinized jobs plus filler type jobs related to meanwhile automatable gaps in the machine system. This indicates that downgrading job skill levels is the forerunner to eliminating respective jobs and, in a context of low economic growth rates, a forerunner to respective redundancies, i.e. unemployment. Past developments in input processing and computer programming jobs clearly illustrate the above relationship. The social dilemma is rooted in the fact that polarization creates such an extremely wide qualifications gap between low and high skill levels because medium-level skills have been eliminated.

A person facing automation induced redundancy and offering nothing but the experience of several years of repeatedly downgraded job skill levels (e.g. a former secretary now working as punching unit operator), has little or no chance of success when competing for one of the relative scarcer high skilled jobs. This indicates that downgrading job skill levels can induce hard-core unemployment. The so-called modernization of work structures appears inhumane when seen in terms of technology induced unemployment figures. For the persons concerned, technological progress is a step backwards in their standard of living and in their social status.

A final judgement of the worth of computerized information processing, however, must also take the following questions into account:

(1)   Are the indicated social developments an inevitable result of technology utilization within the present economic and societal context?

(2)   Are the indicated social consequences universal or incidental phenomena?

In order to answer these questions, two different ideal type forms of technology application may be identified:

3.2.5. Master and Slave Systems - Ideal-Type Forms of Computer Application

Computer technology is by no means the only determinant for the undesirable developments described above, and, although its application does predominantly lead to the type of effects indicated here, other and more desirable effects are conceivable. A comparison of two opposite ideal-type forms of computer application, i.e. master and slave systems, illustrates this. These terms are used in informatics for describing technical differences in man-machine communication.[27] In this context, however, they are employed to distinguish fundamental differences in systems and work design.[28]

In a slave-type system, human work activities are basically machine-controlled, man-performed operations are generally restricted to routine auxiliary tasks. Here, information technology is designed to assume over-all control and monitoring functions. Systems layouts virtually eliminate self-controlled work performance. Instead, work contents, procedures, and the pace of worker-performed tasks are prescribed in detail, the employee's job performance is routinzed and measured. Such systems are typically applied in non-supervisory level clerical areas.

Master-type systems, on the other hand, are typically applied in management, planning, and research areas. Here, information technology is designed to support human activities by performing much or most of the routine work and by helping users handle the constantly growing amounts of information and operate on a higher level of complexity. The application of the SPSS software package for statistical analysis in social science research is an excellent example for this type of computer application. Any systems user who is proficient in statistics and has learned a few basic technical operation standards can master this system and gain from it. In addition, easier programming languages, remote on-line terminals, and precise error-reporting have greatly improved the ease of using the systems.

3.2.6.   Preliminary Conclusions

The above statements illustrate that various realistic technical-organizational alternatives for computerizing information processing tasks do exist. The very high relative number of "slave"-type systems, however, indicates that owners of computer systems are apparently convinced that this is the most appropriate type of system - even at the price of occasional mitigations in efficiency, but for the sake of preserving existing authority structures. Thus, prevailing economic goals and means-ends assumptions generally induce forms of technology application which generate a polarization of job skills. Expected personnel reductions and foreseeable demotions into lower salary brackets as aftereffects of downgraded job skill levels are additional driving forces for polarization.

Such developments are obviously not in the interest of the dependent wage-earner. The basic conflict of interests indicated here is common for all work structure related problems and not only a result of technology application which, however, may intensify it. Therefore, the conflict can not be resolved with the instruments of technology policy alone because it is also generated by the existing societal structure which constantly reinforces the supremacy of interests related to the capital side. The various implemented problem-solving measures, such as restructuring jobs, temporary demotion freezes, or employee re-training programs merely offer some incremental relief which can disguise the basic conflicts, but will not resolve them. Only a fundamental realignment of society's control-mechanisms will successfully resolve this conflict of interests. Examples of indicated realignments are workers' participation/codetermination in systems design, centralized investment control and the collective ownership of the means of production... .

Conclusions of this kind are typical for the closing paragraphs in many industrial sociology research studies. These statements raise a number of questions, the most obtrusive of which concerns the feasibility of depicted changes in the social setting. In terms of research methodology, however, the following question is raised: Are the underlying causal analyses correct and are they actually a suitable point of departure for developing the kind of solutions which will resolve the described conflict? Another consideration which must be accounted for is that changes in the formal societal structure do not automatically induce corresponding changes in an employee's work environment. And technology application and job skill changes in existing so-called socialistic societies have definitely not shown any of the more desirable trends.[30] Considerations of this type indicate that the supporters of polarization theory are perhaps taking an "easy way out" when drawing their conclusions. Theoretically supported conclusions concerning reforms require an in-depth elucidation of polarization theory.

3.3. Criticism of Polarization Theory

Two publications offer a very comprehensive critique of polarization theory. The two groups of authors base their criticism on different theoretical backgrounds and dispraise different elements of the theory. The first group of authors (Fricke and Fricke[31]) especially criticizes the frames of references used in industrial sociology research of having consistently ignored the identification of human choice alternatives. The authors argue that research results describing human choice are a fundamental prerequisite for assessing and improving the quality of working life. Their analysis of human choice alternatives in work design also takes systems related restrictions into account which limit the worker's choice. The authors, however, come to the conclusion that human choice alternatives are large enough to justify comprehensive investigations which, in their opinion, promise important insights and practical solutions. The second group of authors (Project Team "Automation & Qualifications") based its criticism on a Marxist oriented theory concerned with the development of productive forces, i.e. labour[32]. Despite the underlying general position, the criticism of polarization theory here provides both valuable insights into the theory's theoretical shortcomings and practical policy related solutions. Disregardless of their diverging theoretical frameworks, both critiques consistently state that the theoretical confirmation of polarization theory is poor and that the theory does not lead to appropriate reallife solutions. These are the reasons why polarization theory can't reduce the helplessness of policy makers, which was discussed at the beginning of this article.

3.3.1. Polarization Theory and Human Choice Theory

Fricke & Fricke, like Lutz,[33] assume that technology application is the result of social behavior which, when activated by a certain situation "selects one specific technical-organizational solution for implementation from a number of possible alternatives".[34] In particular, a human choice can be made in two stages of the decision-making process:

(1) Mechanization and automation require organizational preparations, i.e. the routinization of work processes whereby standardized procedures for similar and frequent operations are established. "The selection of human performed tasks for future standardization and machine-substitution is based on the following criteria: economic considerations; requisite job skills, either as given by the work force or as desired by the firm; technology related know-how; and worker demands."[35] The listed decision-making criteria represent human choice margins in the selection of operations to be mechanized or automated (technological choice).

(2) The residual non-mechanizable/non-automatable operations which remain after the above selection process has been completed, allow further choice. There are several options for re-linking and re-distributing the indicated residual operations into new jobs (organizational choice).

Technology application, finally, allows a very large variety of hardware and software combinations. These options in technology design offer still other alternatives in technological choice.[36]

In their article, Fricke & Fricke also discuss the investigations by Kern & Schumann[37], who had a significant role in establishing polarization theory as a dominating school of thought. The authors especially dispraise the Kern & Schumann hypothesis which states that standard technological equipment requires a corresponding standard organization of human-performed operations. According to Kern & Schumann, human choice margins and work organization related alternatives are possible but economically infeasible. In the given societal context, downgraded job skills, monotonous procedures, increased stress, etc. are therefore unavoidable results of technology application (social determinism).

Fricke & Fricke accept the empirical findings describing the above results of technology application, but reject their supposed inevitability. In support of this critique, the authors argue that the traditional principle of returns has been enlarged and now includes new kinds of economic considerations. A persistent high level of job dissatisfaction, e.g., generally decreases job performance and thus increases the operation costs of the machine system. Job dissatisfaction also increases absenteeism and labour turnover costs. In this case, more satisfying technological-organizational alternatives will increase returns on investments. Recent investigations, e.g., in personnel costing indicate substantial savings with a reduction of absenteeism and turnover through work restructuring.

Attention must also be directed to the fact that the deterministic effect of the principle of economic returns are only valid in a context of perfect competition, which is non existent. The given economic setting does not allow precise estimates or allocations of returns.[38] Even the very sophisticated methods for calculating returns on investments have problems in identifiying the returns of a computerized information processing system. Progress in calculation methods in this area lags several decades behind technological progress.[39]

Many decisions are apparently based on vague estimates which are probably derived from both economic and authority related considerations.[40] This circumstance supports the conclusion offered by Fricke & Fricke, which states that the existing spectrum of options in technology application can be enlarged and improvements in the quality of working life achieved in step with progress in automation, if the worker's influence on technological-organizational change is increased. Recent legal and bargaining regulations in Scandinavian countries illustrate that workers actually can gain more influence on systems design.[41] This demonstrates the type of perspectives which this criticism of polarization theory offers. The criticism also addresses social research to focus more efforts on identifying and implementing additional options. Thus the transformation of human choice theory into human choice reality could be accomplished and the empirically identified "invariances eliminated".[42]

3.3.2. Polarization Theory and the Interplay of the Factors of Production

The publication of the Project Team "Automation & Qualifications" does not assign much importance to the question of human choice margins. This criticism of polarization theory is much more fundamental in nature. Using skill downgrading theory as their starting point, the authors illustrate and emphasize that the elements of technological development comprising positive effects for workers have been consistently neglected. The authors' critical elucidations are summarized in the following three paragraphs.[43]

(1) Critique of the Vague Concept of Job Skills

The authors begin with a detailed discussion of the vague concept of job skills common in industrial sociology. The vagueness of the concept does not allow a theoretically well supported and precise definition of high skilled and low skilled jobs. As a result, uniform and substantiated standards for assessing job skill changes are not available.[44] From the authors' viewpoint, polarization only indicates divergence.

The standards used in polarization theory and skill downgrading theory are implicitly derived from an ideal-type form of craftsmanship, a historic phenomenon which, by the way, has not yet been investigated very thoroughly. New developments which are assessed with old standards, will obviously be identified as "not old developments". But what are the reasons for using the "old" standard? Is it legitimate to idealize craftsmanship but at the same time reject the societal structure in which this "ideal" has been established? A very simple example illustrates the underlying issues: What theoretical insights and practical conclusions can be drawn from a theory which interprets the emergence of the printing industry as a downgrading of monks' writing skills in the Middle Ages?

The issues indicated above point out some urgent, real-life problems. Technological change has created many new jobs which can not be assessed with traditional standards. Investigations of recent technological innovations in printing industry, for instance, are primarily concerned with the eliminated typesetting skills and neglect emerging new job skills.[45] These changed job skills raise several questions which address both union policy and educational policy. Can prevailing standards for job evaluation and performance appraisal, which were developed in times of a lower degree of automation, be used to evaluate the job skill requirements for machine operating jobs on a higher level of automation? If this is not the case, traditional standards will perhaps automatically interpret skill changes as downgraded skills. This, in turn, establishes a direct and static relationship between requirement profiles and wage brackets. Questions concerning the remuneration of new jobs, however, should be investigated as soon as the respective new job skills begin to emerge. The Project Team strongly emphasizes the importance of future-oriented investigations which, in their opinion, are much more fruitful than backwards-oriented research approaches underlying polarization theory. Otherwise it will be unnoticed that workers in new jobs are performing tasks and employing new skills for which they are not being paid simply because these tasks and skills have not been identified.

(2) Polarization as a Transient Phenomenon

The authors accept the empirical findings concerning polarization trends, although they reject the underlying ill defined concept of job skills. From the authors' viewpoint, however, polarization trends are temporary, i.e. transient phenomena. The authors strongly approve that technological change eliminates routine work from man-performed jobs, and they understand today's new and low skilled technology induced jobs as the target of tomorrow's automation efforts. They argue that the classical example of the punching unit operator (which followers of polarization theory always like to point out) is only a transient phenomenon. Input media operating jobs will disappear at the same rate, as optical scanning devices are installed. Increased numbers of remote terminals will also contribute to eliminating monotonous, low skilled input operating jobs. In this context, the authors dispraise the status quo oriented outlook of polarization theory which neglects future developments.

(3) "Emphasis of Collective Trends" Versus "Neglect of Individual Biographies"

The authors do not deny the human misery resulting from technological progress in any of their statements. But they do not support the reductionistic, or rather individualistic-biographic orientation common to most industrial sociology research. They dispraise that this trend, while depicting the misery, does not indicate possible solutions and only succeeds in concealing whatever desirable corrective incipients may exist in the given societal setting. After all, automation has undoubtedly raised the standard of living for the majority of workers, even in a capitalistic economic setting. Such trends should be reinforced. Automation does eliminate jobs, but isn't the facilitation of human labour its underlying raison d'etre? Ensuing bottlenecks in the labour market, however, do not justify slow-downs in technological change. A more equitable distribution of remaining jobs (e.g. via the reduction of an individual's working hours) should be attempted instead. In this connection, the authors also emphasize that the manifold modern-day obligations in community service and welfare areas offer numerous new job opportunities. It is the educational system, and not technological progress, which must be addressed, if individual workers have difficulties in adjusting to the changed labour market setting. The authors claim that a fundamental realignment of the educational system is necessary in order to provide appropriate and early retraining opportunities and improve employees' occupational mobility. The indicated educational realignments can be synchronized with emerging job skill changes if these are identified early.[46)]

(4) Objections to this Critique

The assumption of an unbroken trend of upgraded skills and increases in the standard of living is a major shortcoming of the Project Team's critical elucidation of polarization theory. Although this assumption has proven true in the past, no proof for its future validity is available. A secular point of view, furthermore, neglects the on-going misery of individuals disconcerted by so-called transient phenomena. The worker does not interpret his lower wages and unemployment in terms of history. And today's worker does not derive consolation from the prospect of improved job opportunities for future generations. This very long-term desirable outlook is questionable, if history disproves the theory of over-all upgraded skills.

This raises the question, to what extent general upgrading trends have occured to date as a result of the fact that workers have not relied on this long-term development but have instead expressed their fears of downgrading through corresponding union action. It should also be taken into account that the severity of the indicated transient problems is rooted in other factors than the existing economic and societal standards for capital allocation. Technological progress itself, or rather the increasing tempo in the rate of progress, could be another such factor.[47] In this case, the realignments in the educational system alone, which the authors proposed as their central problem-solving approach, will not suffice in achieving the desired ends. It is undoubtedly true that, troughout history, outdated professions have disappeared and that new occupations have emerged. In the past, these changes evolved in the course of several generations, and respective adjustments in job skills were successively accomplished with several transitions to following generations of workers. Today, however, individual workers repeatedly experience fundamental changes in job skill requirements in the course of their working life. The present pace in occupational change, which has not yet reached the tempo of changes in job skills, will probably gain in momentun as a result of today's disproportionately high pace in technological change. Thus, a slow-down in technological progress and an adaptation to a feasible pace of change in the educational system, may well be an additional demand which results from this analysis. The above statements, which definitely support the proposed realignments in the educational system as one valuable problem-solving tool, emphasize the need of a multiversant instrument package. In addition to the problems arising from realignments in the educational system, an identification and investigation of anthropological constants, which define the degree of technological progress human beings can contend with, might justify a slow down in the pace of technological change, or at least provide additional valuable insights and perhaps even problem solving tools.

The approach described above also raises the question of whether or not technology is slowly approaching a level of complexity no longer controllable by human beings despite a respective progress in know-how.[48] The assumption that increasing complexity in the economic and social settings can be controlled with additional technological progress is perhaps just as questionable as the assumption that future technological change will resolve the security problems related to atomic energy. Progress in information technology introduces new methods for controlling and monitoring work procedures but, simultaneously, induces increases in levels of complexity which are beyond the control of available monitoring instruments. The increasingly complicated legal regulations governing Social Security illustrate this trend. The Social Security system in the FRG could not have attained its extremely intricate present-day structure without electronic data processing. Nowadays, policy makers prosecuting government employees, and especially beneficiaries are, in fact, confronted with a practically non-penetrable and non-controllable systems structure. The indicated increases in levels of complexity furthermore induce a disproportionate cumulation of impacts resulting from decisional errors. The interplay of data processing systems and communications technology reinforces the above trends. This, finally, can impede safeguards against illegal systems entry and data retrieval, can counteract safeguards against invasions of privacy, and can encourage computer larceny. This illustrates that decision makers who use non-secured computer installations, are in effect employing non-verified data bases, i.e. are basically producing non-validated decisions. Government administration areas are especially susceptible for the type of problems described above.[49]

Such apprehensions lead directly to a third objection. The analyzing statements presented by the Project Team "Automation and Qualifications", like all research in industrial sociology, are only concerned with the production related side of the issue. Automation, however, always implies changes both in production procedures and in products, i.e. concerns both producers and consumers. Whereas the before

mentioned transition from writing monks to the printing industry brought improvements for both sides (upgraded skills and mass access to written information),[50]
the mutual utility of recent innovations in information technology is questionable.
Existing problems in man-machine communication signalize a deterioration in communications between citizen and state and between client and administration. New
mass media signalize similar problems in communications on the societal level. It
can be assumed that the indicated developments may adversely effect lesser privileged persons.

The purpose of this chapter was to pinpoint problem areas requiring further
investigation. Future research should focus on the Project Team's criticism of
polarization theory. Even the brief discussion presented here points out various practical conclusions.

4. Conclusions Addressing Policy Makers, Industry and Research

4.1. Conclusions Adressing Policy Makers and Industry

If the above elucidations are correct, it can be assumed that the discussed problems
and conflicts are most conspicuous on the plant-level, but least solvable in individual firm settings. The pursuance of profit-oriented objectives will be restrained.
The "price" of future entrepreneurial activities are societal-level reforms (especially
in technology policy, employment policy, and educational policy) and plant-level
concessions concerning traditional authority systems. The major worker-side objectives are focused on in-depth realignments in the quality of working life. The
human choice theory points out various improvements which in part comprise a high
potential of industrial conflict. In aspiring the indicated worker-side objectives and
required societal-level reforms, employees and their shop and union representatives
have incured new responsibilities demanding new strategies, new forms of organization and new insights.[51] The ongoing worldwide economic recession makes their
new job more difficult and patented solutions are not available. The fact that
proven traditional strategies are increasingly useless is the only certainty which the
movement can rely on.

The critical analysis presented by the Project Team "Automation and Qualifications"
clearly illustrates that a flat repudiation of technology is inappropriate. In order to
preserve the rational societal elements inherent in technological change and
implement improvements in the quality of working life, the underlying long-term
and formative orientation should be supplemented with a short-term formative and
protective strategy. The coordination of the two component strategies could
synchronize technological and social change. On a short-term basis, the protective
function serves to safeguard the worker against financial loss, on a long-term basis,
to redistribute the reduced number of jobs. A governing system deriving its authority from the existence of a social net and welfare responsibilities can not afford to
load a relative small group of workers with the entire burden of adjustments
incurred by technological change. If unemployment rate forecasts (3 - 6 mio) for
the coming decade should prove true, subsequently emerging social problems could
lead to a dispute questioning the legitimacy of the governing system.

An emphasis of protective functions of trade union policy basically implies slow-
downs in the process of change and can not alone resolve the foreseeable problems.
Therefore, additional formative functions are required. Plant-level and shortterm
measures here, involve the implementation of technologicorganizational options which
minimize transient downgrading trends in job skills. The more work-procedure
related measures, such as job enrichment, definitely comprise a substantial cost-
savings potential, i.e. are advantageous for both the employer and the worker side,
and may therefore be partially realized. The more general, organizational measures,
such as changes in work-design, in personnel planning, in job evaluation or the
expansion of participation in decision-making have very low implementation chances.
Domestic pressures and parallel developments in Scandinavia, Italy and France,
however, will perhaps be a driving force in this process of implementation.

Societal-level and long-term measures are concerned with establishing a technology policy which equally pursues traditional economy related modernization goals and newly established social policy goals. This could eliminate some of those social problems which arise as aftereffects of present modernization - oriented technology policy measures. The same government which initiated technology policy measures is generally addressed to resolve the indicated aftereffects which it has created itself. Other measures here involve the extension of on-the-job training and continuing vocational training plus realignments in general education placing stronger emphasis on skills in abstract and analytical reasoning. Higher skills and an increased social adeptness facilitate the adjustment to changes in work environment. The indicated reforms of the educational system, however, comprise a potential for conflict because the described skills changes are required for reinforcing the economy's position in international competition, but may also endanger existing authority systems. On a long-term basis, however, skill changes nevertheless represent the best and most realistic safeguard for directing work design changes effected by the computerization of information processing away from a one-sided rationalization of working life and towards improvements in the quality of working life.

4.2. Concequences for Research

The various practical concequences discussed above are often based on subjective judgements and appraisals as appropriate validated conceptual frameworks are not available. Research as such, however, will not resolve societal conflicts, even if its findings are used as "weapons" in political disputes. The prevailing short-term and selective form of empirical research actually serves the purpose of exonerating commissioning agencies or of providing incidental proof justifying a specific policy proposal or measure, but will definitely not result in new insights. The chronic lack of theoretical fundaments is the most serious impediment which research faces.

A theory describing e.g. the relations between technological change and work changes can hardly be developed if the underlying theories of technological change and of labour are both missing. In addition, the increasing emphasis of empiricism in social sciences prevents shiftings of research funding in favor of theoretical groundwork. And since the objects of investigation are long-term problems having far-reaching consequences, respective empirical frames of reference should be more concerned with the historical evolution of technological change and labour than with sections of current developments or individual, short-term events. The social history of technology, specifically of information technology, is one of the areas in social science in which the least amount of research has been completed. This indicates that a fundamental redefinition of research objects (and research financing) is necessary for improving the theoretical and empirical foundations which could contribute towards resolving upcoming problems.

Footnotes

1) See the reviews of research in the field of organizational analysis by Kubicek 1979 and in the field of industrial sociology by Brandt et al. 1979 and Projekt-gruppe Automation und Qualifikation 1978

2) See Briefs 1980, Grünwald et al. 1981, Ludwig and Rothweiler 1979, Lutz 1969 and 1979, Wiethold 1978

3) See Vorstand der SPD 1979

4) See Briefs 1978 and 1980

5) Der Bundesminister für Forschung und Technologie 1979a

6) Der Bundesminister für Forschung und Technologie 1979b

7) See Institut für Systemtechnik 1977, Dürrheimer et al. 1980, Grünwald et al. 1981

8) See the reviews by Pauling 1964 and Sadler 1968 in the sixties and those by Brandt et al. 1979, Projektgruppe Automation und Qualifikation 1978, Reese et al. 1979, Grünwald et al. 1981, Dürrheimer et al. 1980 in the late seventies and early eighties

9) See Lutz 1979

1o) See Projektgruppe Automation und Qualifikation 1978

11) See Brandt et al. 1979 as an example

12) See the reviews by Brandt et al. 1979, Fricke 1975, Kubicek 1975 and 1979, Nemitz et al. 1978, Projektgruppe Automation und Qualifikation 1978, Dürr-heimer et al. 1980, Grünwald et al. 1981

13) This also means a change in scope because information technology now is not only viewed as a working technology but also as a control or organizational technology as well in the area of clerical jobs or mental work. See especially Bechmann et al. 1979, Brandt et al. 1978, Brödner and Rolf 1979

14) Projektgruppe Automation und Qualifikation 1978

15) These results have been computed by the author on the basis of a more detailed tabulation in the original paper

16) Pirker 1962, Haas 1961, Lutz et al. 1976, Fuhrmann 1971

17) Especially Kern and Schumann 1970

18) Reese et al. 1979

19) See Reese et al 1979

2o) See Heibey et al. 1977, Brödner et al. 1979 and Rolf 1979 for a more extensive discussion

21) See Kubicek 1980 for a more extensive discussion

22) This issue has only recently gained some attention in connection with the question of appropriate technology for developing countries. See e.g. the contributions to IFIPTC 9 Newsletter No. 7, December 1979

23) There is, however, a dispute on the way and extent that societal factors influence applications of technology and how these factors should be defined. The following discussion draws on the view presented by Reese et al. 1979, which is only one perspective of the ongoing discussion

24) For a more detailed analysis of the objectives in technology application see Altmann, Bechtle and Lutz 1978, Brödner et al. 1979, Kubicek 1980

25) See Bechmann et al. 1979, Brandt et al. 1978, Bravermann 1977, Brödner et al. 1979, Koch 1978, Lutz 1979, Rolf 1979

26) See Koch 1978, pp. 159 f. and Shaiken 1979 and for the production area in general Mickler et al. 1976

27) In the German literature they have been introduced by Mertens and Griese 1972

28) See Kubicek 1980 for a more extensive discussion

29) See the discussion by Lutz 1979 of the specific context in the USA in which the taylorian type of means-end assumptions have originated and the different context in Germany where these assumptions have been adopted

3o) See for example Tatur 1980

31) Fricke and Fricke 1977 as well as Fricke 1975

32) Projektgruppe Automation und Qualifikation 1978

33) Lutz 1969

34) Fricke and Fricke 1977, p. 94

35) Fricke and Fricke 1977, p. 94

36) See also Heibey et al. 1977, pp. 270 ff.

37) Kern and Schumann 1970

38) See Schreyögg 1978 and 1980. In a more recent study, Kern himself emphazises historical changes in the interpretation and application of the principle of economic returns. See Kern et al. 1976, p. 109

39) See for example the analysis presented by Grochla 1970 more than ten years ago which still applies to the present state of the art

40) For a more detailed analysis of the authority related aspects, see Blau 1970, Blau and Schoenherr 1971, Briefs 1980, Brödner et al. 1979 and Shaiken 1979

41) See Kubicek 1980

42) For a discussion of this methodological principle, see Galtung 1977

43) Projektgruppe Automation und Qualifikation 1978 and Gottschalch and Ohm 1977

44) See also Ludwig and Rothweiler 1979, Nemitz et al. 1978 and Wiethold 1978

45) See Bürger 1978 and Ludwig and Rothweiler 1979

46) Similar conclusions are drawn by social scientists in the eastern European countries. See Tatur 1980

47) For an analysis of the consequences of the assumed acceleration of technological change, see Reese et al. 1979. This assumption, however, is not undisputed

48) For a more detailed discussion of this assumed increase in complexitiy see Reese et al. 1979 and in particular Weizenbaum 1980

49) See the several papers in Hansen et al. 1979

50) Projektgruppe Automation und Qualifikation 1978

51) See Briefs 1980

References

/1/ Altmann, N., G. Bechtle und B. Lutz, Betrieb-Technik-Arbeit. Elemente einer soziologischen Analytik technisch-organisatorischer Veränderungen. Frankfurt/M. und New York 1978.

/2/ Bechmann, G., R. Vahrenkamp und B. Wingert, Mechanisierung geistiger Arbeit. Eine sozialwissenschaftliche Begleituntersuchung zum Rechnereinsatz in der Konstruktion. Frankfurt/M. und New York 1979.

/3/ Blau, P.M., Decentralization in Bureaucracies, in: Zald, M.N. (ed.), Power in Organizations. Nashville 1970, pp. 150-174.

/4/ Blau, P.M. und R.A. Schoenherr, The Structure of Organizations. New York 1971.

/5/ Brandt, G., B. Kündig und Z. Papadimitriou, Qualitative und quantitative Beschäftigungseffekte des EDV-Einsatzes, in: Hansen, H.R. et al. (eds.), Mensch und Computer. München und Wien 1979, pp. 167-184.

/6/ Brandt, G. et al., Computer und Arbeitsprozeß. Frankfurt/M. 1978.

/7/ Braverman, H., Die Arbeit im modernen Produktionsprozeß. Frankfurt/M. 1977.

/8/ Briefs, U., EDV-Einsatz und Arbeit im Betrieb. Zur Veränderung der Produktionsbedingungen für die menschliche Arbeit durch die EDV, in: Hansen, H.R. et al. (eds.), Mensch und Computer. München und Wien 1979, pp. 243-256.

/9/ - Neue Technologien als Herausforderungen für die Gewerkschaften, Blätter für deutsche und internationale Politik, Vol. lo 1978, pp. 1179-1197.

/lo/ - Arbeiten ohne Sinn und Perspektive? Gewerkschaften und "Neue Technologien". Köln 1980.

/11/ Brödner, P., D. Krüger und B. Senf, Automatisierung der 'Kopfarbeit'. Veröffentlichungen der Fachhochschule für Wirtschaft Nr. 3. Berlin 1979.

/12/ Bürger, H., Einsatz neuer Technik in der Text- und Daten-
     erfassung und Verarbeitung.   Betriebliche Erfahrung und
     Interessenvertretung der Arbeitnehmer. Arbeitsmaterial Nr.
     2, Projekt Arbeits- und Lebensbedingungen der Arbeitnehmer
     als Gegenstand der Hochschulforschung, Universität Biele-
     feld, Bielefeld 1978.

/13/ Der Bundesminister für Forschung und Technologie, Bundes-
     bericht Forschung VI. Bonn 1979(a).

/14/ - Soziale Folgen der Mikroelektronik dürfen nicht bagatel-
     lisiert werden. BMFT-Mitteilungen 6/1979(b), p. 61.

/15/ Dürrheimer, A., G. Hartmann und A. Sorge, Qualitative
     Veränderungen der Arbeit durch neue Informationstechnik.
     IIM Papers 80-3, Internationales Institut für Management
     und Verwaltung, Wissenschaftszentrum Berlin, Mai 1980.

/16/ European Trade Union Institute, The Impact of Microelec-
     tronics on Employment in Western Europe in the 1980's.
     Brussels 1980.

/17/ Fricke, E. und W. Fricke, Industriesoziologie und Humani-
     sierung der Arbeit. Über Möglichkeiten und Schwierigkeiten
     industrie-soziologischer Forschung, einen Beitrag zur
     autonomie-orientierten Gestaltung von Arbeitssystemen zu
     leisten, Soziale Welt, Vol. 28 1977, pp. 91-108.

/18/ Fricke, W., Arbeitsorganisation und Qualifikation. Ein
     industrie-soziologischer Beitrag zur Humanisierung der
     Arbeit. Bonn-Bad Godesberg 1975.

/19/ Fuhrmann, J., Automation und Angestellte. Frankfurt/M.
     1971.

/20/ Galtung, J., Methodology and Ideology. Theory and Methods
     of Social Research, Vol. 1. Copenhagen 1977.

/21/ Gottschalch, H. und Ch. Ohm, Kritische Bemerkungen zur
     Polarisierungsthese bei Kern und Schumann. Soziale Welt,
     Vol. 28 1977, pp. 340-363.

/22/ Grochla, E., Automation und Organisation. Die technische
     Entwicklung und ihre betriebswirtschaftlich-organisatori-
     schen Konsequenzen. Wiesbaden 1966.

/23/ - Grundfragen der Wirtschaftlichkeit automatisierter
     Datenverarbeitung. Zeitschrift für Organisation, Vol. 39
     1970, pp. 329-336.

/24/ Grünewald,U., R. Koch und H. Lehmann, Informationstechnik
     in Büro und Verwaltung. Studie über Entwicklung und Anwen-
     dung der Informationstechnik in den Tätigkeitsfeldern
     kaufmännischer und verwaltender Berufe. Bundesinstitut für
     Berufsbildungsforschung, Heft 32, Berlin 1981.

/25/ Hansen, H.R., K.T. Schröder und H.J. Weihe (eds.), Mensch
     und Computer. Zur Kontroverse über die ökonomischen und
     gesellschaftlichen Auswirkungen der EDV. München und Wien
     1979.

/26/ Heibey, H.-W., B. Lutterbeck und M. Töpel, Auswirkungen der elektronischen Datenverarbeitung in Organisationen. BMFT Forschungsbericht DV 77-01. Eggenstein-Leopoldshafen 1977.

/27/ - Organisatorische Konsequenzen des EDV-Einsatzes, in: Hansen, H.R. et al. (eds.), Mensch und Computer. München und Wien 1979, S. 261-273.

/28/ Hoos, I.R., Automation in the Office. Washington 1961.

/29/ Institut für Systemtechnik und Innovationsforschung der FHG und Institut für Angewandte Systemanalyse der GFK, Der Einfluß neuer Techniken auf die Arbeitsplätze. Eine Analyse ausgewählter Studien unter spezieller Berücksichtigung der neuen Informationstechniken. Karlsruhe 1977.

/30/ Jaeggi, U. und H. Wiedemann, Der Angestellte im automatisierten Büro. Stuttgart 1963.

/31/ Kern, H. und M. Schumann, Industriearbeit und Arbeiterbewußtsein. Frankfurt/M. 1970.

/32/ Kern, H. et al., Neue Formen betrieblicher Arbeitsgestaltung. Der Bundesminister für Arbeit und Sozialordnung. Bonn 1976.

/33/ Koch, R., Elektronische Datenverarbeitung und kaufmännische Angestellte. Frankfurt/M. 1978.

/34/ Kubicek, H., Informationstechnologie und organisatorische Regelungen. Berlin 1975.

/35/ - Informationstechnologie und Organisationsforschung. Eine kritische Bestandsaufnahme der Forschungsergebnisse, in: Hansen, H.R. et al. (eds.), Mensch und Computer. München und Wien 1979, pp. 53-80.

/36/ - Interessenberücksichtigung beim Technikeinsatz im Büro- und Verwaltungsbereich. Grundgedanken und neuere skandinavische Entwicklungen. München und Wien 1980.

/37/ Ludwig, J. und W. Rothweiler, Entwicklung von Qualifikationsanforderungen durch den Einsatz neuer Technologien der Text- und Datenverarbeitung. Forschungsdefizite zur Entwicklung neuer beruflicher Qualifikationen am Beispiel der Druckindustrie. Projekt Arbeits- und Lebensbedingungen der Arbeitnehmer als Gegenstand der Hochschulforschung, Universität Bielefeld, Bielefeld 1979.

/38/ Lutz, B., Produktionsprozeß und Berufsqualifikation, in: Adorno, Th.W. (ed.), Spätkapitalismus oder Industriegesellschaft. Stuttgart 1969, pp. 227-25o.

/39/ - Einführungsreferat zum Arbeitkreis II "Bildung-Beruf-Technik". In: Vorstand der SPD (ed.), Forum Zukunft SPD. 1. Forum "Arbeit und Technik", 1./2. Februar 1979 in Essen. Bonn 1979, pp. 85-95.

/40/ Lutz, B. et al.,Rationalisierung und Mechanisierung im öffentlichen Dienst. München 1976.

/41/ Mertens, P. und J. Griese, Industrielle Datenverarbeitung. Bd. II.: Informations- und Planungssysteme. Wiesbaden 1972.

/42/ Mickler, O., E. Dittrich und U. Neumann, Technik, Arbeitsorganisation und Arbeit. Eine empirische Untersuchung in der automatisierten Produktion. Frankfurt/M. 1976.

/43/ Nemitz, R. et al., Forschung, Entwicklung und Einsatz neuer Technologien in der Text- und Datenerfassung und -verarbeitung. Arbeitsmaterial Nr. 1, Projekt Arbeits- und Lebensbedingungen der Arbeitnehmer als Gegenstand der Hochschulforschung, Universität Bielefeld, Bielefeld 1978.

/44/ Pauling, N.G., Some Neglected Areas of Research on the Effects of Automation and other Technological Changes on Workers, The Journal of Business, Vol. 37 1964, pp. 261-273.

/45/ Pirker, Th., Büro und Maschine. Tübingen 1962.

/46/ Projektgruppe Automation und Qualifikation, Band III: Theorien über Automationsarbeit. Argument Sonderband AS 31, Berlin 1978.

/47/ Reese, J. et al., Gefahren der informationstechnologischen Entwicklung. Perspektiven der Wirkungsforschung. Frankfurt/M. und New York 1979.

/48/ Rolf A., Zur Maschinisierung der Arbeit in Büro und Verwaltung durch Informationstechnik. Diss., Universität Osnabrück 1979.

/49/ Sadler, Ph., Socical Research on Automation. Social Science Research Council, London 1968.

/50/ Schreyögg, G., Umwelt, Technologie und Organisationsstruktur. Eine Analyse des kontingenz-theoretischen Ansatzes. Bern und Stuttgart 1978.

/51/ - Contingency and Choice in Organization Theory, Organization Studies, Vol. 1 1980, pp. 3o5-326.

/52/ Shaiken, H., Impact of New Technologies on Employees and Their Organizations. IIVG Papers dp/79-202. Internationales Institut für Vergleichende Gesellschaftsforschung, Wissenschaftszentrum Berlin, Berlin 1979.

/53/ Tatur, M., Qualifikation von Industriearbeitern in Osteuropa. Ein Beitrag zur Frage des Verhältnisses von Bildungs- und Beschäftigungssystem in der Sowjetunion, der CSSR und Polen, Soziale Welt, Vol. 31 1980, pp. 88-112.

/54/ Vorstand der SPD (ed.), Forum Zukunft SPD. 1. Forum "Arbeit und Technik", 1./2. Februar 1979 in Essen. Bonn 1979.

/55/ Weizenbaum, J., Human Choice in the Interstices of the
     Megamachine, in: Mowshowitz, A. (ed.): Human Choice and
     Computers, 2. Amsterdam 1980, pp. 271-278.

/56/ Wiethold, F., Hypothesen zum Zusammenhang von technisch-
     organisatorischer Entwicklung des Arbeitsprozesses und
     Entwicklung der Qualifikationsanforderungen, WSI-Mit-
     teilungen, Vol. 31 1978, pp. 321-332.

Computerized Information Systems in Personnel

Some Results of an Investigation Among the 220 Largest Industrial Enterprises in West-Germany

Wolfgang Kilian
University of Hannover, D-3000 Hannover, FRG

In the highly developed industrialized countries computer-assisted information systems in personnel have been set up for many reasons and purposes. My research study showed empirically how and to what extend the large German enterprises are introducing computerized systems for administration and planning. The individual data on each employee serve basically for accounting, but more and more for statements about capabilities, achievements, promotions, and profiles. Chances and dangers with respect to decisionmaking, communication, data privacy, and participation arise and should lead to a legal framework.

I. Aims and scopes of computerized information systems in personnel

Computer assisted information systems in personnel have been set up in the highly developed industrial countries since the beginning of the 70's[1]. Governments, states, local authorities, private and public insurances, hospitals, credit bureaus, and industrial groups use automated systems, containing data on persons. This technological development is due to several reasons:

1. In business and administration there is pressure to rationalize in order to save expenses and - in business - to obtain or safeguard competitive advantages. By means of automation above all costly workforces are freed from routine work.

2. There is a desire to have more comprehensive information available more quickly in order to improve internal administration and planning. As a result all phases preceding a decision as well as the organization of the decision proceedings gain in significance. Therefore the systematic efforts to reduce informational uncertainties become an important driving factor for the establishment of automated systems.

3. The growing interdependence between private and state authorities increase the information network and demand a quick and accurate communication. In a highly sophisticated industrial society large enterprises could scarcely be in a position to accomplish their duties without the aid of a computer because the external requirements are growing in leaps and bounds. It is well known that more than 1oo laws on the federal level in Germany require the passing on of data regarding persons from business enterprises to other places. Among the addressees are tax administrations, national insurance institutions, courts, labour authorities, churches, employers' associations, unions and many others. Already as far as that goes in

the Federal Republic of Germany at least 50 individual data on each employee must be compiled and kept up to date[2]. To this are added above all proficiency data for personnel planning. All individual data represent combinable variables which are available for many purposes and can portray each employee in qualities which constitute his personality. For example, computercontrolled statements about capabilities, achievements, personal development, reliability and creditability are possible.

Even if for the reasons named practically all enterprises in Germany having more than 5,000 employees use computers for the personnel sphere, every EDP-based personnel data file cannot be classified as "information system in personnel". There is still uncertainty, however, regarding the definition of an information system in personnel: Some authors already call an automated payroll accounting an "information system in personnel", although the payroll accounting is not in the management sense within the responsibility of personnel planning but that of financial accounting. On the other hand, an automated payroll accounting effectively forms the basis for planning methods. This may be the reason why different development stages of an information system in personnel are differentiated, extending from accounting systems, statistical decision aids to planning methods with dialog mode.

It goes without saying that developments in communication technology are leading to new problems in social relations. As soon as one ceases to treat the development solely as a function of technical possibilities and of financing and instead starts to view it as an affair of public, management, and employee interests, the social effects come to the fore. Wherever information is better selected and more purposely processed it will produce changes in working or behaviour patterns, attitudes and organizational structures of the persons and institutions concerned. Varying with the structure of the information model, information will be interpreted either positively as enrichment or negatively as surveillance and manipulation. Chances and threats are close together. Implications and repercussions of the computerisation process will result first and foremost from the way in which people organize the communication field. The further development depends on how to identify, understand and utilize the information available.

The question is to whom is it to lay down, with what means and under what conditions the use of new technologies will occur and how social control will be organized. It is readily possible that, depending on the organization, different classes of informed persons will result, which will not remain without influence on relative power conditions in society. The possibilities of the new technologies, which in many respects bring to mind George Orwell's novel "1984", may open up a new era offering greater chances of participation and greater freedom, or, on the contrary, inhuman organizational forms are taking shape which will make it even harder to find answers to man's individual problems and those of society as a whole. It is not without reason that in critical commentaries the question is more and more often being asked whether in the development of new systems we should not first of all examine just who will profit by them, what consequences they will have and just how people presumably will get along with them. Only quite gradually the awareness is growing that any technological development has its social cost as well. This is reflected most clearly in the world-wide efforts that are being made to draw up legal conditions and restrictions for the collecting, processing and transmitting of data.However, these efforts are more in the nature of an attempt to belatedly bring past technological developments under control than of an attempt to anticipate future developments and to design strategies for controlling them. To be able to design such strategies, the problems must be known and several alternative solutions must be available.

II. The IPIS-Project

Decisions on alternative solutions require empirical data. Except for some case studies mostly published by the computer industry or their customers no well-founded large scale empirical investigation into organizational forms and functions of information systems in personnel has been published[3]. Therefore, the author started research of what functions existing information systems in personnel have and how they affect individual rights, collective bargaining, decisionmaking, and behaviour in the employment system. A two years' grant from the Volkswagen Foundation (Stiftung Volkswagenwerk)[4] enabled me to organize a research group for analyzing the integrated personnel information systems (IPIS) in private enterprises. Together with two full time assistants (an economist and a lawyer) I started in 1977 on the basis of existing case studies and the results of a special international seminar attended by experienced practioneers and representatives (managers, trade unionists, system analysts) to develop a detailed questionnaire.

We put forward the following questions:

1. What functions do existing computer systems in personnel have?
   - How are the systems to be described?
   - What functions are taken over by computers?
   - What functions are expected to be computerized?

2. What data have been processed by computers and how?
   - What job related data exist?
   - What employee related data (qualifications, skills, health care) are used for what purposes?

3. What alterations of organizational structures are caused by computers?
   - What effects on the quantity and quality of personnel data management can be observed?
   - To what extend does the computer become an instrument of social control?

4. What measures to protect workers' rights and participation are taken into account?
   - What minimum conditions are set up with regard to computerization (data privacy, data security)?
   - What standard control mechanism does exist with respect to individual and collective rights?

The pretested questionnaire included 229 questions. During summer and autumn 1978 the questionnaire was successfully administered and introduced by interviews to all 220 industrial and trade corporations with the highest rate of annual turnover in the Federal Republic of Germany. A list of these enterprises is published annually in correspondence with disclosure law and business reports.

The rank of the top ten enterprises runs thus: VEBA, DAIMLER-BENZ, HOECHST, BASF, THYSSEN, VOLKSWAGEN, BAYER, SIEMENS, RWE, RUHRKOHLE.

Among the other 21o enterprises are well-known transnational corpo-rations, namely ESSO, TEXACO, BP, IBM, UNILEVER, METALL-GESELLSCHAFT, FORD, LUFTHANSA, which participated in our investigation.

According to our efforts to establish contacts with the enterprises in our sample prior to the actual questioning the quota of return was first rate: Only 39 of the 22o enterprises refused participation, sometimes assigning considerable reasons. The overwhelming majority cooperated in an excellent manner: 67 filled up the questionnaire completely (hereinafter: "respondents"), 34 answered a reduced questionnaire (but only three of them possessed an information system), 8o participated in the investigation but had no information system installed. Among the top 2o enterprises, the results were even better: 14 filled up completely, 2 answered a reduced question-naire, 3 had no information system installed and one gave no share to the questionnaire. From an economic point of view, it might be interesting that our respondents have together 2,2 million employees and a summarized annual turnover in Germany of 448 milliard DM (equals 2oo billion US Dollars).

Normally, the interviews based on the elaborated questionnaire were given by the top manger in the personnel department, assisted by the leader and/or a member of the EDP staff. Parallel to these inter-views segments of the questionnaire were requested to the works' council (Betriebsrat) and the indoor physician (Betriebsarzt). We assured the investigated of treating their information like business secrets. Therefore, we established internal code systems, security measures, and anonymity for computation and presentation.

Because of the richness and extensiveness of the data resulting from the interviews the coding and analysis has only recently been completed. Subsequently, I would like to present some frequency distributions estimated to be of general interest.

III. Level of Improvement and Functions of Information Systems in
     Personnel

The respondents using information systems in personnel chiefly be-long to the following branches: iron and steel industry (32.9 %), energy/oil (16.4 %), chemical industry (14.9 %), trade (16.4 %), food (1o.5 %). The rest spread on traffic, building, electrical engineering, and consumption.

The questionnaire asked for the level of improvement of the informa-tion system in personnel. Respondents assessed their system as:

Answer	Percentage
planned	11.9
designed, but not yet tested	9.o
partly in use	55.2
completely in use without further implementation intended	o.o
completely in use and further imple-mentation intended	23.9

It appeared that no respondent assessed his system as definitely installed. Only 23.9 % run their system completely in accordance with the designing process, but even those intend further developments.

Informative were the answers concerning the origination of the system. It is well-known, that the computer industry is highly concentrated and in Germany dominated by IBM (6o % market share) and SIEMENS (25 % market share). Every big manufacturer of computers sells software packages for information systems in personnel (e.g. IBM-IPERS, SIEMENS-IVIP). In the Federal Republic of Germany, there is a strong tendency for inhouse designing fit up for special purposes:

Answer	Percentage
system was designed inhouse	71.6
system was designed by a soft-ware-house on special demand	1.5
system was purchased as infor-mation system in personnel	11.9
the system purchased was essen-tially modified inhouse	14.9

Another question asked respondents to indicate the completely computer assisted functions in their enterprises. The results:

Answer	Percentage
only payroll system	3.o
personnel statistics and personnel administration	43.3
part of personnel planning	44.8
most of the administrative and dispositive functions	9.o

The IPIS project was eager to know the perceptions of the investigated corporations on the important utilizations of an information system in personnel. Respondents were asked to classify 1o possible aims in a preference list. The answers resulted in the following four preferences (frequency distribution):

1. Improvement of the data base for concern related planning.

2. Application of rational methods.

3. Acceleration of information flow for decisionmaking in personnel.

4. Better and more comprehensive disposal for improvement of company related administration and planning.

We can say that to a great extent information systems in personnel fulfil administrative and disposable functions. Administrative functions serve to cope with the legal and business requirements such as

payroll accounting, appointments, transfers, promotions and dis-
missials. Planning methods improve on the other hand above all the
personnel planning, for they make it possible to calculate and organize the employee requirement, their procurement, placement, re-
lease, training and further education as well as to develop wage and
salary codes or promotional and training programmes. In any case,
the exchange between administrative and planning methods are fluent.
For the most part the information systems in personnel do not consist namely of one single data bank but of several self-contained
but interlinked sub-data banks. Thus it is possible to link up data
from the personnel data bank, e.g. data on education, advanced
training, development, capabilities, achievements, performance rate-
ings and medical fitness of an employee with the assistance of a
method data bank not only with an accounting data bank but also
with an employment data bank. The latter contains mainly data about
work vacancies, job functions, job organization and security requirements.

IV. Input/Output Data

It appeared interesting to investigate the sources of input data.
We asked the question: Out of what internal sources originate the
individual data inside the information system in personnel? (mul-
tiple answers were permitted).

Answers	Percentage
personnel questionnaire	1ó0.0
tests	9.0
judgements by supervisor	58.2
information by inhouse police	3.0
information by inhouse physician	32.8
information resulting from utili- zation of inhouse equipment	46.3
information by health insurance	38.8
information by works' council	1o.4

The main source of input data originate in the personnel questionnaires and judgement by supervisors. The number of data built into
the data base structure for describing the position requirements and
the employee qualifications was found to be very numerous and
sophisticated.

Technical progress has been achieved first and foremost in the procedures for the streamlining and further utilization of the input
data. An objective of the project was to investigate whether and
tc what extend the manpower planning activities are computer assisted. The data stored are available in the form of a quantity of combinable variablesfor a wide variety of purposes in future. In order
to have "the right man in the right place at the right time", 3o %
of our respondents establish job profiles and ability profiles for
each of the job/employee involved. Moreover, additional 2o % of
respondents are going to implement their information system in personnel towards profile methods. Sooner or later, every second enterprise of our sample will utilize job and employee profiles to identi-

fy positions which correspond to the individual development needs of selected employees. In the software systems of large computer manufacturers, there are already possibilities of a so-called "profile matching". The evaluations may also be combined into interest or personality profiles and may be made the basic for company decision on specialized training, promotion, transfer, or dismissal of an employee.

The problems of automated profile matching are obvious: performance, workload, and aptitude profiles are based on a certain number of criteria. They only deal with one section of the whole personality. So-called "hard facts" such as character traits, behavior, and motivation are neglected.

Another problem and a decisive prequisite of the effectiveness of the information system is the actuality of input data and data profiles. The input data have to be updated in shorttime intervals. Updating routines are very seldom to be found. On the contrary: Even personal data concerning retired or dismissed employees are stored in separated data banks by 44.8 % of our respondents.

V. Economic and Social Implications

The functions of information systems in personnel shown make it clear that there are numerous opportunities but also risks for those concerned upon installation. As far as industrial management is concerned information systems in personnel facilitate new and speedy data linkages for many purposes, even for the purpose of humanization of work. Sociologically, the new technical possibilities might lead to an increase in the power of those who can use or supervise them. The programming of the communications presumably favours a centralizing of the decision responsibilities at the top of the organization hierarchy because previous planning duties of the middle decision authorities are automated. Thereby, the organizational significance, the co-decision and co-management possibilities of the middle and lower authorities are diminished.

Hitherto, information systems in personnel are normally regarded as a modernized personnel file administration. In reality, it represents a qualitatively new means of organization which produces not only influences of rationalization but also change accession processes, supervisory processes, decision processes, and co-management processes in business.

The IPIS project investigated chances of employees to participate in system designing and data processing. We asked the questions: Was the works' council (the representatives of the employees) engaged in the designing process for the information system in personnel?

Answer	Percentage
no	19.4
works' council was informed about planning and designing models	31.3
models were discussed and conferred with works' council	31.3

Answers	Percentage
systems designing team included representatives of works' council	13.4
there exists no works' council	3.o
no statement	1.5

The result shows only a minor fraction of the respondents made the works' council play an active role in the designing process.

Prerequisite to individual control of personnel data is the chance to get information about the data collected in the data bank. We asked the question: Is the employee allowed to demand information in the data bank related to his person?

Answer	Percentage
yes, he is furnished with information about all data stored relative to his person	71.6
yes, but some data are excluded from information	22.4
no, employee has no right of getting information	3.o
no statement	3.o

There is, in accordance with the German Works Constitution Act (sec. 83) a high degree of information disclosure. Contrary to that in the U.S.A. all enterprises testified by the Privacy Protection Study Commission had policies limiting the disclosure of information about employees[5].

VI. Legal Aspects

Information systems in personnel are a valuable and necessary instrument for rationalizing business information processes. It is to be expected that the scope of the administrative and planning functions exercised as well as the degree of integration with other partial data banks will still increase. The industrial law coverage of information systems in personnel is limping especially far behind the practical interpretation, because lawyers until now have hardly preoccupied themselves with automation points of view. It will be an important task to develop legal solutions which comply with the legitimate interests of those concerned.

The legal problems are usually grouped under the heading "data privacy" and "data security". They have been discussed in numerous publications and official reports. Minimum standards for many problems are contained in the national data protection laws of Austria, Canada, Federal Republic of Germany, France, Denmark, New Zealand, Norway, Sweden, and the United States of America. It is evident that the viewpoint, determined by a liberal tradition, of individual sovereignty and integrity is increasingly shifting toward a discussion of the conditions under which the protection of individual rights appears to be possible at all. Elementary preconditions for the exercise of individual rights are transparency of the stored data and knowledge about the gathering and processing.

The German Federal Data Protection Act (Bundesdatenschutzgesetz) of 1977 asserts the rights to everybody, also to every employee, to

- information regarding the data stored about himself
- correction of the data should it be incorrect
- stoppage if neither correctness nor incorrectness is determined
- cancellation if the storage was inadmissible.

Most employees will, however, not be in a position to actually exercise their rights. It may therefore well be argued that in the long run the development of social control instruments will prove to be much more effective than individual rights of enquiry and access. Such social control instruments include first of all the following and other technical security measures that can in principle be applied unrestrictedly within the sole limits dictated by their costs and efficiency: restrictions of access and use (badge reader, password, fingerprints), the recording of enquiries, programmed barriers in hardware and software, or internal agency regulations. Any further measures taken should be first and foremost of an organizational nature. Thus it is being contemplated to establish public registers on the functional scope, internal processing programmes and control procedures of data banks and to appoint data protection commissioners.

In the sphere of collective rights decision structures and industrial democracy come to the fore. The German Federal Works Constitution Act (Betriebsverfassungsgesetz) of 1972 specifies in many sections (27, 28, 87, 90, 92, 94, 98, 99, 102, 106, 107) participation rights on the works' council, e.g. the need to consent personnel questionnaires, the right to participate in personnel planning or the right to co-determine the introduction of new technical devices. These rights must be transferred cautiously and properly to computerized systems. I think it is necessary to stipulate collective safeguarding of interests with respect to the dimensioning of the data bank, the data framework, the methods of computing the validity and reliability of data collected. On the other hand, it is necessary to limit disclosure of concrete employee data to the works' council as far as sensitive information is concerned[6].

In Germany, interesting developments are arising at present from collective agreements. They offer itself as flexible control instrument for clarifying the following problems:

- the exact purpose of the information system in personnel
- the process for collecting the basic data
- the positive and negative lists of merits and groups of merits to be stored
- the setting up of a register of the computing programmes used
- the participation of the works' council in the conception of new computing programmes
- the settlement of arising conflicts.

VII. Conclusion

The development of legal criteria is still only beginning. This
is clear from the fact that "the same kind of imaginative thinking
and systematic programming and planning must be applied to this
problem as went into the development of the technology for the
information systems themselves"[7].

Notes

1. H.G. Bächler, Einführung eines Personal-Informationssystems
   bei der IBM Schweiz, in: DSWR 1974, 194-200 und 234-241; F. Bla-
   misch u.a., Personal-Verwaltungs-System (PVS). Ein EDV-gestütz-
   tes System zur Verwaltung des Personals und der Stellen der
   Hochschulen, Pullach 1973; J. Bleil/H. Korb. Das computerunter-
   stützte Personaldateninformationssystem der Volkswagen AG, in:
   IBM-Nachrichten Nr. 234 (Februar 1977), 23-27; R. Bunselmeyer,
   Datenbank-Konzepte in der Versicherungswirtschaft, Karlsruhe
   1975; Control Data GmbH, Integriertes Personaldaten- und Ab-
   rechnungssystem. Einführungsinformation. Frankfurt a.M. (o.J.);
   M. Domsch, Personal-Informationssysteme. Instrumente der Per-
   sonalführung und Personalverwaltung, 2. A. Hamburg 1973;
   H. Gebert, Das integrierte Personalinformationssystem (IPIS)
   der Ford Werke AG Köln, in: IBM-Nachrichten 1969, 919-924;
   R. Hackstein/F.W. Meyer, Die Abspeicherung und Auswertung von
   Arbeitsplatz- und Personaldaten mit Hilfe einer EDV-Anlage, in:
   Arbeit und Leistung 1973, 113-123; R. Hackstein u.a., Ein Analy-
   se-Instrument zur Erfassung und zum Vergleich von Arbeitsplatz-
   Anforderungs- und Personalfähigkeitsdaten, Forschungsinstitut
   für Rationalisierung an der TH Aachen 1975; L.J. Heinrich/
   M. Pils, Personalinformationssysteme: Anspruch, Realität, Kon-
   zepte. Arbeitsbericht Nr. 4 des Instituts für Fertigungswirt-
   schaft und Betriebsinformatik der Universität Linz, Linz-Auhof
   1976; B. Hentschel, Einrichtung von Personalinformationssyste-
   men, in: Personal 1975, 191-193; IBM-Deutschland GmbH, IBM-
   Personal-Informationssystem (PERSIS). Ein modulares Anwendungs-
   konzept, IBM Deutschland 1971. IBM Form E 12/1143-0; W. Sämann,
   Personalinformationssysteme, Struktureller Aufbau und Leistungs-
   breite bestehender Personalinformationssysteme in: AWV-Fachbe-
   richt, Frankfurt a.M. 1976; H. Schmidt, Computergestützte Per-
   sonal- und Arbeitsplatz-Informationssysteme, in: AWV-Schrift
   Nr. 126 (1974), 7-27; Siemens AG, Integriertes Verarbeitungs-
   und Informationssystem für Personaldaten (IVIP, München o.J.);
   M. Terasaki, Personaldatenbank im Computer. Beispiel des Fach-
   kräftebestand-Systems der Nippon Electric Company Tokyo, in:
   Industrielle Organisation 40 (1971), 569-571.

2. W. Kilian, Melde- und Auskunftspflichten des Arbeitgebers im
   Personalbereich, in: BB 1977, S. 1153-1159.

3. W.-M. Esser/W. Kirsch, Die Einführung von Planungs- und Infor-
   mationssystemen, München 1979; Information Privacy Research
   Center, Krannert Graduate School of Management, Purdue University (ed.) Working Paper No. 5, Some Employee Perceptions of Information Practices in Large Organization Propriety, Comfort,
   and Invasion of Privacy, Lafayette/Ind./U.S.A. 1979; The Report
   of the Privacy Protection Study Commission (ed.), Personal
   Privacy in an Information Society, U.S. Government Printing
   Office Washington D.C. (1977).

4. Grant No. 140238.

5. The Report of the Privacy Protection Study Commission (note 3),
   p. 269.

6. U.S. Supreme Court, Detroit Edison Co. v. National Labor Relations Board, No. 77-968 (Mar. 5, 1979).

7. A.F. Westin, Information Technology in a Democracy, Harvard University Press, Cambridge/Mass. (1971), p. 301 (307).

Section III

Some Prerequisites for Systems Design in the Interest of the Workers

The profile of overwhelmingly negative consequences of computerization for the workers - that is the actual state of the art -
unfortunately cannot be met with a corresponding set of solutions.
The Section III, instead, concentrates on two major prerequisites
to ameliorate workers' conditions in this process.

The first direction is participation, i.e. the deliberate option for
a strategy in the development of computerized systems jointly operated by workers, systems designers, management.

The first paper - that of Bjørn Anderson and Kjaer - starts from empirical findings in the service industries to derive the necessity
for a broad and efficent workers' participation. It was unfortunately
not possible to find from the realms from which this reader was compiled a comparable study for the productive lines (industrial activities, blue collar-work a.s.o.). This, too, reflects a deficiency of
the state of the art in the debate on social aspects of computerization. It is, of course, also partially due to the fact, that computerization in the service industry now has a longer and better
established history than in the productive realms of our organizations and economies.

The second paper - the paper of Fjalestad - reflecting the Norwegian
model of trade union participation puts the debate on participation
on a general and more theoretical level, thereby somewhat remedying
the deficiencies mentioned before.

The third paper - that of Mende and Ofner - deals with one of the
most urgent new directions for controlling computerization in the
interest of the workers: the need to educate workers.

They also clearly point out that this cannot mean to convey and
extend the existing computer specialists' knowledge to the workers,
but that much broader and deeper concepts of knowledge and of education will have to be elaborated and transferred to the workers. It
ist not raised the question whether it is not expecially the computer specialists who have to learn an enormous series of lessons in order to be really competent to deal with the complex reality which
they are now changing - in not too few cases even to their own detriment.

With this in mind the matter will be handed over to Section IV -
within this volume - and thereby to the presentation of approaches
in technical systems design directly, approaches which try to better
safeguard workers' interest by imposing certain criteria upon these
design processes.

Individual and Social Implications of Data Processing and Office Automation in Service Industries

Niels Bjørn Andersen[1] and John Kjaer[2]

[1] Information Systems Research Group, Copenhagen Buisness School, DK-Copenhagen, Denmark

[2] Royal Chartered General, Fire Insurance Co.Ltd., DK-Copenhagen, Denmark

1. Towards the Automated Office

During the last twenty years we have witnessed changes in working conditions in service industries (i.e. banking, insurance, etc.) more profound than at any time before. Furthermore, we know that the next ten years are going to bring changes even more profound. These changes are primarily due to the trivial fact that the only product within this sector is information.

Without going into information technology to a great extent, we should like to summarize some aspects of the developments of information technology which appear most important to the job situation of clerks and middle managers.

Three developments are especially important - terminals, word processing (which is a buzzword for the growing use of electronic devices for everything else but traditional data processing), and the development of operating/managerial systems based on a new philosophy of control.

The first development is the spreading of terminals. Especially the portable ones make it possible to distribute data entry and data retrieval functions to places where it has not earlier been feasible/economically justifiable. Accordingly, we see today that terminals are placed/used

- in all divisions/departments of a company

- in district offices and in sales situations in the homes/offices of the customers

- in the work of insurance claims agents directly on the spot where the accident has taken place or where the vehicle is to be repaired

- in the homes of the employees.

These terminals are linked to large data bases and large integrated systems.

The second major development is the gradual application of electronic devices to traditional clerical/managerial functions related to manipulation of text, i.e. word processing. Originally word processing is a natural extension of the typewriter. However, the main effects of the word processing are not to be seen before this is integrated with data processing. In other words, traditional stand-alone word processors are not likely to have any significant impact on the job content, but as soon as data processing and word processing are integrated via telecommunications, electronic mail, data retrieval programs, etc., we shall witness tremendous changes in working conditions in service industries. The concept "Image processing" portends the disappearance of paper and a strong utilization of terminals. The third development is covered by the concept "CWIP" - Control Work in Process. This is a continuation of the automation of office work made possible during the sixties and seventies through data bases and integrated application systems.

Monitoring of clerks' work in insurance and public services is now one of the ways of increasing productivity. The idea of CWIP is that the terminal continually informs the clerk what he has to do next. It keeps track of his outstanding cases, it presents new cases/transactions to be dealt with and so on. Even the method of work and its sequence are controlled by the computer. Individual decision making is reduced to defaults and standard answers. "Automation of this kind of work is impossible", we said in the sixties. "It is a necessity", we are told in the eighties.

In this paper we are going to question whether this is a desirable development. We shall do that by discussing the effects of computerization in general and especially highlight the possible changes in working conditions by examples from the insurance and banking sectors. Finally, we shall point out some of the activities taking place in the trade union movement today in order to control and avoid any negative consequences of computerization.

2. Changing Role of Employees

A major problem when studying the impact of computer technology in office automation is that its character as a knowledge technology makes it less concrete than other technologies. It has many potential applications. Accordingly, its effects will, to a great extent, be determined by the objectives set for the computer system, by whoever is involved in the processes of design. Weizenbaum, (1976) puts it this way,

> "...the computer, as presently used by the technological elite, is not a cause of anything. It is rather an instrument pressed into the service of rationalizing, supporting, and sustaining the most conservative, indeed, reactionary, ideological components of the current Zeitgeist".

It is, however, important to realize that it is not an easy matter to identify the members of this technological elite. In our opinion, it would be a mistake to equate the management of a company with this elite, although in many instances there will be a strong agreement amongst both technological experts and management that profit maximization and rationalization shall be major system objectives.

It must be recognized that it may be extremely difficult for even management and experts to control computer developments within the enterprise. A knowledge of the likely consequences, so far as these can be identified, may be a step towards better control.

Ancient philosophers have put forward three ideals for human endeavour: truth, goodness, and beauty. Modern philosophers have added a fourth: prosperity (Ackoff, 1962), p. 430-431. These four ideals can be defined in the following way:

" 1. The scientific ideal of perfect knowledge (i.e. complete attainment of truth): the ability of every individual to develop and select instruments and courses of action which are perfectly efficient for the attainment of any end.

2. The politico-economic ideal of plenty or abundance: The availability to every individual of courses of action and the instruments necessary for them which are perfectly efficient for the attainment of any end.

3. The ethical-moral ideal of goodness: (a) the absence of contrary and contradictory objectives within each individual (i.e. peace of mind), since no state of plenty or knowledge can make the attainment of such objectives possible, (b) the absence of conflicting objectives among people (i.e. peace on earth, good will toward man), since only in the absence of such conflict can every individual attain his objectives.

    These three ideals would be vacuously attained if no one wanted anything. The universal wish for the ability to attain any objective itself presupposes that

	FRENCH BATCH		DANISH BATCH		BRITISH ON-LINE		DANISH ON-LINE		SWEDISH ON-LINE	
	INC	DEC	INC	DEC	INC	DEC	INC	DEC	INC	DEC
I TASK VARIETY	24	44	9	57	42	23	42	8	67	25
FREEDOM FROM REPETITION	11	27	35	26	32	14	21	21	17	58
II ERROR DETECTION BY PEOPLE	22	41	0	43	0	89	8	46	4	92
RAPID ERROR FEED-BACK	47	4	17	17	71	12	58	0	92	4
III PACE OF WORK	54	6	9	22	76	3	21	13	33	37
OWN CONTROL OF WORK PACE	13	12	13	17	0	20	21	13	12	56
STEADY WORK PACE	37	5	63	4	14	29	13	17	32	40
CONVENIENT HOURS	5	1	65	0	83	0	0	62	32	14
IV FREEDOM FROM CLOSE SUPERVISION	2	26	17	9	43	29	8	8	23	5
SUPERVISORS KNOWLEDGE OF JOB	26	9	4	4	0	38	17	33	4	57
V METHODS CHOICE	11	32	9	57	4	42	0	29	8	48
SEQUENCE CHOICE	13	21	0	9	5	29	4	8	8	40
FREEDOM FROM WORK INSTRUCTIONS	22	50	0	30	0	69	0	37	12	52
VI RESPONSIBILITY FOR DECISIONS	6	6	0	13	57	0	8	0	33	4
USE OF TRAINING	4	12	22	26	32	24	25	0	44	22
LEARNING IN THE JOB	45	6	22	22	73	9	58	0	80	0
VII WORK INTEREST	6	9	17	26	71	0	50	4	76	0

Figure 1: Percentage of the clerks in each bank having perceived an impact by the computer system. INC: Increased, DEC: Decreased.

there are desired ends (i.e. unfulfilled objectives) and that they continuously expand. Hence, the last ideal:

4. The aesthetic ideal of beauty: the existence in every individual's environment of stimuli which inspire him to raise his aspirations, to enlarge the scope and meaning of his experience."

In order to make explicit the way in which electronic digital technology influences man's behaviour and attitudes as an office worker, we shall use these ideals as the basis for a classification of the impact of this technology on employees as found in a number of empirical studies.

For each of the four ideals we shall discuss the extent to which computer technology has influenced the role of clerks and managers.

2.1 Influence on Politico-Economic Values

Electronic digital technology came into operation at a time when communication and control problems were the major impediments to the concentration of capital. The economic benefits of large-scale operations (low costs per transaction) were often lost through poor control and an inability to adapt to new market opportunities. Decentralization, divisionalizing, profil centres, etc. were attempts to overcome these problems. The alternative approach was an improvement of horizontal and vertical information system (Galbraith, 1973) and electronic digital technology turned out to be restricted or even reversed and the technology made it possible for the management of large organisations to re-centralize.

2.1.1. Changes in Degree of Structure

An increased control of the use of production resources is intended to improve profitability. Often this is accompanied by altered job functions where the most pronounced change is an increased structuring/programming/planning of the work performed by the individual. All buffers are reduced or disappear, and an increased dependence between productive units (groups or individuals) is established.

This may be illustrated by showing the results obtained in a large international study carried out in five banks in Denmark, France, Great Britain, and Sweden.
These banks had introduced different computer systems. The impact of the computer systems on the role of the clerks was analysed, using interviews. Some of the results are shown in figure 1 (Bjørn-Andersen et.al., 1980).

Especially, if one looks to the variables in group V it is important to note that in all banks we see a decrease in the number of work instructions. This all points towards a higher degree of structuring of the job.

Similar results were obtained by Whisler (1970) in his study of the impact of computer systems on insurance companies. He states that "... it is critical in computerized systems that employees perform precisely as the system demands. Greater reliability in performance is required."

In a study of the consequences of an on-line system in a Danish insurance company (Kjær, 1977) it is concluded that the production-oriented goals of the system

- easy to use
- rapidity
- a high degree of security against errors
- no time constraints from edp

had been obtained.

However, in order to achieve these objectives the designers of the system have had to introduce a higher degree of structuring and control of the work processes. This has caused a perceived decrease in task variation, more repetitious work, more sedentary work, and less communication with colleagues. A change from group work towards more isolated, individual performance-oriented work.

The same tendencies towards a higher degree of structuring holds true for managers as constantly greater parts of the managerial job are taken over by the computerized systems.

In a recent study carried out by one of the authors (Bjørn-Andersen & Pedersen, 1980) we investigated the impact of a production planning and control system in a Danish radio and TV production company on the discretion (autonomy, self-control of the job) of three groups of managers, production planners, factory managers and shop stewards. The results are shown in figure 2.

Change in: Number of respondents	Planners (9) .	Factory Managers (3)	Shop Stewards ·(5)
1. Dependence on the work of others	1.3	0.7	1.4
2. Rules, procedures, methods	1.6	1.3	1.0
3. Goals, policies, plans	0.8	1.0	1.2
4. Supervision of task	1.1	0.7	1.2
5. Orders and advice from subordinates	0.8	0.0	0.6
6. Orders and advice from superiors	-0.3	-0.3	-1.2

Figure 2:   Average changes in limits of direction within the day-to-day task perceived by the three groups as caused by the computer system. Scale from +2 (large increase in limits) to -2 (large decrease in limits).

It is interesting to note that everybody perceived limitations in their discretion as a consequence of the introduction of the computer system on all dimensions except orders and advice from superior. The restrictions imposed through more dependency on others, more rules, more procedures, more methods, more goals, more policies, and more plans confirm the hypothesis that computer systems function as impersonal control - mechanisms designed in order to improve the overall efficiency of the factory by limiting the discretion of the individual managers. This is even supported by the fact that there has been a decrease in the number of orders and advice from superiors.

These are no longer as necessary as because the computer system has taken over parts of the control task.

A second interesting aspect of the results is the high degree of similarity between the three groups. The limitations in discretion have not exclusively been confined e.g. to the line managers (shop stewards and factory managers) but are also felt by staff managers (planners), who obtained the role as gatekeepers to the technology.They were the ones who actually got a new and better tool. Even though the planners had gained in general influence (which normally happens to gatekeepers) they too had lost discretion.

In insurance companies the same tendencies appear. Stymne (1966) found in his study in insurance companies "extensive changes more directed towards the creation of a more rational structure, where insurance-professionel orientation was replaced by conscious planning and control of production". On the other hand, Whisler (1970) found that "the number and variety of responsibilities were increased for most superiors".

We do not see any contradiction here. The likely general trend is that the routine tasks are automated "from below" leaving the managers more time to get involved in middle to long range planning. As a matter of fact that is the general trend throughout the company, and the consequence is that the job of everybody gets more structured as the planning of yesterday is limiting the discretion of today.

2.1.2 Change in Degree of Control

Closely linked to the question of structure is the opportunity for control. If jobs get more routinized this will often create a decrease in job satisfaction and a need to control the job and the performance of the individual in order that production may be maintained at a reasonable level. This again may cause the need for routinizing the job even more to make it more susceptible to tighter controls. We have started what Culowsen calls a negative spiral, illustrated by the following figure.

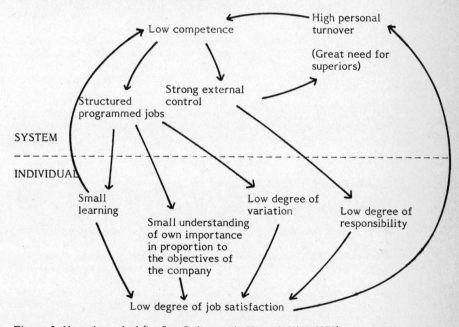

Figure 3: Negative spiral (by Jon Gulowsen in Haug & Kjær 1978).

One must bear in mind that the most important function of information technology is to control the utilization of resources. If the production resource is labour, and this is true of almost all administrative computer systems, this will mean a higher degree of control of the individual in his work situation. Especially, this is true in fairly routine jobs where only a fraction of all human skills are utilized.

Terminals and microprocessors built into cash registers and production equipment offer opportunity for second-by-second registration of the activities of the operator, for comparisons with standard norms and with the performance of other operators.

This means that management may increase the pressure on the individual either through direct intervention (everything from the polite request to sacking) or through pressure from colleagues in the work group.

Attitudes of this kind were behind the proposal of introducing an advanced computer system in a Paris-based insurance company. All traditional keys were substituted with identity cards and every door including the door to the lavatories was furnished with card readers. Only if the computer system accepted your card would you be permitted to enter. Obviously, such a system could also be used for all kinds of very detailed control of the individual, and the trade union called out a strike until the system was abandoned.

2.1.3 Changes in Ergonomic Factors

Although the introduction of computer technology has removed many strains, a number of ergonomic problems, reduced eyesight, headaches, back pains, stress, etc. have been caused by the introduction of terminals. The reason for this should by found in the fact that design of dialogue-based terminal systems will always be subject to a series of constraints, for instance demands from other system, demands on economy, productivity, privacy of customers, etc. These demands often recoil upon the individual user. Average workplace layout is used instead of tailor-made, and systems intended for the average user, who only exists in theory, are designed. Accordingly, many systems are generally bad for everybody.

However, in the design of on-line systems, many, but not all, Scandinavian corporations have shown extensive ergonomic considerations when deciding on special workstations, lighting, etc. Better VDU screens, detailed keyboards, etc. have been developed. It is our opinion that most problems of this type are trivial ones if they are dealt with in the design process. Very often it is a question of investment in better individualized workstations.

One of the ergonomic problems which is not dealt with that easily, is the stress problem. A study done in the insurance conpany Skandia, Sweden, by The Psychological Institute for The University of Stockholm (1979) shows that insurance clerks working with terminals experienced a higher degree of stress than clerks doing non-terminal work. The study also showed that the higher stress level measured by blood pressure and the level of adrenalin, remained with the clerks for several hours after they had finished the day's work and returned home.

The absolute stress level at terminal work is considerable even though it does not belong to the so-called "stress top", namely bus drivers during rush hours.

Factors influencing stress are,

- the kind and amount of work
- the time length of each terminal session
- response times
- system breakdown
- external interruptions, e.g. noise, phones, customers, etc.

The more routinized, the greater amount of work, the longer work at the terminal, the more fluctuating response times, the higher incidence of system breakdowns, and the more frequent the external interruptions - the more stressing is the work at the terminal. Guidelines for the design of terminals in order to avoid these kinds of problems may be found in Haug & Kjær (1978).

2.1.4 Change in Economic Efficiency

The main objective of introducing new computer technology is of course to increase productivity and efficiency. In spite of the fact that many investments in systems have failed, there is no doubt that the technologly has contributed substantially towards a higher standard of living in society. To a great extent this has been achieved through the substitution of manual labour with machines, and substantial savings in labour have taken place within many corporations. If computer systems were to by abandoned, the volume of work carried out in, for instance, insurance companies and banks today could not be accomplished without large increases in staff. A conservative estimate would be at least a doubling of the staff. Furthermore, by no means are we today at the end of the road as regards labour savings. As an example, the Nora and Minc report (1978) to the French president estimates that there will be a 30% decrease in staff in service industries in the eighties.

Therefore, there is no doubt that technology has contributed substantially towards the attainment of economic and material prosperity. However, this raises two questions. Firstly the technology has no characteristics which lead to a more equal distribution of wealth, either between those with jobs and those without, or among countries. The contrary seems to be the case. Secondly our breathless striving towards the economic ideal of wealth seems to sacrifice our attainment of the other three ideals mentioned previously.

2.2 Influence on Epistomological (knowledge) Values

2.2.1 Change in General Skill Levels

This section concerns changes in knowledge and skill. One might raise the questsion whether, in general, technology puts higher demands on staff or whether we shall see a tendency towards employment of more unskilled labour.

Jaffe & Froomkin (1968) report that insurance companies which have experienced high increases in worker productivity show a corresponding growth of skilled positions. Crossman & Laner (1969) show that because of computerization, skill requirements immediately essential to job performance tend to increase, while skill requirements in maintenance and support functions tend to decrease. This is consistent with Mowshowitz (1976) who observes that "... in insurance, computer systems eliminate many jobs connected with support functions, while introducing new operating jobs with higher skill require-ments".

In spite of the obvious consistency in the results, several reasons could be found to explain why there could be disagreement about whether or not skill demands have changed. On the one hand it can be argued that computerization will lead to higher demands on skills, as

- the most routinized jobs are the ones to be automated first, leaving the most demanding tasks for the clerk and manager
- when new systems are introduced one must learn how to use the new system, which is an extra skill to acquire

However, certain aspects point in the opposite direction, i.e.

- new routine tasks (often related to control of the performance of the system) are introduced
- more structure is introduced in the job, making the total job more routinized as the man-machine interface has to be very formalized
- some more demanding tasks disappear as the knowledge of the clerk is transferred to a computer program.

In order to evaluate the balance of these diverse developments it all comes back to the key question of specialization, where it is necessary to differentiate between vertical and horizontal specialization.

2.2.2. Change in Specialization

The electronic technology demands a certain amount of knowledge for it to be evaluated and exploited. Large groups do not possess this knowledge or are not allowed to possess it, and this means that a vertical specialization between the planning task and the performance task has taken place.

This has been taken to mean that in future it would be impossible for users and clients to participate in the formulation of system objectives. Therefore, the influence of users/clients has not been found in most systems' designs. Typically, the technology has been introduced in such a way that a division between planning and operation has taken place. The system planner defines the need for information, designs the system, handles the programming and implements the system. The user is often an astonished spectator. For many reasons, this is unacceptable. The knowledge and understanding of solutions to administrative problems are generated with the system planner and not with the person carrying out the task. The accumulation of knowledge takes place away from the user/client who will have only limited opportunities for handling errors in the system and for modifying it.

Another typical problem related to the introduction of electronic equipement is horizontal specialization. Terminals and other peripheral equipment are still so expensive that viewed from a narrow efficiency perspective it is economical not to purchase a terminal for each employee but to train a small number of employees and make them operate a limited number of terminals all day long. One example of this type of specialization was found in the international study of the impact of computer systems on bank clerks. Three banks were studied which had systems on three different levels of technology. 23 dimensions in the jobs were measured, using interviews, and an index of job quality was calculated for the two user groups, direct users (directly operating terminals) and indirect users (primarily only using output from the computer system). The results obtained are shown in figure 4.

	A Batch	B On-line data entry	C Real-time
Direct users	179	233	270
Indirect users	158	177	170

Figure 4: Job index for direct and indirect users in the three banks. The higher the figure the poorer the job.

Looking at the job index we can see first that there is a difference in the level of job content within each bank. In all three banks the job of working directly with the computer system either as a terminal operator, or as a clerk filling in punching vouchers and controlling output, is poorer than that of working indirectly with the computer.

Secondly, the figures in figure 4 illustrate the fact that the difference in job content between direct and indirect users becomes larger as the technology becomes more advanced. The index for the indirect users of the computer systems is approximately the same in all three banks, but there is a clear indication that the direct users in bank A have a better job than the direct users in bank B and these again a better job than the direct users in bank C. One might argue that there is an accumulation of effects resulting in very large differences between direct and indirect user jobs in the technologically most advanced system. The better job content is especially obvious on variables such as more task variation, fewer written instructions, more opportunity for selection of one's own work methods and more opportunity for showing initiative.

And now history repeats itself with the computer technology being used in different kinds of equipment. For instance, we have seen how word processing systems are introduced with the recommendation that the best "typist" be selected to take care of all the keying functions, regardless of the consequences this may have for her job satisfaction.

2.3 Influence on Ethical/Moral Values

One of the first changes introduced by this technology on ethical (moral values was already observed by Whisler (1970). He found that the introduction of computer systems caused a <u>decrease in the communiction</u> between employees and that personal communications and the man-computer interaction were dominated by giving and receiving impersonal informations to and from the computer system. In our opinion there is no doubt that technological deveopments since the study of Whisler have contributed further in the direction of impersonal communication, and this is indeed also confirmed by later studies of companies working with on-line systems, Kjær (1977).

A second important question concerns whether there is a change in <u>human relationships</u> and in the way we handle complex interpersonal interaction. An even more critical question is whether, as a result of computer systems, we make decisions in a way which is less compatible with our ethical/moral values. There are strong indications at present that we are experiencing a shift in the premises on which decisions are made. Qualitative premises are replaced by quantitative premises, and only those factors which are possible to specify exactly, and consequently to computerize, are taken into account. Decisions based on rules will then tend to replace decisions based on desired consequences as more precise prescriptions are applied to individual jobs and more efficient control mechanisms become available to ensure the observance of the rules.

One of the latest applications of terminals is to place terminals in the homes of the employees in order that they may carry out (part of) their work at home. Among other things this would mean reduced transportation time and energy saving in society, and the employee will get more freedom to carry out the task when he/she is motivated for doing it. As a matter of fact, some time ago one of the authors received a request from the office of the German Bundeskansler. The question was whether there was any research done on the impact of home terminals, as the use of home terminals was seen as a solution to the problem of having a shortage of kindergartens in the Federal Republic. Home terminals would allow mothers to stay at home and take care of the children and at the same time carry out the work via the terminal. We strongly recommend not viewing home terminals as "the solution" to that problem.

Firstly, the job at a terminal at home does not give any kind of social contact with other human beings, which is one of the prime reasons for most women for taking jobs in the first place. Secondly, it invites a higher degree of stress than experienced in most jobs today as the work place is always there, even in one's spare time. Thirdly, the tasks at the terminal demand a high degree of accuracy which does not seem compatible with taking care of children.

Finally, we shall mention the influence of technology on job satisfaction and alienation. Almost always the impact of technology on job satisfaction in office work is positive. Concern about the effects of computer systems is normally most pronounced before implementation but it usually transpires that employees prefer to work with the new system and do not want to return to the old one. However, in spite of this, systems often contribute to feelings of alienation with work. Several studies show increased alienation and a higher degree of instrumentality in job relationships.

2.4.4. Influence on Aesthetic Values

So far as we know, no scientifically well-founded empirical studies have been made of the impact of electronic digital technology on aesthetic values. The technology seems to offer enhancing potential in music where analogue signals are transformed to digital ones in order to make them better suited for editing before they are transferred back to analogue signals. However, it is highly doubtful whether this technology contributes to our attainment of aesthetic values by being applied in electronic music or in computer graphics, any more than plastic has contributed by being used in artificial flowers.

3. User participation in Systems Design

3.1. Trend Towards Democratization

In the last few years there has been a clear tendency for users/employees/trade unions to become more hostile towards computerization in general. In our opinion this is a reaction to the fact that computer systems have been designed with a negligible concern for the human aspect. The reason for this cannot be a lack of normative guidelines for taking human aspects into account. Several guidelines exist for designing socio-technical systems in general (Mumford & Henshall 1979, Bjørn-Andersen & Hedberg 1977, Bjørn-Andersen 1980), for designing terminal dialogues (Haug & Kjær 1978) and for designing computer systems in insurance in particular (Haug, Wines & Forfang 1979, Næsborg etal. 1979). These are just examples.

However, when these guidelines/recommendations are not followed, we see this as an indication that technical/economic objectives are dominating the design process. Therefore, it is to be expected that the employees will demand some influence on the system design process in order to make sure that their interests are taken into account.

In a study from 1977 employees in Danish savings banks were asked about the extent to which their interests were taken into account when the recent system was introduced. 60% felt that only to a slight extent or not at all were the interests of the employees taken into account. Furthermore, no less than 79% of all the employees wanted influence on the design of future systems in the bank. The significance of these figures is emphasized by the fact that only 30% of the employees requested influence on systems design when the same group was asked exactly the same question in a similar study in 1974 (Bjørn-Andersen & Jappe, 1979).

This tendency is supported by the general development in society towards a higher degree of democratization. Sometimes objections are raised to democracy, e.g.

- It takes longer
- It is more inefficient to have more people and more groups
- It invites systematic manipulation of individuals and groups
- It increases opportunities for polarization and obstructionism
- It invites mediocrity and superficiality
- It limits creativity, as a vast amount of the social science literature has shown that the committee approach is more likely to be unimaginative
- It politicises the design process which can be dangerously counter-productive
- It represents a higher risk of not arriving at the best solutions, as we all know that majority opinion can often be wrong
- It particularly needs professionally trained change agents who know how to run groups effectively. You cannot just get people together and have them work smoothly without their first getting to know one another.

However, these points do not reflect reality, and as Sackman points out, "...I believe, with Winston Churchill, that democracy is the least worse form of government. It is our job to improve it as best we can." (Bjørn-Andersen, 1980).

Although management in many companies strongly resist direct user participation in systems design, in some companies there are already good results of user participation. According to empirical research the main benefits to be achieved seen from the point of view of management are

- lower costs
- increased productivity
- easier implementation
- improved quality

while the main benefits seen from the point of view of the users are

- better work environment
- reduces alienation
- stepping stone to industrial democracy

However, in spite of these obvious advantages management seems reluctant to allow for a greater degree of user participation and as a result we see strong pressure from users and trade unions.

If user interest is still not taken into account through real user participation in systems design, we are going to see an increased radicalization of the industrial relations climate.

3.2. Role of Trade Unions

Trade unions in the Scandinavian countries became seriously interested/involved in evaluating and trying to control technological developments in 1971 when the Norwegian Iron and Metal Workers' Union received a grant from the Norwegian Technical Research Fund for investigating the consequences of introducing computer technology and for formulating demands and plans for controlling this technology.

Since then more than twenty trade union research projects have been launched in the Scandinavian countries.

The main characteristics have been

- one party projects, i.e. no involvement of management, and the trade union is the only group controlling the project

- clear conflict perspective, i.e. it is assumed that the objectives of workers and management are not compatible

- action oriented, i.e. aims at increasing knowledge within the trade union, building central power for decentral action, analysing consequences of systems solutions, and at formulating demands on system.

A large number of systems has been investigated and many trade unions have formulated demands to guide future developments of computer systems. This has taken place on two levels. First of all there have been attempts from trade unions to get agreements/laws giving them the right to participate and secondly there have been a number of demands raised in relation to specific computer applications.
Today there are a number of laws/agreements already granting employees influence and participation in system design.

Most far-reaching is the law about co-determination, which has been in effect in Sweden since January 1977. This meets most of the demands raised above. According to this law,

§11   The employer must initiate negotiations when he plans "important changes".

§12   The union has the right to demand negotiations on issues not covered by §11.

§19   Employers have the duty to continually inform workers about
- personnel issues
- budgets
- plans
- prognoses
- work and production methods

§38   Employers must negotiate before engaging consultants or subcontractors (union veto).

However, one must realize that this is only a framework law, and that within each industry employers and employees must negotiate in order to establish the details of an agreement.

In Norway, a general agreement between the Norwegian TUC and the Employers' Federation has been established, covering the areas mentioned above, even though it is weaker in the sense that it gives the employees less influence. This is also a framework agreement, and within this each company or industry must make its own detailed agreement. Up till now more than 7oo separate agreements have been established and some of these meet all the demands raised above.

In Denmark parts of the demands are covered by The Work Environment Act. Furthermore several data agreements (banking, insurance, public telephone services, etc.) have been established.

4. Conclusion

We have seen a very significant impact of computer technology on service industries and the work role of the individual employee. Furthermore, this development is going to accelerate in the next ten years to come. Employees and their representatives are becoming more and more aware of the risks involved in this development, and we are going to see increased demands for influence and participation. Today these demands are strongest in the northernmost part of Europe (Norway and Sweden), but the demands are also strong in Denmark and there are signs of trade unions also preparing themselves to move into this area in the Federal Republic, in the United Kingdom and in Holland. In our opinion it is high time that managers and computer specialists start preparing themselves for a situation where the users have the right of participating in all decisions influencing their own work situation.

Bibliography:

ACKOFF, R.L. (1962). Scientific Method. Wiley, N.Y.

ANDERSEN, H. (1980). New Edp-Report from the Danish Insurance Employees' Union. Forsikringsfunktionaeren. No. 1, March. (In Danish).

BJØRN-ANDERSEN, N. and RASMUSSEN, L.B. (1980). Sociological Implications of Computer Systems. In: Hugh Smith and Thomas Green (eds.). Man-Computer Research. Academic Press, London.

BJØRN-ANDERSEN, N. (ed.) (1980). The Human Side of Information Processing. North-Holland, Amsterdam.

BJØRN-ANDERSEN, N. et al. (1979). The Impact of Systems Change in Organisations. Sijthoff and Noordhoff, Alphen aan den Rijn.

BJØRN-ANDERSEN, N. (1983). Information Technology and Power Change in Organizations - Prospects of Technology Agreements and Technology Assessments. In: K.W. Grewlich and F.H. Pedersen (eds.). Power and Participation in an Information Society.

BJØRN-ANDERSEN, N. and PEDERSEN, P.H. (1980). Computer Facilitated Changes in the Power Structure. Accounting, Organization and Society, vol. 5, no. 2.

BJØRN-ANDERSEN, N. and JAPPE, L. (1979). Computer Impact and the Demand for Participation. In: A. Niemi (ed.) A Link Between Science and Applications of Automatic Control. Pergamon Press, Oxford.

BJØRN-ANDERSEN, N. and HEDBERG, B. (1977). Designing Information Systems in an Organizational Perspective. In: P.C. Nystrom and W.H. Starbuck (eds.). Prescriptive Models of Organizations. TIMS Studies in the Management Sciences, 5, North-Holland, Amsterdam.

CROSSMAN, E.R.F.W. and LANER, S. (1969). The Impact of Technological Change on Manpower and Skill Demand: Case-Study and Policy Implications. Berkeley, California.

GALBRAITH, J.R. (1973). Designing Complex Organisations. Addison-Wesley, Reading, Mass.

HAUG, T., WINES, S. and FORFANG, E. (1979). A Temporary Attitude to Computer Technology and Work Places within Insurance. Oslo. (In Norwegian).

JAFFE, A.J. and FROOMKIN, J. (1968). Technology and Jobs. Praeger, N.Y.

JOHANSSON, G. and ARONSSON, G. (1979). Stress-Reactions in Work with VDU's. University of Stockholm, Report no. 27. (In Swedish).

KJAER, J. (1977). On-Line Production and Job Content in Insurance. NordDATA 1977. proceedings pp. 272-275. (In Danish).

MOWSHOWITZ, A. (1976). The Conquest of Will. Information Processing In Human Affairs. Addison-Wesley, Reading, Mass.

MUMFORD, E. and HENSHALL, D. (1979). A Participative Approach to Computer Systems Design. Associated Business Press, London.

NORA, S. and MINC, A. (1978). L'Informatisation de la Société. Vol. 1, Paris.

NAESBORG et al. (1978). Edp-Report. The Danish Insurance Employees' Union. Copenhagen. (In Danish).

SKANDIA (1979). Stress-Report. Stockholm. (In Swedish).

STYMNE, B. (1966). EDP and Organizational Structure: A Case Study of an Insurance Company. Swedish Journal of Economics, 68, 4.

WHISLER, T.L. (1970). Information Technology and Organizational Change. Wadsworth, Belmont.

Participation in Technical Change

Jostein Fjalestad

Norwegian Computing Center, P.O. Box 335, Blindern, N-Oslo 3, Norway

1. INTRODUCTION

This paper is mainly adressing issues related to information
technology. I feel, however, slightly uncomfortable about this.
Information technology has, however, become such a "hot" topic
that in many cases technological change is interpreted as change
involving information technology. This is unfortunate as technological change (of course) is vastly more diversified. There are
other important major trends, in Norway the obvious example is
the development of off-shore oil-exploration and petrochemical
industries. On the local level less "exotic" technologies often
cause greater changes in work organization and employment than
the installation of new computer systems. In fact technical
change in organizations often appears to have less dramatic
impacts than both technological optimists and pessimists "crying
wolf" at every point of change like to think.

But: Information technology remains one of the major trends of
technological change. It is a gift of fire that can be used for
better or for worse, depending on the intentions and abilities of
those who control development and use. This paper will examine
strategies and conditions for enhancing influence from employees
in this game.

2. SOME EMERGING TRENDS

The information technology is changing rapidly, so rapidly that
we constantly have to update our conceptions of its nature.
Without such adjustments it will be difficult to plot schemes for
influencing the development.

Most large and middle sized organizations have by now to some
extent automated their administrative routines, at least the
large "bulk" operations yielding the easy profit. The future
development will consist of updating existing systems and pursuing new targets like office automation where the gains may be
less obvious and often other than simple savings in man-power.

Small firms are now entering the bulk-automation phase, made
possible through the introduction of cheap microcomputers with
reliable, easy to use application programs. In a way they are
going through the same development as large firms were ten or
fifteen years ago, but more rapidly and with less problems and
relatively less costs.

Sinking costs are accelerating the diffusion of information

technology, not only because it becomes more easy to invest, financially speaking. Because of this the investment analysis becomes less serious, even sloppy. To many people it seems no point in using more resources to evaluate an investment than the investment itself takes. One simply buys it if one feels like it. Diffusion becomes more rapid, less planned and the impacts even more difficult to predict.

This development may contradict the traditional role of EDP-departments in larger firms, but the centralized systems will still play an important role as the "information technology core" of the firms. The large computer is not being killed by the mini or micro. It is being supplemented. But there is growing power struggle and diversification among different technologies. The proliferation of personal computers and similar technologies will to a considerable extent change the way firms introduce new applications. This again will have implications for the design of strategies for participation.

Another important development is the growing use of application oriented software packages (often running on dedicated hardware), the obvious example being text-processing and new user-oriented programming tools, so called application generators. The latter will in many cases allow the users to program their own applications - to a certain extent. Again this will change the relations between the edp-department and the way projects are organized.

Communication is becoming an increasingly important feature of computerized systems. Both are new ways of communicating established and traditional applications of edp are being interconnected. Again one byproduct is more rapid diffusion. In some sectors like trade and travel, connection to a sentralized information system seems to be one of the most important drives behind computerization. This may make information technology less managable from a user point of view as important decisions are taken outside the organization of the single user. It also makes interorganizational impacts more crucial. Information technology makes the operation of multinational cooperations more efficient and centrally controlled. Market control by monopolies or oligopolies may be facilitated.

3.   PARTICIPATION IN TECHNOLOGICAL CHANGE

The introduction of information technology into organizations seems, in many cases, to lead to or intensify tendencies to arrange the work place in ways which often are in conflict with the interests of groups of employees and their trade unions. This applies to working conditions and employment as well as the balance of power in the organization, and hence the possibilities of influencing decision-making.

The proliferation of computerized systems emphazising formalized, structured and hierarchical procedures may be described as neo-Taylorism. It need not be so. Information technology could just as well be used to support more satisfying ways of organizing work, but it is not likely that the continued development of information technology will of its own accord counteract the undesirable tendencies. It is possible, however, that a greater variety of technological alternatives and a more flexible technology might provide a greater range of choices, thus making a better final solution from the employee's point of view more likely. The extent to which this will happen depends on the ability of the employees to influence the development of information technology as well as the local choice of technology.

The choice of technology in an organization will often involve conflicts of interests. Typical is the case where the technology is used to introduce forms of organization that improve efficiency and control at the expance of reduced autonomy and increased work load onthe part of the workers. In such cases the introduction of information technology will appear as a game of power. The interests with most power attached will determine the course of events. This power game need not be experienced as such by those who put the technology to use. Their aim may simply be to improve efficiency. Likewise, the people who are affected may not feel as though anyone in particular is opposing their interests. What they feel is just impotence in the face of a development which seems inevitable.

The edp-experts have tended to grossly underestimate the complexity of organizations and the difficulties inherent in the process of reproducing human systems by automatic ones. Not only are system development projects often behind schedule, the systems produced leaves much to be desired regarding administrative and technical qualities, and they are met by reactions among the employees involved ranging from reluctance to downright hostility. As a result of this, cooperation between experts and the organization to be changed, has become more common. A normal form of such cooperation is the use of user-representatives in project groups. At least in Norway this has also coincided with pressure from the trade unions for representation in project groups. User-representatives have thus become the most common form of participation in systems development, but representing different motivations and not necessarily resulting in the same appointment of persons. From a management's point of view, representation is seen as means for providing the project group with crucial information about the functioning of the organization, evaluation of proposed solutions and contact with the rest of the potential users of a future system. Participation is, in other words, used as some sort of organization development. From a trade union's point of view participation is regarded in another fashion. Here it is seen upon as an instrument for democratization through greater influence on systems development. But even if priority is given to specific trade union interests, it is evident that the employees also will welcome better working systems.

Considerable experience has demonstrated that user-representatives often play a loosing game seen from the democratization angle. At the same time as being very valuable as providers of information on technical or administrative matters, they are not able to exercise any influence regarding working conditions, employment and similar matters, conserning the interest of the employees. We have a one-sided cooperation where the representatives have become "hostages of the technology".

So far I have somewhat vaguely mentioned "trade union interests" and "social impacts" affecting these interests. There is much current research demonstrating real problems in this area which deserve serious attention. It is an interesting fact that negative social consequences often are called "unexpected", at the same time as it is quite evident that in most cases where such impacts occur, those who label them as unexpected did not invest much time, money or energy on predicting what specific social consequences could be expected or avoiding the unwanted ones.

However, it should not be forgotten that there also are impacts that are very much "expected". Those are impacts like improved productivity, control or other things that, in most cases, can be labeled as management interests, constituting the explicit objectives of system development projects, and attracting most resources available. As a rule new systems are able to give a positive contribution to such goods.

It is most tempting to conclude that we have a situation where the management's interests are the ones that are the most explicitly formulated, having the most resources at hand, and therefore are best off when counting the "unexpected" and the "expected" consequences.

In some cases, removal of unwanted social consequences will "only" be a question of developing better knowledge of possible problems, and how to avoid them by using better methods for system development, cooperation with users and the like. Even if this may be difficult enough, the most serious cases will be those where there are conflicting interests. Conflicts will occur where better systems regarding the users interests are more expensive to buy or to develop, and in many cases having a potential for conflicts of more ideological nature. In such cases the management's philosophy, regarding, for instance, control or division of labour, may collide violently with the wishes for a more autonomous working situation and more challenging jobs. So, if we want participation in systems development to be a step in the direction of a more democratic society, it must be developed in such a manner that it will increase the workers' ability to defend their interests, also in cases of conflicting interests. Thus, the power attached to trade union interests will be an important condition for achieving technical solutions better suited to the needs of people.

4.   THE CONTEXT OF PARTICIPATION

Much discussion of participation in systems development is limited to the internal routines of the single company or organization, hardly surprising, since we are dealing with the question of local decisions conserning technological choice. It must not be forgotten, however, that in our societies the choice of technology within the single organization remains rather limited. The actual techniques eligible have already quite a number of important decisions built into them.[1]

Then the choice, adaption and use of techniques will be heavily influenced by factors external to the single organization. Technology is not an independent variable which can be chosen and adapted by wish as it appears to be assumed in some of the current work research. Given the present situation regarding participation, there seems to be, however, considerable space for increasing influence for the workers within the existing limits. Along with the exploration of the possibilities within these limits, researchers should also start to consider if and how these limits can be moved.

External limits consist on the one hand of acts and agreements, on the other hand of economical and political factors. From a trade union's point the first are limitations which often protect and give possibilities, and then should be further developed, while the second are the real limitations that should be removed. Local trade unions can, of course, not be expected to exercise any perceptible influence on external limitations. Such influence should be channeled through higher levels of the trade union movement, directed towards the political system.

The central level of the trade unions have also an important support function towards local action. This support is partly general in nature as e.g. education and diffusion of methods for local organization. Support may also be specific in nature as assistance in negotiating conflicts or providing expert consultance in complicated technological matters.

To have efficient participation, it has to be tied to some organizational structure being able to manage problems of the kind discussed in this paper. Today the trade union movement seems to be the only realistic alternative, but this is not an entirely satisfying solution, as several groups are left outside. Such groups, e.g. females working part-time, are often those who most heavily are exposed to problems related to information technology, still they often are not unionized. I would also like to mention that trade unions not automatically are well equipped to deal with the problems of participation, there seems, among other things, to be an inherent tendency of centralization which do not well conform the ideals advocated in this paper.

5.   THE NORWEGIAN CONTEXT

In Norway there is a strong tradition within the last 20 years emphasizing the question of industrial democracy. Research and practical experiments have had considerable influence on general attitudes as well as day to day workings in Norwegian industry. An important step forward was the new "Act relating to worker protections and working environment", effective from 1977. An important aspect of this act is, that is does not only state which harmful factors should be removed from the working environment, but also factors which should be introduced. These factors apply to physical, psychological as well as social factors. The system development is of course covered by the act and it is also mentioned in particular. It is explicitly stated that employees must participate in developing "systems employed for planning and affecting the work". The existence of this act does not in itself produce participation. Even if the act seems to have had some influence on attitudes and also on actual practice, there still remains to be developed an apparatus of more detailed regulations and a set of working procedures that can bring more substantial changes.

Norwegian Trade Unions were quick to develop concern for the potential consequences of information technology. One result of this concern was a series of research projects from 1970 and onwards, these projects were conducted in cooperation with various trade unions and the Norwegian Computing Center. The aim of the projects was to evaluate the consequences of information technology for the trade unions and at the same time develop a strategy for dealing with the proliferating information technology.

The use of research, not a traditional tool of the trade unions, can be understood as a result of the tradition which had been created through earlier work research in Norway, socio-technical collaborative experiments with new forms of organization of work (i.e. semi-autonomous groups). In this case, however, the trade unions departed from the collaborative approach and chose to work on the problem giving exclusive consideration to the interests of the labour movement.

Partly as a result of these projects, technology agreements have spread and by now, virtually all sectors in the Norwegian economy are covered by agreements between the major trade unions and the employers federations. The agreements state that social impacts shall be considered as equally important as the technological and economic, when designing information systems. The agreements also define the rights for the employees to receive all relevant information on planned technological changes, to elect representatives (data shop-stewards) to take care of special problems concerning information technology, the right to participate in projects and to negotiate local agreements.

The existence of acts and agreements on technical change in the local organizations have been an important step forward, and much has been achieved on the local level. Still there seems to be, however, much confusion regarding the application of such instruments.

6.   CHOICE OF STRATEGY

Further development, using of the acts and agreements as well as the general development of participation in systems development, will necessitate a balanced combination of three different strategies, the strategy of regulation, the strategy of local development and the strategy of negotiation. Today these strategies for controling technological change are often advocated as competing strategies.

The strategy of regulation represents the traditional approach to the protection of the workers interests. The chief instruments being acts and agreements. True enough, there will still be a great demand for more or less detailed rules and regulations. But considering the nature of the system development process, it will not be possible to develop all the necessary rules and keep them updated in such a way so that all relevant cases are covered. Perhaps even more imporant, this strategy is contradictory to basic ideas of democratization and participation as it defines a passive role for the employees themselves.

Within the trade union movement there seems to be a certain bias in favour of the strategy of negotiations. In this, even more traditional approach, problems concerning the interests of the workers are to be solved through negotiations between union and management or often on a still higher level. This strategy may be efficient and is often necessary to make the issues involved explicit enough, or to avoid progress through "non-decision". Considering once more the nature of the system development process, we are, however, forced to conclude that the issues to be negotiated and relevant information about them, often have to be produced by local activities within the system development process itself. Without this, negotiation will distance itself from reality, as it often does.

Local development and participation within the single project
seems to be the strategy which conforms best to ideals of democratization as well as the idea that people, who are exposed to
problems are the ones who are the best qualified in finding
solutions to their satisfaction. I myself, am much in favour of
such a strategy, but I also find that those who defend this
strategy often have unrealistic assumptions about its possibilities for an independent existence without outside support.

Necessary support for local participation will on one side be
well defined rules that defines procedures or solutions whenever
such definition is relevant or needed. On the other side it is
also necessary to have an apparatus for negotiation of the conflicts which often occur in a system development process. In fact
we are left in a combination of strategies.

7. CONDITIONS FOR PARTICIPATION

Experiences from different schemes of participation in systems
design, indicate no easy solutions to the problem of taking
better care of the interests of the employees when designing and
implementing information technology. Our own results at the NCC
verify this, but at the same time it is also possible to deduct
certain conditions that are crucial for obtaining influence
through participation. Wether it will be possible to obtain real
influence from trade unions, depends on how powerful they are,
defined by the seven conditions that follows:

Base of power, consciousness, options for action, information,
organization (3).

Base of power

Traditionally, the trade unions' base of power has been the
solidarity between their members that can be used for collective
sanctions. Much of what we have seen of improvements of working
conditions and democratization, has been a product of pressure
based on this. Gradually, however, the base of power is changing
its nature and is becoming institutionalized through legal regulations or agreements between workers and their management. Such
a change is a necessary operationalization when trying to gain
influence on complicated technical matters. The traditional
collective actions is a too coarse instrument when dealing with
complex problems of organizational design. It may be like limiting
birds with a cannon. Collective actions may on the other hand be
well suited for obtaining the more delicate instrument of acts
and agreements. Thus these may be said to represent an operationalization of collective action. Acts and agreements can also
contribute to a more even distribution of power among so-called
strong and weak trade-unions. Here the weaker trade unions will
benefit from the stronger position of the pioneering efforts (as
long as we are not talking exclusively of in-house agreements.

In Norway it has been found necessary that acts and agreements
define both desired properties of systems to be developed, and
the rights of the employees in connection with the system development process.

Consciousness

If a base of power is to be transformed into influence that can be used for a specific purpose, the first condition to be met, is that the persons who are to use this potential for influence, are conscious about possible areas for influence, and what can be achieved. In my cooperation with trade unions I have often found ideas as the one expressed in the following quote from an old worker: "Automation is like the sun, there is nothing we can do to influence its coming and its course". Such an attitude will not foster offensive action.

It is also a problem that many technical changes within an organization, isolated from another, may seem small and have insignificant consequences, while in the long run, they may add up to a development of serious proportions, and have a negative impact on the interests of the employees. There may even be cases where the sum of small positive changes regarding working conditions may have unexpected negative implications.

Consciousness can, to a certain extent, be developed through information from outside. Practical experience have, however, demonstrated that to go beyond a certain point, it is necessary that consciousness is developed through practical experience at the local level.

This is a time-consuming process that very much depends on proper organization and also on support and advice from outside. The operational manifestation of a developed consciousness on technical change, will be the formulation of objectives to be used in the participation process. Without such objectives it will not be possible to relate to the choice between different options for action to the interests of the employees. Power will be blind, not able to defend any cause. It may be easy to formulate loose objectives that shows the general interests of the employees regarding system development, but it is much more difficult to make such objectives operational so that specific demands can be put forward to the systems designers. If these demands become too general, they will give too much space for interpretation and make it difficult to evaluate whether the finished systems correspond to the demands. Again it is difficult to rely extensively on guidelines from outside, which easily are lending themselves to mechanical reproduction and application. Local practice and experience will be necessary.

Options for action

To exercise influence, it is necessary to have a choice of options for action. Depending on the situation, the requirement for options will range from completely different system designs to minor modifications. Within the local organization, the option for action may be severely limited by the designs available on the market, economic or other external obligations and the abilities, imagination and values of those who are designing the systems. It is evident that some of these limitations could be changed through systematic influence, but only to a certain extent, and in many cases this would require political mechanisms and political consensus which do not exist today. Still, within existing limits there exists a considerable potential for enhanced influence which should be exploited.

An increasing proportion of systems is bought "ready-made"
either as standard software packages or as products with integrated microprocessors. This may further restrict the possibilities for participation in local adoption. On the other hand this
may in some cases also provide a wider range of alternatives for
investment, and also a wider range of choice for those who are
participating in the design process. Further, limitations due to
the skills or perspectives of the involved technicians may become
less serious. In fact technological development in this field has
to a large extent made obsolete the traditional fear of software-
packages among trade unions.

Another limitation is found in organizations that have to adopt
certain systems because they are parts of a larger economic or
administrative unit. Such systems may, however, also present
interesting possibilities if they are combined with some sort of
participatory process for designing the surrounding organization
of work. In this case they may, in fact, serve as a remedy for
diffusing certain forms of participation. It is nevertheless
evident that the opposite is the normal case today.

Information

To formulate possible options for action it is necessary to have
information about them. To choose between them, there will also
be necessary to have information that can relate them to the
relevant objectives. There is a floating borderline between
information as something given in a specific situation, and
information that comes from knowledge already established.

Information in the first sense of the word is normally coming
from the management or from professionals working with system
development. In order to be useful, such information must have a
content that is relevant, it must be given in an understandable
form and it has to be received at the right time. These requirements are incorporated in Norwegian technology agreements. Here
it is stated that the representatives elected by the employees
shall have the right to have all relevant information about
planned systems, information must be given about social consequences of such systems, the information has to be understandable
for people without a specialist's education, and it has to be
given early enough so the employees will be able to influ-ence
the plans.

Such requirements are not trivial. Determining what is relevant
information will easily become a matter of conflict, and it is
also a serious question what level of quality it is realistic to
expect. Those who have to inform about social consequences will
often be less qualified for this task and biased by attitudes
typical of management and technical experts at the same time as
this is a very complicated theme. "Understandable form" will
often be confused with oversimplification or, as we have seen it
in Norway, simple concerns about how to translate English termi-
nology. Finally, what is "early enough"? Today, information is
often given too late. Changing this, can only partly be accomplished by simple administrative measures, which will not remove
the cases where late information stems from bad planning or bad
project management. Often information will be tied to the formalization of a project. But in many cases the formal project will
only be the last step in a long informal management process. This
process will determine important design variables without the

decisions being so formalized that it is possible to apply any
acts or agreements to them. In order to extract information or
exercise influence.

Information, in the second sense of the word, knowledge, is
necessary in order to evaluate and utilize information of the
type just discussed. There has taken place much discussion about
what type of knowledge will be necessary to participate in system
development. Often the need for more knowledge of technology will
be perceived as urgent, due to the complicated nature of information
technology and the difficulties that come from efforts to communicate with EDP-specialists. Even if it may be necessary to have a
working understanding of the information technology in order to
know what to demand from it, it is my conviction that it would be
unvise to move too far into that direction. Those who are to
participate, will never be able to compete with the experts of
technology in their own field of competence. Knowledge and education will in most cases be scarce goods, therefore knowledge
about working conditions and strategies for participation should
be given priority.

If we pursue the strategy of education indicated here, this will
have important implications also for the methods of participation.
The employees should not involve themselves too much in technical
specifications, instead present their own demands based on their
knowledge of the issues where they are the real experts, their
own interests. In later stages the design made by the EDP-specialists, have to be evaluated and new demands formulated, if
necessary. Such strategy has, of course, to be supported by a
sufficient strong base of power, but one is less likely to fall
into the trap of becoming a hostage of the technology.

A third type of knowledge may also prove useful or necessary, the
assistance of experts, external to the organization and possessing
sufficient knowledge of the values and the problems of the trade
unions. Such experts are scarce today.

Organization

The actual procedures of participation serve a dual function.
First, the choice of procedures and organization will be a condition for exploiting the possibilities defined by the other conditions discussed in this chapter. Secondly, the choice of organization also have to reflect the dynamic aspect of participation.
It should be possible to establish participation as a process of
learning, starting from simple cases, gradually moving on to the
more complicated ones along with the simultanious development of
consciousness, objectives and knowledge. Such development of
experience seems to be a necessary path to go, in order to achieve
meaningful participation, but it is important to realize that it
will be a long and cumbersome process. Sensational results are
not to be expected in the first run.

Our experiences at the NCC demonstrate that it is difficult to
start and maintain such processes. Initially, there has to be a
strong enough motivation to start, a feeling that participation
will be worth-while, and the necessary activities must be given a
high priority and support. Finally, outside support will often be
necessary both to initiate activities, and in case of special
problems. What will happen next, depends on the chosen form of
organization.

Our experiments have involved traditional representation in
project groups. We have recommended that representatives form a
support group together with at least one representative from the
board of the local union. This group discusses decisions to be
talken in the project groups, thus supporting the representatives
who, without such support, easily participate in decisions without
seing the consequences. There must also be possibilities for
transferring problems to higher levels for negotiations of conflicts that cannot be solved on the project level. Without such
possibilities, the group will easily turn into a pure discussion
group, without any real power.

I would like to emphasize strongly that models of organization
that are too detailed and too complicated seem to be difficult to
diffuse. We try to suggest very simple guidelines for organization,
that can be locally adapted, and further developed as local
experience and ability will grow.

Research of the kind discussed here, may bring interesting
results if it gets started, to diffuse the necessary principles
to a greater number of organizations is, however, a serious
problem, which is not yet satisfactorily solved. This is a problem
well known from other research that resemble ours. There was a
time when diffusion was believed to be spontaneous, only maintained by way of successful examples. This is proved not to be
the case or at best too slow.

8.   CONCLUSION

Action research has to be both realistic and ambitious - although
the two qualities are not always consistent. This must also be
kept in mind when evaluating the results of such research. Facing
the formidable task of improving the present situation with
regard to participation in systems design, most contributions
will seem modest compared with the ambitious goals it is necessary
to keep in mind. The conditions presented in the last chapter
represent an effort to analyze what constitutes the difference
between success and failure. Even if they have grown out of our
own action research, these conditions could also be used as a
framework for the analyzis of other experiments with participation
in systems development.

We are often asked whether our research has produced any significant
changes in systems designs. In some cases where our groups have
been active, the answer is indeed yes. We do feel, however, that
our work should not be judged by these few cases.

First of all I feel it is a wrong way of putting the question. If
you ask for specific changes, you also have to compare with
something. But, if you get into a design process so late that you
already have a defined alternative to compare with and to compete
against, then you have probably come on the scene too late. Too
many things have already been settled and only minor changes can
be achieved. Consequently we are not aiming so much at design
features of defined systems. Instead we try to influence the
design procedure in such a way that the employees can advocate
their interests before a technological alternative is fixed. As
mentioned earlier we try to achieve this by education and by
organization which again is complemented with legal support.

Another reason why one should not look too closely at our pilot
studies is that they are too special. Not every local union in
Norway is able to cooperate with a research project. Research is
also expensive and time-consuming. One of our research objectives
has thus been to make ourselves obsolete. We have tried to implant
processes that can spread out methods to other local unions and
run without us. The establishment of such processes constitutes
the research. To make them continue should be part of the normal
day to day trade union activities.

It should be noted that in our projects we have dealt primarily
with problems of working conditions. Problems of employment have
not been dominant in our research. This is partly due to the fact
that Norway until recently had practically speaking full employment. On the other hand employment problems will in many cases be
impossible to solve within the realm of the single company exposed
to external economic conditions. In these cases our methods will
be less suited.

Notes.

1.
Several publications describing our projects exist in Norwegian.
In English an overview is given by Pape, A., Fjalestad, J.:
Research on Social Aspects of Computerization and Democratization
of Working Life.
EURO IFIP 79, P.A. Samet (editor), North-Holland Publishing
Company, Amsterdam 1979.

In German a more extensive description is given by Kubicek, H.:
Interessenberücksichtigung beim Technikeinsatz im Büro- und
Verwaltungsbereich,
R. Oldenburg Verlag, München 1979.

2.
A more extensive discussion may be found in Fjalestad, J.,
Nygaard, K.: Group Interests and Participation in Information
System Development, Paper presented to Special Session on Micro-
electronics, Productivity and Employment. OECD, Paris 1979.

3.
The following discussion will be based on Fjalestad, J.: Techno-
logy and Participation. Report to The Norwegian Ministry of
Labour, Norwegian Computing Center 1980
(In Norwegian).

Footnotes.

1)   An example of this is automatic monitoring of work-
      performance in text-processing systems.

Computerization and Education

Franz Ofner

Department of Economics and Sociology of Education, University of Klagenfurt, A-9020 Klagenfurt, Austria

In this paper reflections have been made on the
following: Is there a possibility to make a contribution to cope with the existing societal problems
caused by automation, by means of reforming the educational system and introducing specific training
measurements? It has been proposed to overcome
employees' adaption to automation process on the one
hand and to gain certain perspectives for their interests on the other hand. The starting point of these
reflections is to characterize the change of requirements of qualification conditioned by automation.
These problems are understood to be societal problems.
The answers to these social problems are found in the
areas of retraining personnels, adult education, vocational and general education.

INTRODUCTION

The intensified use of computer-controlled technologies leads to a
greater automation in many fields of employment such as in production,
construction, administration, trade and banking. This process is
associated with a basic change of work and also with many social
problems. In this situation, "the impacts" of the technical development are mentioned frequently as if this development would be an
autonomous process deprived of human activity and control. As a
matter of fact, this conception of technilogical determinism is even
found with employees, work-councils and trade-unions. The predominant
opinion is to avoid only the worst impacts of technical development:
to reduce dismissals by early retirements of employees and without
replacing the retired employees as well as to stabilize wages. This
system constitute pessimism, resignation and lack of incentives. It
does not encourage industrialization nor social advancement. In other
words, it is not possible to obtain a positive perspective from automation.

These experiences were derived from different businesses and companies
when it came to the process of technical change. The essence of this
experience is that within capitalism, no planned social development
exists where wage-earners are participating as active and decision
making persons. And they are not able to bring to their interests
some constitutive elements. Due to the inability of the employees to
make decision, they are confronted with strange decisions. Therefore,
they are forced to adapt themselves to the decisions made. If these
circumstances are interpreted technically, it means, that the technical development is conceived as an autonomous and quasi natural pro-

cess, it is concealed that within this process there are acting persons who assert on their economical rule interests, and that the position of impotence is conditioned on societal structures which can be changed.

The persons concerned will have to give up their fears and make their points very clear, and this will be of crucial significance for a satisfactory solution to the societal problems emanating from automation. The range of the problems caused by automation are so extensive to such a degree that isolated defensive measures have to stop. The questions previously raised in this paper such as the change in occupational structure, development of qualification and vocational training, represent only a small part of the problems caused by automation. Further elements within these complex range of problems are the increment of unemployment, intensified possibilities of supervision, control and manipulation by business and national personnel information systems, the increase of work intensity as well as the rise of the new forms burdens.

CHANGES OF WORKING ACTIVITIES CONDITIONED BY AUTOMATION

From technical point of view, the automation consist in the transfer of working functions, which till now have been performed by mankind into the technical system. This transfer of working functions has the consequence, that traditional working activities cease totally or are reduced considerably. But at the same time, new fields of tasks arise which are necessary for the application of automatic systems. These changes together with increases of productivity within the field of application which can reach for more than 100 percent, and the increase of branches which are occupied with the production of computers, automatic technologies and software, lead to a change of the occupational structure, - a process which is already in full swing, though with different intensity within the single countries. In Austria for example the specturm of occupational categories, which are concerned by such processes, have a quota of 46 percent at the dependent employees (1).

What kind of activities are these supposed to be? Which activities originate from automation? These questions raised in this paper are important enough to change the qualification requirements conditioned by automation and also it calls for the necessary consequences within the educational system.

Working procedures which ought to be executed by automatic system, have to be organized in form of programms. These programms have to include all important informations about constellations and changes of working procedures and instructions about the kind and quantity of work to be performed. As a matter of fact, the working conditions which have to be automated should be described within the frame work of mathematical and symbolic concepts (2). The automateable working activities are a question of physical and mental process with a limited grade of variability of working conditions and a high degree of repetition. Therefore, automateable activities are above all activities demanding a relatively low level of qualifications which are untied from single areas of tasks and transfered to automatic system. Also activities with a very low level of qualification such as assembly activities at the assembly line and technical drawing belong to it.

As for the activities which arise newly from the application of automatic systems that are in two categories have to be distinguished. One category can be summarized as where the content consists in the preparation and in the purposive use of the systems, which means development, construction and installation of plants and software, preparatory activities such as to design, test and optimize programms, the computer-aided design and documentation of papers for manufacturing, supervising, controlling activities and maintenance and repaire activities. These activities can be defined as "specific for automation" (3). Together with the automation, a category of activities rises which has the function of preparing the 'working materials' in its breadest sense (material things as well as data and informations) and adapt it for processing of the systems and to feed the plants respectively. These activities bring the products away, and also 'assist' them with correcting motions when faults appear in the sequence of operations. Examples are: feeding and unloading activities with the automatic machine tool, punching of data respectively text input at video terminals, reading and reporting measuring data, manual intervention at the interruptions of packing processes, the coating of wooden boards, the tearing of yarns at the automatical weaving machines etc. These new activities are characterized by a high degree of repetition and monotony, especially because they are separated by taylorism. But there are those distinctive marks and simple structures which make it possible to control these activities by taking further technical steps or by reducing them so that they can be integrated in to higher qualification requirements. Therefore, they can be specified as 'residual activities conditioned by automation' which possess in the course of the technical development a 'transitory character' (4). In review of the existing process of automation, a great number of such residual activities, which are restraining and disappearing, can be noticed due to the decentralized use of video terminals in offices, publishing houses and banks and due to the use of programmable machine tools and industrial robots etc. (5).

It is obvious that the restructuring processes which take place in the course of the automation cannot be seen to be independent of organizational measurements, particularly as EDP and the automation-technics are also a question of arganizational technology. For economic reasons, wage- and training costs, and the interest in securing the domination over production, and exploitation process, the tendency of employers have been existing before automation in order to split the fields of activities and competences by division and decomposition of labour, and by separation of planning and execution, and by organizing from above to enable to keep the average standard of qualification as low as possible.

In the course of the introduction of computer controlled technologies as a re-organisation, new distribution of work takes place. The attempt should be made on one hand to separate activities, which are specific for automation, from residual activities, and on the other hand to organize hierarchically structured spheres of competences within the activities which are specific for automation. This type of organisation makes it easy to controll from the above and restricts a horizontal cooperation. The process of re-organisation of work in the course of automation represents at the same time a situation of 'instable balance', which offers the possibility to carry through such models of vocational competences where the aim is the removal of the isolation and restriction of the work force (6). Of course such an intervention has to be initiated and held by the employees and their organizations and would have to be enforced against the interests of the employers. This would necessitate a strategy which exceeds the mere defence of rights which have been gained in the past, and tries to be engaged creatively in the process of the re-organisation of labour. On the level of the educational system, this strategy ought to be included in the creation of new occupations and training activities, and where extensive competences will be provided for the working force.

QUALIFICATION REQUIREMENTS OF ACTIVITIES, WHICH ARE SPECIFIC FOR AUTO-MATION

From the process of automation, a positive view can only be won, if those developments are made in the right way, the orientation and starting point for an intervention which advances the working process in the direction of an expansion of competences for all employees. Such positive developments can be found within the activities speci-fied by automation, and these qualification requirements will be shortly defined in the following (7).

Due to the automation work-planning activities do not only increase quantitatively, but also change qualitatively. The qualitative change states, that the complete process has to be pre-planned and thought over in detail, technically and properly organized. Problems have to be analysed, scheme of sequences and designs of programs have to be provided, tested, modified, optimized and co-ordinated with others. This means a) logistization, b) mathematization and c) "practical scientification" of work. Recent empirical surveys show that it can-not be avoided that skilled workers and referees are incorporated in the process of the working preparations, even under the present con-ditions. The reason for this fact has to be seeked in the following: these groups of employees dispose of important practical experiences, formal knowledge in analysis and making programms are not capable enough to get some practical experiences, but the knowledge in EDP has to be combined with the practical knowledge about production methods, manufacturing operations, functioning of technical systems etc.

As for the activities for supervising and controlling automatic sy-stems, as well as for the correcting interventions in the technical control system, it is important that the system of measuring instru-ments and data shows the complete production process and gives infor-mation about its state. Accordingly, the technical connection, which has to be understood, becomes more complex and abstract. As a matter of fact, in order that one is able to estimate the state of the pro-cess, one has to establish connections between a lot of data. This necessitates the theoretical knowledge about the process as well as the operating manner and the manner of function, because activity by trial and error is not enough. As the manner of the function of elec-tronic systems is rather abstract - the processes are not perceptable by the sense-organs -, the maintenance is influenced too. When searching for obstruction, auxiliary instruments have to be used. Also construction, circuit diagrams, technical and circiut-logical knowledge are required. And to find the reason of obstructions, it is unalterable to propound and examine different hypotheses.

The integration of many processes into one system, the increasing ten-dency of scientification as well as the variety of tasks to be solved and coordinated, necessitate the junction of different professional knowledges and a universal exchange of informations. Situations where a smooth cooperation is essential are interruptions, detecting sources of error, repairing activities and changing of shifts. Therefore, high requirements are made to coordinate and distribute the total work, to design a common action programm, to consider a working result at dif-ferent places, to know the working organisation and the competences

of others, to be able to inform in a precise, methodically structured
form, to absorb observations and intentions of other persons.

Operators of systems and programmers are confronted with economical
tasks in form of optimizing problems. This is remarkable because tra-
ditionally no economical requirements are made on skilled workers.
Optimizing tasks is to be understood as follows, the proportion of
costs, expenditure of raw material, time of production, type of
employment, the capacity of the systems and the production-output
should be arranged most economically with regard to the quality of
production and possibly the selling price too. The solution of optimizing problems is only possible by conscious considerations of conditions and connections as well as exact methodical proceedings.

Connected with the increase of cognitive requirements is a increase
of the readiness to work correctly and reliably as well as to learn;
the cooperative connections require a critical attitude towards one-
self and towards the working activities of others, but without en-
dangering the cooperation. Also, the high value of the systems as
well as the high standstill-costs at false operations represent factors, which raise the responsibility of workers and staffs compared
with the level of the mechanical production.

To avoid misunderstandings, it has to be emphasized, that this statement is not a representation characterizing the real working situation of automation-workers altogether. Moreover, the new positive
elements ought to be accentuated in a one-sided way, - on the one
hand these elements are - at least partly - noticeable and on the
other hand it is possible to have them as a mark for unionist activities by distributing the work at automatic systems to work-organi-
sational measurements in a way that many may take part in these positive trends of development, and by acquiring the necessary competences
to educational system. Those possibilities which are opened to the
automation process, shall be confronted with the real conditions and
problems. The contribution which can be made by the educational
system to solve the problems, shall be demonstrated. Of course, it is
not possible to generalize such measurements, but they depend on the
particularity of the concerned educational system. This article only
refers to the Austrian educational system (9).

CONSEQUENCES OF THE EDUCATIONAL SYSTEM

If the educational systems are interpreted as a means of making a
contribution to the solution of existing problems in accordance with
the interests of the employees, it has to be distinguished between
three fundamental areas of problems which have to be considered dif-
ferently. First of all, the problems are different when it is a
question of persons who are already in the working process, or when
it is a question of the education of the future generation and who
is going to enter the social reproduction process. These persons have
to be prepared. In the second place it has to be asked whether it is
enough to restrict educationals systems to vocational education in a
narrow sense in view of the far-reaching and complex changes, or
whether the primary and secondary schools ought to have an important
preparatory function. Clearly, the question is whether the existing
separation of general and vocational education can be maintained. And
finally it has to be asked, whether the transmission of qualifications
in a narrow sense - of knowledge and skills - enables the accomplish-
ment of work-responsibilities and is sufficient. Also, whether the
consciousness about the social, economical and political problems as
well as the possibility of an intervention which change things, have
to be developed.

The treatment of all these questions would require a close and comprehensive analysis about the changes on automation which is beyond the
question of changes of qualification as well as the educational system.
The last but not the least is the political system, the state-machinery,
the parties, organisations of employers, unions etc., especially if
the succeeding with reforms is involved. The following statements are
far away from such an analysis. They only include the thoughts of the
author, and some suggestions as answer to the asked questions. Moreover, the following fields have been excluded due to the difficult
problems: the university, the secondary schools for vocational training (10), and the education of teachers.

FIELD OF PROBLEM: RETRAINING AND CONTINUED EDUCATION

It has already been discussed that with the introduction of EDP and
automatic systems, a re-organisation of work takes place. It is not
only important that the existing work has to be devided in quantity,
but the problem also reveals that the existing qualifications are not
required any more and new qualifications are required. Characteristic
for such transpositions is the situation of competition in which the
employees are brought mutually, provided that they do not offer resistance by showing a deliberate solidarity.

The acquisition of the new qualifications can either be organized by
the companies or it can be left to the private initiative of the
employees by attending seminars and courses out of the working hours.
When companies make retraining and continued education-measures, always a strict selection takes place - with the help of tests, certi-
ficates about performance are administered by the companies themselves. Qualified and younger candidates are accepted, because the
period of courses and the quota of failures can be kept low, and
those workers still remain in the working process for a long time.
Low-qualified and older employees are either discharged or they are
forced to undertake residual activities which are often below their
educational standard and are even paid less wages. This refers especially, to uncertain working places, because they render superfluous
by further automation. Moreover, these persons lose connection with
the general development of qualification and their chances at the
labour market decrease at the long-term. Unqualified, unemployed
juniors are exposed to this danger too. In this connection women represent an especially discriminated group. As a matter of fact, they
belong to the low-qualified workers, however, the employers need for
retraining their workers a high engagement and willingness to have
them to learn out of their working hours, which is not demanded from
women due to their social condition as mother and housewife.

In Austria external retraining and possibilities for continued education are offered on one hand by establishments of the 'social partners' (organisations of employers, trade-unions) and on the other
hand by private schools with partly rather unreliable business practices. The participation mostly depends on the private initiative of
the employees wło also have to bear the fees themselves. The administration of employment placing bears the fees for unemployed people.
These evening classes are again especially for women a considerable
strain. Additionally, the background of education and the working
conditions form a considerable barrier for the access. Altogether, in
Austria the vocational adult education is rarely developed, the adaptation to the demand for manpower at short notice is dominating.

A very difficult problem presents the arrangement of the retraining
and advanced training courses. Especially, in the companies where
courses are in many cases thightly restricted and specialized requirements, they only have the character of instructions and learning
by doing. The process of automation still is at the beginning, even
more extensive and complex systems are created, the theoretical requirements of qualification are increasing, therefore it would be
necessary to impart a fundamental knowledge which is as broad as
possible and represents the basis for specialization and enables a
further vocational advanced training. A satisfactory solution can
only be obtained if the interests of the employees are made to the
pole of retraining and continued-education-measures. The union educational commitees, which can be organized in the nationalized industry, represent a first start: They try to organize and coordinate
the educational activities with regard to the working and living conditions of the staff and getting agrreable conditions from the management concerning leaves and financial aid. The increase of productivity on automation enables the insertion of periodical educational
offers during the working hours. The influence ought to be concerned
with the development of substance to avoiding a cut in specification
in favour of the development of a political consciousness and questions
of the change of the complete occupational field.

FIELD OF PROBLEM: TRAINING OF SKILLED WORKERS

In Austria, the training of becoming a skilled worker predominantly
takes place in form of a dual system: about 80 percent of the training takes place in a company, the rest has to be absolved in a vocational school, which has only a complementary function. Therefore,
the access to an apprenticeship depends on an article of apprenticeship with a company and subsequently on the economic development.

The weakness of the dual system of the apprenticeship has been criti-
zised vehemently during the last 15 years, but it could not be re-
dressed with the effected reforms. It has to be apprehended that
these weaknesses will be greater to the disantvantage of the trained
persons in connection with a progressive automation.

Small workmanlike businesses are dominating quantitatively in the
apprenticeship, but they are not provided with the necessary technical
equipment enabling a qualifying training and usually they have a small
specialized production programm. These businesses do not possess workshops for training, but the apprentices are introduced into the
working process by collaborating - sometimes like a labourer. Workshops for training are to be found only in bigger businesses. In
smaller businesses the trained persons who finished their apprenticeship are exchanged by new apprentices, because they represent cheap
workers. The trained persons wander away into other spheres of employment, especially to industry, - but they usually have the wrong qualification and they will be employed as unskilled workers or they undergo a new training. Moreover, in the dual system the practical and
theoretical training are separated from each other: the theoretical
training takes place in the vocational school, the practical training
takes place in the business. Theoretical and practical training are
not united, the curriculum is not coordinated. At the moment, the
occupations are strongly disunited: In Austria, there are 225 occupations, that can be learnt.

To impart qualifications which are relevant in the future to apprentices, the vocational training ought to take place at new machines
and systems, but usually they are not present in workmanlike businesses.

The present separation of practical and theoretical training is problematic due to automation, and the theoretical knowledge for work
becomes dominant and the knowledge conerning automation has to be
added. Furthermore, due to automation, the tendency of fusion of related occupations can be realized in many fields (e.g. in the metal
working process). It would be necessary to create new occupations
with extensive competences, enabling to oppose an extrem division of
labour by the businesses. Consequently a redifinition and restructuring of substance would have to be done at the occupations that can
be learnt. The things which are relevant for the fields of retraining
and vocational advanced education, is to impart a basic knowledge
which is as broad as possible and which can be used as the basis for
further specialization and for advanced educational requirements.
These are relevant more than ever for the training of skilled workers.

A further problem faces the general education, which deals only with
a small part of the apprenticeship. Besides the expansion of this
part, the development of the general education ought to be orientated
in such a way that the prospective skilled workers are enabled to
have a critical discussion about the technical, economical and political development regarding a qualified participation in the processes of decisions making within business and society.

FIELD OF PROBLEM: GENERAL SCHOOL SYSTEM

The Austrian compulsory school system is distinguished by a strong
vertical structure and by a social selection. Moreover, it is distinguished by a general education in the traditional sense as well as
by a strict division of subjects. The compulsory education requires
nine years.

Right after the elementary school which takes four years, the children
are divided at the age of ten to get different kinds of a general education. The majority (about 80 percent) attend the Upper Primary
School; about 20 percent of this age-group start in an Arts Grammar
and Science Grammar School, which takes eight years. The completion
of this school enables them to enter the university. The possibility
to change from the Upper Primary School to a Grammar School exists
formally, but in fact, it seldomly happens. Only about half of the
pupils who enter at the age of ten an Arts Grammar and Science Grammar
School complete this school. The limitation with regard to a general
education in the traditional sense means above all that there are
scarcely relations to the "field of work" and that a Fundamental view
of the social connection and development is hardly offered. The division of subjects leads to the cutting up of knowledge and to empty-
ing of contents (formalization). It impedes to comprehend social,
historical, political, scientific and technical connections.

The tendency to make production processes theoretical and scientific,
which is caused by the increasing automation, makes the present organisation of school system of 10 to 15-year old pupils with the division in a higher and lower general education dubious. An extensive
and scientific wellgrounded general education for all strata of population makes a unification of the compulsory school system and a
prolongation of the compulsory education appear sensible. Together
with this, a restructuring of the curricula and a change of the organisation of instruction ought to take place. Above all, a vocation
orientated basic education - which makes an insight in the reality
of the "field of work", with regard to social and scientific-technical
problems possible, - ought to be integrated in the field of the general education. The natural scientific subjects including mathematics,

ought to be reconsiled and coordinated with a group of subjects - which would have to be organized and called 'polytechnic education'. It establishes a connection to the field of production. In the social scientific subjects, the real steady social changes, problems and contrasts of interests should be conveyed, enabling to get a differentiated and universal view of the social processes. A restriction on technical information, without social and human questions, put pupils under restraint and makes the technical development appear an autonomous process which can only be accepted. With the reconception of the curricula, new problem-oriented and cooperative methods of instruction, with regard to the 'project-instruction' would have to be added, enabling to overcome the existing separation of subjects.

FINAL OBSERVATION

This statement ought to show, that with the help of educational activities an important contribution can be made to the solution of the problems effected by automation. Measurements to avert social deterioration and the worst consequences of the technical application may be very important, but they are not enough to solve the manifold problems and to win a positive perspective. This implies in the field of education, that measurements which have in mind only a short-dated adaptation to the labour market, have to be exceeded. Educational processes have to be formulated with a long-term perspective. Children, which enter the school system now and appear on the labour market after nine years of schooling at least and the greater majority who completed schooling after 12 years, require an education which prepares them for their total occupational activities and qualifies them for further educational processes. The drastic social changes which are stated by the scientific-technical development within the educational system have to be attached. These changes within the educational system must have the target to make the employees become active and conscious creators of their own and of the society as a whole. Who else than the employees themselves and their organisations are able to set these initiatives and to succeed with them?

The developments and the use of techniques are not possible without science, the natural, and technical sciences including an increasing extent of the social sciences. But this means, that without these sciences the existing problems cannot be solved. Investigations show that often employees and shop committees are overcharged in estimating the importance of the consequences which are initiated by the introduction of new systems. Scientists and technologists are confronted by the employees with mistrust and scepticism, but not with complete injustice. It will be of great importance if the trade unions can gain the scientists support and the scientists can commit themselves to the trade unions.

NOTES

(1) cf. Mende, J. & Ofner, F., 1981, p. 153.
(2) cf. to this Fuchs-Kottowski, K. u.a., 1976, p. 22 ff.
(3) cf. Projektgruppe Automation und Qualifikation, 1978, p. 15.
(4) cf. Projektgruppe Automation und Qualifikation, 1978, p. 16.
(5) cf. Mende, J. & Ofner, F., 1981, p. 84-85.
(6) To characterize the 'work action' more exactly with the help of the categories 'isolationship' and 'restrictionship' cf. Volpert, W., 1974, p. 56-62.
(7) For a preciser presentation cf. 3), 6), 7), 8).

(8) Projektgruppe Automation und Qualifikation, 1981, p. 306.

(9) A preciser presentation can be found at Mende, J. und Ofner, F., 1981, p. 157-298.

(10) The secondary schools for vocational training are characteristic and specifical for the Austrain educational system; these schools educate pupils to become qualified technical (mechanical, electrical and construction engineering, etc.) and commercial workers beyond the system of higher education (universities); this qualification is adjusted to the direct application in the economic system, while the graduates of universities get a scientific education.

LITERATURE

1) Bechmann, G. u.a.: Mechanisierung geistiger Arbeit (Campus, Frankfurt/Main, 1979).

2) Fuchs-Kittowski, K. u.a.: Informatik und Automatisierung, Band 1 (Akademie-Verlag, Berlin 1976).

3) Littek, W. und Heisig, U.: Kaufmännische Berufstätigkeit und Bürorationalisierung, Zeitschrift für Berufs- und Wirtschaftspädagogik 7 (1981), S. 483 ff.

4) Mende, J. und Ofner, F.: Automation und Ausbildung (Verlag für Gesellschaftskritik, Wien 1981).

5) Projektgruppe Automation und Qualifikation: Theorien über Automationsarbeit (Argument-Verlag, Berlin 1978).

6) Projektgruppe Automation und Qualifikation: Automationsarbeit: Empirie 1 (Argument-Verlag, Berlin 1980).

7) Projektgruppe Automation und Qualifikation: Automationsarbeit: Empirie 2 (Argument-Verlag, Berlin 1980).

8) Projektgruppe Automation und Qualifikation: Automationsarbeit: Empirie 3 (Argument-Verlag, Berlin 1981).

9) Volpert, W.: Handlungsstrukturanalyse als Beitrag zur Qualifikationsforschung (Pahl-Rugenstein, Köln 1974).

Section IV

Approaches in System Design for a Defense of Human Work

The section contains two contributions written by researchers in Computer Science from the Federal Republic of Germany and Canada.

H.W. Heibey et al. analyse "How to design information technology". They state that generally accepted strategies of technological and organizational design to avoid undesirable impacts of the use of EDP hardly can be seen.

Further they claim that one reason for this is - in Germany - that Computer Science which is able to show the scope of technological design pretends to be a basic science not willing to analyse the practical and organizational problems resulting from the use of its own technology. The paper does not deal with alternative methods or organizational design as part III of this volume but it is a necessary completion from the view of the Computer Science.

The authors have found five aims of design of EDP-based systems. The use of EDP has to help:

1. to reduce the cost of information and of data processing in organizations

2. to improve the quality of the information processing processes and the products and services offered by organizations

3. to advance the adaptability of the organizations to the change of requirements in the environment

4. to increase the transparency of organizations and of organizational processes

5. to improve working conditions of the members of the organization.

Recognized negative organizational impacts are caused by the exclusive concentration on the first aim and the simultaneous neglection of the other aims.

The causes are further analysed and in order to reduce or eliminate the negative impacts the paper suggests the following approaches:

- cooperation between Computer Science, Organizational Science and Ergonomics

- participative methods of design

  - further development of the concept of "social"
    information technologies.

The technology offers the scope to solve the problems and Computer
Science has to be a decisive instrument in this development -
although it still has to go through many a learning process in
view of the problems.

Theodor D. Sterling's "Guidelines for Humanizing Computerized
Information Systems" were developed in a series of workshops
sponsored by the Canadian Information Processing Society.

Based on the Stanley House criteria for humanizing information
systems he discussed especially methods for making systems
courteous, for making systems relieve the users from unnecessary
difficulties and for providing systems with human information
interfaces.

The author stresses the important point that the utility of humanizing procedures will not be revealed in ordinary cost benefit
calculations but in the quality of life. Two very conscious
questions are asked:

  1. Should we burden ourselves and future generations
     with dehumanizing practices designed and implemented
     today?

  2. Must not the wish to keep systems human and dignified
     take its place with the desire to keep the air and the
     water patable as a necessary counter motive to the
     drive of government and industry to be as efficient
     and cost conscious as possible?

The Canadian guidelines are certainly a step in the direction of
a design and an implementation of systems in a way that they
create a more human setting.

Organizational Consequences of the Use of EDP – How to Design Information Technology

Hanns-Wilhelm Heibey[1], Bernd Lutterbeck[2], and Michael Töpel[3]

[1] c/o Der Berliner Datenschutzbeauftragte, Hildegardstraße 29–30, D-1000 Berlin 31, FRG

[2] TU-Berlin, Fachbereich 20 – Informatik, Sekretariat FR 5–10, Franklinstraße 28–29, D-1000 Berlin 10, FRG

[3] Ostpreußenweg 5, D-2150 Buxtehude, FRG

1. Introduction

The discussion about the technological progress is increasingly held in a critical manner. Expecially the broad expansion of information technologies has caused impacts, which by no means have
been approved by all applying or afflicted people. For a long time
the analysis of these phenomena was only made by a few, mostly interdisciplinary research groups. In the meantime the necessity of
work in this field has been reflected in research policy. The so-
called impact research in the field of information technologies was
officially initiated in different European countries. Here we
mention the German study [17], French studies (see [6], [16]) and a
British study [2] . All these studies are surveys and attempts to
show potential future developments and their risks in a prospective
and theoretical way. In the Federal Republic of Germany these
studies had some predecessors which dealt empirically with the
impacts of EDP use in organizations. Here we have to mention the
important work of Kubicek (see [13] , [14]), which helped to reinte-
grate the human requirements and interests into the science of organizations and industrial management. The Research Group on Automation in Public Administration in Kassel (see [10], [15]) has
analysed strategies and mechanisms of impacts of automation in
public administrations.

In spite of this a unique orientation, especially according generally accepted strategies of technological and organizational
design to beware of undesirable impacts of the use of EDP can hardly be seen. One reason for this is that in Germany Computer Science
as the only science which is able to show the scope of technological
design pretends to be a basic science not willing to analyse the
practical and organizational problems resulting from the use of its
own technology. This contribution can also give only one element of
a concept of human design of the use of EDP technology. It is based
on works made by the Research Group on the impacts of EDP at the
Department of Computer Science of the University of Hamburg ([11],
[12]). The basic aims of these efforts were to get hints how to reduce negative impacts by modification of the technology. We analysed the causes of the impacts of EDP on organizations and human
individuals working with them implied by properties of the techno-

logy. This way of precedure was no alternative to different methods of organizational design, especially not to the participative approaches 1), but a necessary completion from the view of Computer Science.

One of the basic assumptions is that by improvement of the technology negative organizational impacts can be reduced and positive impacts have been considered as being negative if they are inconsistent with the following aims of design, which are <u>totally of equal priority.</u> The use of EDP has to help

1. <u>to reduce the costs</u> of the information and data processing in organizations

2. <u>to improve the quality</u> of the informations processing processes and the products and services made by the organizations

3. <u>to advance the adaptability</u> of the organizations to the change of requirements of the environment

4. <u>to increase the transparency</u> of organizations and the organizational processes

5. <u>to improve the working conditions</u> of the members of the organization

Looking at this system of aims we can explain the recognized negative organizational impacts of the use of EDP as being caused by the exclusive concentration on the first aim and the simultaneous neglecting of the other aims.

In this paper we want to work out the system of aims to deduce the scope of technological design. In chapter 2 we describe the problems of the use of EDP in organizations differentiated by problems of data processing, of organizations and of the work in organizations. Further we trace them back to the general problem of the adaptation between technology and organization. Chapter 3 contains thoughts about the analysis of the causes of the impacts, differentiated by general causes, which are an implication of the social utilization of the technology, and by technological causes, which are an implication of the conditions of use of EDP. The last chapter 4 contains a constructive approach to design the EDP technology and to define new aims of technological development.

2. Problems of the use of EDP in organizations

2.1. Problems in the field of EDP

Problems directly within the scope of EDP in organizations are all problems which concern

- the <u>representation</u> of data
- the <u>relevance</u> and <u>topicality</u> of data
- the <u>representation</u> of data, problems and processes by <u>programming</u>
- the man computer interaction
- the formalization and automation of <u>complex</u> information processes

The representation of data concerns the special syntactical requirements, which data have to meet in EDP. Problems connected with this
are for example

- unforeseen mistakes by rounding up numbers during the execution
  of arithmetical programs

- unsufficient mappings from structured informations to data used
  as input of computerized data processing

Another aspect of the characterization of data is their value for
the benefit of derivation of informations from them (interpretation
of date). We distinguish the data properties topicality
(opportuneness), i.e. the availability in time, and relevance
(usefulness), i.e. the applicability of the data for the derivation
of the needed information in the correct moment. Faults of the
topicality or relevance of data lead to different specific problems
of the use of EDP:

- anonymity of the selection of data for those persons who want
  to use the data

- deficient und badly supported updating and therefore missing
  adaptation of the data to changing environments

- use of data for purposes other than originally intended (data
  protection problem).

In addition to those problems concerning data, there are impacts
caused by the substitution of human information processes by processes of EDP. This substitution presupposes the programming of
those processes. From this the following problems result:

- unsufficient possibilities to transfer complex data structures
  by programming with available programming languages

- missing flexibility of the user in representing data and problems
  and in man computer interaction

- programming languages which are not adequate to the tasks they
  are needed for, which are too difficult to learn and which hinder
  the structuring of programs

- missing utilization of the potentials of programming languages
  caused by unsufficient education of the programmers.

The last two points leed to less possibilites for software
maintenance, to missing flexibility and transparency in the use of
software in organizations.

The increasing importance of interactive systems leads to problems
which are results of the unequality of the interaction "partners"
man and computer (see [7], [8]):

- stress of nerves caused by various faults of the design of
  interaction as for example ergonomical problems, overcharge by
  too many data, too fast or too slow reactions of the system

- dependence on rigid interaction schemes and therefore inflexible
  integration of the user into the interaction processes.

The formalization and automation of complex information processes
for the use in data processing were tested before there was enough
knowledge about the character of these real processes. So it was
not suprising that complex information, decision and planning
systems (f.e. MIS) failed (see f.e. [1], [15]). This problem splits
into different parts:

- missing adaptation of the offer of data to the user´s demand on
  data

- anonymity of the selection of data, of the structuring of data
  and the determination of processes

- restrictions of the possibilities being at the user´s disposal
  during interaction.

These problems caused by technical faults have impacts on the organizational task accomplishing processes and working processes.
These problems will be discussed in the next two sections.

2.2. Problems of the organization

The use of EDP has considerably changed the organizational processes
and the relations of organizations to their environment. We can
consider three kinds of organizational problems:

- change of the relations to the environment

- change of organizational rules in the task accomplishing process

- dispersing of information processing and data processing

The change of the relations to the environment are especially
concerning new relations of dependence between organization and
other instances and between customers and organizations:

- dependence on producers of hardware and software.
  This problem ist especially a problem of smaller organizations.
  It results from the missing compatibility of products of
  different producers, from the necessity of contracts of
  maintenance and from use of standard software,

- dependence on the public offer of communication infrastructure,

- additional laws (f.e. data protection laws) and therefore more
  influence of public authorities,

- dissatisfaction of customers caused by obscure computer output
  and by formalized processes at the interface between organization
  and customers 2).

The change of the organizational rules concern their contents as
well as the processes of their definition and their execution:

- change of the traditional division of labour and of the contents
  of labour, staff reduction, new places of work, construction and
  reduction of organizational authorities,

- change of coordination methods, especially decrease of individual
  coordination and increase of coordination by contitional programs,

- <u>centralization</u> of the EDP processes and tendencies of centralization of decision making 3),

- <u>centralization of instances which define the rules</u> of task accomplishing. Decrease of purpose oriented rules in favour of formal conditional rules,

- <u>de facto delegation of rule definition</u> to the EDP departments without delegating responsibility. This effect is called "evaporation of responsibility".

The transfer of information and data processing activities from special departments to the EDP department or newly created departments has the following consequences:

- <u>conflicts</u> between EDP and other departments,

- new potentials <u>to carry through new organizational aims and strategies</u>,

- change of the <u>organizational view of the environment</u>, decrease of the importance of individual experiences to the credit of stored models of environment.

2.3. Problems of work in organizations

After considering the whole organizations we now continue considering the individual situation of the persons working in the organizations. This aspect got importance in the last time only, because the science of organization and industrial management only now discovered the man as an important object of its researches and because the researches in the field of "humanization of working life" have difficulties to consider more than pure ergonomical problems.

We consider the following aspects:

- Change of <u>working conditions with respect to man computer contact</u>

- Change of <u>working conditions caused by the change of the organization of work.</u>

We can adjoin the following problems to the first category

- <u>Ergonomical problems</u> caused by missing adaptation of hardware tools and the equipment of places of work to human requirements

- <u>Restrictions of psychological potentials</u> of man caused by restrictions during man-computer interaction

- <u>Restriction of the possibilities</u> of the employees <u>to make</u> their <u>time disposition.</u>This concerns man´s dependance on the machine´s rhythm in interacting as well as the schedule of the EDP department and the shiftwork of the staff of the computer center.

The changes of the organization of work lead to

- <u>Discharges</u>, internal <u>shift of jobs</u>, <u>reductions of jobs</u> caused by changes of division of labour and automation of functions. This leads to <u>impairments of the employee morale</u> and <u>industrial peace</u>, to forced willingness to resign, to worse conditions of work and to increased pressure to obtain better qualifications.

- Reduction of <u>autonomy of work</u> connected with a decrease of motivation of work caused by the increase of the number of orders and the range of possibilities to <u>control the employees</u> in a stronger and more subtle manner.

- Restriction of <u>social interaction</u> at work.

- Change of the demands on qualification according to the tasks of the staff in the administrative area. This problem is intensified by the limited adaptibility of the employees to these demands of qualification. This problem especially concerns the older employees.

2.4. The adaption of technology and organization

The broad spectrum of impacts of the use of EDP in organizations indicates that the technology has by no means been integrated smoothly into organizations. Evidently the conditions for the use of the organizing instrument "computer" are not yet known sufficiently. The substitution of traditional information processing by information processing supported by EDP does not succeed without undesirable side effects. Until now two contradicting basic positions are in the foreground of discussions. On the one hand it is stated that the best integration of EDP into organizations is made by adapting the organizations and all processes in it to the technological requirements. On the other hand it is stated that the computer is an unlimited flexible instrument which can be adapted to all conditions of an organization.

We deny both opinions. The computer technology is no exception to the set of technologies within the fact that it is a technology without any technological requirements. On the other hand it is flexible enough that it must not rob the applying organizations of their individual characteristics.

In reality there is a <u>double problem of adaptation:</u>

(1) There are specific properties of the computer technology, which determine its potentials, its restrictions and the limits of its design flexibility. Only within these limits organizational task accomplishing processes and working processes must be adapted to the technology.

(2) The computer technology has a sufficient scope of designing it flexibly. It can extensively be adapted to organizations by suitable further development and also suitable design of the use of existing technologies. It is possible to adjust the design of organizational task accomplishing processes to other criteria than criteria determined by the technology. Such criteria can be derived from the system of aims described in chapter 1.

It must be the main goal to minimize the portion of organizational adaptation to technological requirements instead of the technological adaption to the applying organization. For this we need an technology oriented analysis of the causes for negative EDP impacts, which can give hints for the pithy utilization of the scope of technological design.

3. Analysis of the causes

3.1. General causes

Of course, the various undesirable impacts do not only result from bad technological design. Certainly we will consider them especially, but it is not correct, if the background for the fact, that the full scope of technology has not been utilized so far, will not be mentioned.
Social scientists see this background exclusively in the social conditions of the utilization of the technology. They say that the information technology is an instrument, "which is used for the benefit of special interest groups and is adapted to the established social conditions.
Since the development of the use of technologies is being controlled by established interest groups, the use of the technologies is normally designed in that way, that existing trends in the concerned application field are growing stronger. So the information technology becomes a 'trend supporting technology'" 4). From the view of Computer Science it must be questioned whether the pursuit of these strategies for computer application follows rational calculations. The Computer Science as a "science of the systematical processing with digital computers" [3] considers the denying of technological compulsions as precipitate and unfounded.

An important index for the assumption that the use of information technology could not always be submitted to its underlied social strategies, is the fact that there are a lot of impacts mentioned in chapter 2, which must be judged negatively from different points of interest. There often is a gap between application strategies and application reality.

The general spectrum rather is stratified. Belonging to it are

- the problematic using strategies which are oriented to certain interests and therefore against other interests, especially against the interests of the employees concerning better conditions of work in every respect,

- helplessness in using the EDP technology caused by gaps of research especially in Computer Science, Organizational Sciences and Working Sciences,

- unsufficient degree of maturity of the used technologies, imperfection of technological design and insufficient state of training of EDP staff,

- frequently missing possibilities of participation for the applyers and the employees concerned by the use of EDP in designing and implementing the EDP systems and processes,

- specific properties of information technologies which have not been considered for application.

The contribution of Computer Science now has to be the defining of the scope of technological design and the transposition of the scope to aims of research, development and education. Computer Science has to be based on the fact that because of exactly stated properties of its technology the relation between the technology itself and its application is not in free dispositon for every interest.

Instead of this there is an exactly stated, optimal, to some extend dialectical balance, which determines scope and direction of alternatives of technological design.

3.2. Technological causes

For an exact analysis we first have to agree upon some conceptions:

- with a process we mean the change of an object caused by activities by an acting instance in the lapse of time and controlled by rules.

- Informations are acoustically or optically represented chains of signals, which are built up in a well defined manner (syntax), which have well defined meanings for sender and receiver (semantics) and which are combined with a purpose with which the sender transmits them and with which the receiver uses them (pragmatics). With this interpretation informations are connected with subjective targets and sometimes subjective interpretations of their meaning. That implies that informations cannot be transmitted without changing them.

- Data are words over a symbol set which can be read, stored and processed by a technical medium. This condition requires that data have to be represented by a final number of symbols over a final symbol set and by using additional syntactical rules for formatization.

- With the word computer we only mean the available hardware of an EDP system. A so defined computer can generally be used for all tasks for which we can use EDP systems if we perform suitable and complicated operating activities. With this meaning the production of software is an activity to operate (adjusting) the computer.

Such a computer has three basic properties:

(1) It is a data processing machine. That means: It can only be acting authority of data processing processes.

(2) It is a final machine. That means: In addition to the finiteness of storage capacity, of the capacity of a storage cell and of the instruction set especially the finiteness of the instructions which can be processed in a final period of time.

(3) It is an universal machine. That means: With the properties (1) and (2) all restrictions of the efficiency of the computer have been stated.

From these basic properties we can derive the following technical conditions for the use of computers:

- Processes of EDP must be procedures. That means:
  They have to be determined uniquely by giving a finite set of processable instructions and there must be conditions on which the process has to stop.

- Therefore they are deterministical, that means, that at any time during the process the following state is uniquely determined, and they are discrete.

- The operating activities must describe these procedures
  exactly (programming), because the universality of the computer
  and the needed determination imply that one element has to be
  determined from an infinite set of possible processes.

So we get the fundamental and indispensable requirement for the use
of EDP: Each method to accomplish a task by using EDP processes has
to be divided into a finite number of discrete single steps which
can be executed by a machine.

The impact of this requirement forced by the technology becomes
clear, if we look at the context in which this requirement works.
This context is given by the places of the occurrence of the
impacts:

- the task accomplishing processes of the organizations which are
  directly concerned in reaching the goal of the organization

- the working processes of the individual members of the organization as part of the task accomplishing processes 5)

- the human information processes as parts of the working processes

- the organizational information processes as parts of the
  organizational task accomplishing processes including the human
  information processes

- the data processing processes supporting the organizational
  information processes.

The impacts of the use of computers can so be interpreted as
changes of the characteristics of the process elements (objects,
activities, acting instances, rules). These changes which first
of all concern the data processing processes affect also the other
processes as a result of the correlations between all mentioned
processes.

Data processing processes support information processes. Information
processes are involved in the controlling or organizational task
accomplishing processes and individual working processes. Changes
of data processing processes by using new technologies lead to
changes of the information processes and all other processes,
particularly caused by the substitution of former information
processes by data processing processes.

This substitution must have consequences for the organizational
information processing and so for the task accomplishing and working
processes, because data processing processes and information
processes are different:

- Objects of these processes are data resp. informations. In
  contrast to data informations have a pragmatical component and
  are so dependent on the purpose giving man. Moreover the
  syntactical component of informations is mostly not adapted
  to the requirements of processing by machines.

- Therefore the acting instances of information processes are
  always men, those of data processing computers in this context.

- The rules of information processes are characterized by the
  potentials and methods of human thinking, human methods of

receiving or transmissing impulses. The rules of data processing
are given by algorithmic computer programs.

- The activities of men processing informations and the activities
  of computers processing data can be differentiated into input,
  transportation, storing, combining and output of informations
  resp. data.

The equality of the activities, the so-called formal identity, and
the neglecting of the differences between the objects result in the
illusion that information processing can be substituted by data
processing without consequences. Opposite to the formal identity
there is the qualitative difference, which comes from the different
competence of the acting instances, especially from the human capability to be subjective and the availability of flexible methods for
him. So the substitution of information processing by data processing
must necessarily cause changes. These changes of the organizational
information processing, which are produced by the substitution of
parts of them by computerized data processing, are called information changes. They are the graver the more the substituted information processes are depending on potentials of men and his
own model of the world (f.e. planning, deciding). They are the
slighter the more men themselves have to use formal algorithmic
methods (f.e. mathematical calculations). Because of the
property of information processing to be able to regulate task
accomplishing processes and working processes these processes are
also concerned by information changes. These changes of task
accomplishing and working processes are called impacts of information changes.

The structure of 2.1., 2.2. and 2.3. bases on these reflections.
2.1. contains the information changes, 2.2. resp. 2.3. contain the
impacts of information changes on task accomplishing processes
(organization) and working processes (work in organizations).

4. The scope of technological design

The specification of negative impacts and the analysis of their
causes raise the question for the possibilities to reduce or
eliminate them. Most of impact research studies consider the
answer to this question to be an open problem which now has to be
taken up. We also can't answer the question exactly in this paper.
We can see the following approaches:

- Giving isolated designing suggestions to eliminate one single
  undesirable impact. On the one hand this can be done by definition
  of research aims in Computer Science, Organizational Science and
  Working Science which can give exact hints for directed support
  of researches. On the other hand this can be done by more or less
  immediately practicable actions to design the use of EDP in
  organizations [12].

- Participative methods to design applications of EDP in
  organizations seem to be more effective. By using participation
  the employees can influence the criteria and directions of the
  design of the use of EDP. This approach is followed by Kubicek
  [14] and the Norwegian impact research [9].

- The demand for so-called "social" information technologies must
  be discussed critically. This conception can only get a meaning
  if it helps not only to veil strategies of special interest groups.

The further explanations are intended to plot the scope of technological design, in which the three approaches can range. For this
we use the theoretical discussion of the causes explained in 3.2.

One of the properties of the computer is its universality, i.e. its
capability to be acting instance of all data processing processes
which are not repugnant to finiteness. This means that the user can
select processes from an arbitrary number of different EDP processes
performing suitable operating activities, i.e. programming in a
broad sense. So the computer has a big using flexibility. The more
system and application programs are available to the user, that
means, the more operating activities are taken off his shoulders
by other authorities, the more his choice within contents and
methods of EDP processes is restricted. He only has a smaller using
flexibility than the technology can make available on principle.

Using flexibility could be measured by the number of the EDP
processes, which the user can "adjust" at the computer. The bigger
the using flexibility the more efforts are necessary to choose a
definite process. That means, that a user can only use big using
flexibility if he is able to do the more complicated operating
activities. He must be able to get over big objective operating
complexity, if he wants to use this using flexibility 6). The
improved adaptation of computer and man and of design of the use
of EDP and the organization is pre-condition for the reduction
of undesirable impacts. All activities which design the technology and its use in a way, that the organization and people working
in it are able to use the technology competently, flexibly
and in their free discretion, follow that aim. So it is desirable
to make big using flexibility available to each user.

The dilemma of the proportion of desirable big using flexibility
and undesirable big operating complexity seems to make the problem
unsolvable. But there is another way: Men perceive operating
complexity very much if the operating activities as usual are
optimized exclusively to the requirements of the machine and if
it is proceeded on the arbitrary adaptability of man. Evidently
there is a subjective operating complextiy, which is not only
dependent on the objective operating complexity but also on the
conditions of work at the man computer interface, the physical
and psychical capabilities of the user and his qualification. So
the abstract aim of designing is to get an optimal compromise
between using flexibility und subjective operating complexity
within the respective criteria of use and criteria of well
designed working places. That means: to get a maximum of using
flexibility by using the subjective capabilities and requirements
of men designing the man computer interface (MCI), i.e. the
adaptation of the machine to men. We give two examples which
stand for others:

- Improvements of the ergonomical conditions at the MCI facilitate
  the work with the computer without an amount of software.

- An important step is the development of universal program
  languages which began 20 years ago. These program languages
  are certainly formal but they approach to the human faculty of
  speech without restricting the using flexibility essentially.
  The optimum - but unfortunately not realizable - would be the
  totally unrestricted user of the natural colloquial language
  of the user. This language is very complex from an objective
  point of view and so able to describe every possible data

processing process, but it is very little complex from a
subjective point of view, because the user is master of it
anyhow.

The abstract scope of designing can be differentiated in simple
operations at existing systems on the one hand and the search for
so-called "social" information technologies on the other hand.

In spite of all "technological compulsions" the technology offers
the scope to

- design work <u>more human</u>, i.e. to realize qualitatively demands
  on working processes to accomplish entire tasks (to work against
  increasing taylorism and estrangement of activities aided by
  computers)

- make the accomplishing of tasks <u>more transparent</u> for employees
  and customers

- <u>destruct</u> organizational or external <u>dependencies</u>

- make the organization and the staff able to react <u>more
  flexibly</u> (to work against the increasing fixing of methods
  of task accomplishing when using computers)

- guarantee competent participation and codetermination of
  afflicted persons during the system design process.

To utilize these aims for the technological development Computer
Science has to be a decisive instrument - although it is even
near its learning process according this problem.

FOOTNOTES:

1) Such participative approaches are usual methods of Scandinavian
   impact research [9]. In these approaches the afflicted
   employees are competently integrated into the analysing and
   designing processes of the organizations. In the Federal
   Republic of Germany expecially Kubicek [14] is engaged in the
   testing of these emancipatorical designing methods.

2) This problem has particular importance for the relation between
   citizens and public authorities. We can not only see the
   increase of the distance between citizens and government but
   also a shifting of work from the public to the citizens. See
   f.e. [5].

3) The centralization of the EDP will hardly be influenced by
   distributed systems. Mostly (but not necessarily) these systems
   are characterized by central processing and storage capacities
   and distributed access only. Concerning the centralization
   of decision making there are different and contradictory
   empirial results. See the summary of Kubicek ([13], p. 158)
   and the results of Brinckmann [4] concerning the public
   administration.

4) This is the theoretical background of the German study on
   impact research (see [17], translation of p. 36).

5) The distinction between task accomplishing process and working
   process ist an analytic one and helps to differentiate
   perspectively the complex "task accomplishing in organizations"
   into organizational and individual aspects.

6) An example: A referee who does his work at a terminal using an
   interactive application program with only a small set of
   instructions can not do very much more with the computer. So
   he has only a small using flexibility and he must not be
   instructed very much to be able to use it. A system programmer
   certainly needs a highly specialized education to be able to
   use big using flexibility and so to make sure about the
   latitude of how to choose his methods.

REFERENCES:

[1]   Ackhoff, R.: Management Misinformation Systems.
        Management Science 14, 147-156 (1967)

[2]   Barrow, I.; Curnow, R.C.: The Future of Information
        Technology. Internal Report of Social Policy Research
        Unit, University of Sussex, Brighton 1978

[3]   Brauer, W.; Haacke, W.; Münch, S.: Studien- und Forschungs-
        führer Informatik. GMD/DAAD Bonn/Bad Godesberg 1978

[4]   Brinckmann, H.: Verwaltungsgliederung als Schranke von
        Planungs- und Informationsverbund. ÖVD 5, 239-248 (1975)

[5]   Brinckmann, H.; Grimmer, K.; Lenk, K.; Rave, D.: Verwal-
        tungsautomation. Darmstadt: S. Toeche-Mittler 1974

[6]   Danzin, A.: Die gesellschaftlichen Auswirkungen der Daten-
        verarbeitung. Birlinghoven: GMD-Eigenverlag 1978

[7]   Dehning, W.; Essig, H.; Maaß, S.: Zur Anpassung virtueller
        Mensch-Rechner-Schnittstellen an Benutzererfordernisse im
        Dialog - dargestellt am Beispiel von Datenbanksystemen.
        Report of the Department of Computer Science of the Uni-
        versity of Hamburg, IfI-HH-B-50/78, 1978

[8]   Dehning, W.; Maaß, S.: Kommunikative Aspekte der Mensch-
        Computer-Interaktion. Note of the Department of Computer
        Science of the University of Hamburg, IfI-HH-M-43/77, 1977

[9]   Fjalestad, J.; Pape, A.: Social Impacts of Information
        Technology, Norwegian Strategies for Research. Lecture
        of the Conference on Social Impacts of Information
        Technology, Schloß Birlinghoven, 1978

[10]   Forschungsgruppe Verwaltungsautomation: Forschungsberichte,
        11 Volumes. Gesamthochschule Kassel: Eigenverlag 1975-1978

[11]   Heibey, H.-W.; Kühn, M.; Lutterbeck, B.; Töpel, M.: Techno-
        logische Gestaltung der Mensch-Computer-Schnittstellen.
        Report of the Department of Computer Science of the
        University of Hamburg, IfI-HH-B -61/79, 1979

[12]   Heibey, H.-W., Lutterbeck, B.; Töpel, M.: Auswirkungen der
        elektrischen Datenverarbeitung in Organisationen. Research
        Report DV 77-01 of the German Secretary of Research and
        Technology, Eggenstein-Leopoldshafen: Centrum of Nuclear
        Power-Documentation 1977

[13]   Kubicek, H.: Informationstechnologie und organisatorische
        Regelungen. Berlin: Duncker und Humblot 1975

[14]   Kubicek, H.: Humanisierung des DV-Gestützten Büros durch
        partizipative Systemgestaltung. Angewandte Informatik 8/78,
        331-342 (1978)

[15]   Lucas, H.-C., jr.: Why Information Systems Fail. New York-
        London: Columbia University Press 1975

158

[16]   Nora, S.; Minc, A: L'informatisation de la societé.
        Rapport a M. le President de la Republique. Paris: La
        Documentation Francaise 1978

[17]   Reese, J.; Kubicek, H; Lange, B.P.; Lutterbeck, B; Reese, U.:
        Bestandsaufnahme der Wirkungsforschung im Bereich Informa-
        tionstechnologie, Final Report with 2 additional volumes,
        Institut für Planungs- und Entscheidungssysteme of GMD,
        Bonn-Birlinghoven: Eigenverlag 1978

Humanizing Computerized Information Systems

Guidelines developed in a series of workshops are presented and their Implications are Discussed

Theodor D. Sterling

Computing Science Program, Simon Fraser University, CDN-Burnaby, British Columbia, V5A 1S6, Canada

The accumulation and control of information is a critical function for government and private, industrial and non-industrial organizations. Yet the role of information as an organizational resource is not very well understood, especially as it is related to the organization's environment. What does appear is that computerized information systems have become a facilitating technology that interacts with organizational, historical, and environmental pressures and goals to shape not only the internal structure of an organization but also its interactions with society (1,2). There is little doubt that the computerized or automated information system is revolutionizing the management of most, if not all, systems by which goods and services are produced or information is accumulated. This should be a source of great concern.

Weizenbaum (3) asked whether large computerized systems can be used by anybody except governments and really large corporations and whether such organizations will not use them mainly for antihuman purposes. The power of computerized information systems to control large enterprises answers the need to manage large systems and make them amenable to human control. By any criteria of management performance, computerization of a system permits its detailed control, and thus the computer is the ideal management tool. But the cost of the control is high. Start-up costs to redesign and computerize large-scale enterprises are immense. In concentrating on feasibility and workability and simultaneously minimizing costs, few systems designers seem to have been concerned about whether their products will be used for antihuman purposes.

In many ways, it is immaterial whether control over the management network is exercised by manual means or by automation. As long as official procedures are detrimental to human dignity, nothing is changed in converting to automation — except that individuals may shift the blame for their oppression from the human cog to the computer cog. It may be necessary, therefore, to clarify the dehumanizing components of a management system, which may be present whether or not the system has been automated, and to provide relief for any suffering they may have caused.

In a previous analysis (4) I pointed to two design strategies that account in large part for the presence of dehumanizing features in a management system. First, the efficiency of an enterprise is commonly increased by treating the recipients of the service and participants in the system as unpaid components whose time, effort and intelligence do not appear in the cost accounting. Then, in order to maintain the efficiency of procedures once they have been established, the system is made exceedingly rigid, permitting freedom of action at only a few, usually hidden, focal points of real control. Dehumanizing features are thus already ingrained in most systems of management, and automation of such systems simply transfers the dehumanizing practice from one means of exercising control to another, codifies it in computer programs, and expands its influence to a larger circle of recipients and participants. To provide for the smooth and efficient operation of a largely computerized management system, the automation process makes demands of its own on all participants which decrease the area of free action remaining to the individual. Rules of procedure are thus dictated by the growth of machines and not by the needs of man. As a consequence, it is possible for the machine to capture the prerogative to formulate questions important to man. If we take such developments as inevitable we are surrendering our humanity.

The point is that an intelligent understanding of a machine mode of control may be delayed until long after this control has been exercised. Wiener (5) argued that although procedures laid down to satisfy a process of automation are subject to human criticism and modification, such criticism may be ineffective because it may not surface until long after it is relevant. It may be too late then to correct the damage to the human condition. Systems are not detached from the people they interact with and the settings they create, and people strive for a sense of dignity, have needs that should be taken seriously, like to be treated with consideration and courtesy, and occasionally act as individuals – in short, they are entitled to be treated as human beings.

Despite the overriding importance of a person's dignity and humanity, little is known in terms of "scientific" specifics about the operational meaning of these concepts or the antecedent conditions that enhance or diminish them. Relatively few analyses have been devoted to systems features that may humanize organizations (6,7). We know of only one attempt to incorporate humanizing features in a system and to evaluate their effects (8). Yet we cannot afford to wait for knowledge to accumulate about the procedures to be incorporated in information systems or information parts of systems to help avoid dehumizing or add humanizing qualities to them. We live in a time of active proliferation of new and revised management procedures, and designers of information systems are organizational designers as well, who cannot avoid changing organizations (7,9). This is especially true of the proliferation of management information systems, which are more than information systems in the technical sense, as they include all bureaucratic procedures and perhaps all systems components that enter into the production and distribution of goods and services and so dominate the economic, political, and social management of society.

Organizational design should be taken on as an explicit activity and management information systems implemented in such a way that they create a more humane setting.

Gouldner (10) showed how rules and regulations respond to the self-interest of those who govern and are governed. But to influence the shaping of new bureaucracies and other management systems, it is first necessary to isolate the crucial categories of design features that may make manifest humanizing or dehumanizing qualities of information systems. The analysis presented here is based on the guidelines developed by the Stanley House workshop on humanizing computerized information systems (11,12) in a serious attempt to isolate such design features. The guidelines are grouped into five broad categories, as shown in Table 1.

Many of the Stanley House criteria make sense as procedures for softening a bureaucracy as well as making an information system less rigid. There is no real distinction between manual and automated systems, and guidelines apply whether or not computers are used.

Table 1. Stanley House criteria for humanizing information systems.

A. Procedures for dealing with users

1. The language of a system should be easy to understand.
2. Transactions with a system should be courteous.
3. A system should be quick to react.
4. A system should respond quickly to users (if it is unable to resolve its intended procedure).

5. A system should relieve the users of unnecessary chores.
6. A system should provide for human information interface.
7. A system should include provisions for corrections.
8. Management should be held responsible for mismanagement.

B. Procedures for dealing with exceptions

1. A system should recognize as much as possible that it deals with different classes of individuals.
2. A system should recognize that special conditions might occur that could require special actions by it.
3. A system must allow for alternatives in input and processing.
4. A system should give individuals choices on how to deal with it.
5. A procedure must exist to override the system.

C. Action of the system with respect to information

1. There should be provisions to permit individuals to inspect information about themselves.
2. There should be provisions to correct errors.
3. There should be provisions for evaluating information stored in the system.
4. There should be provisions for individuals to add information that they consider important.
5. It should be made known in general what information is stored in systems and what use will be made of that information.

D. The problem of privacy

1. In the design of a system all procedures should be evaluated with respect to both privacy and humanization requirements.
2. The decision to merge information from different files and systems should never occur automatically. Whenever information from one file is made available to another file, it should be examined first for its implications for privacy and humanization.

E. Guidelines for system design having a bearing on ethics

1. A system should not trick or deceive.
2. A system should assist participants and users and not manipulate them.
3. A system should not eliminate opportunities for employment without a careful examination of consequences to other available jobs.
4. System designers should not participate in the creation or maintenance of secret data banks.
5. A system should treat with consideration all individuals who come in contact with it.

DISCUSSION OF GUIDELINES

By and large, the Stanley House guidelines are self-descriptive. This discussion is designed to illuminate their less obvious aspects and point to special problems that arise in connection with their implementation.

Criterion A2 is not a commonly encountered consideration in systems design. And indeed, courtesy is not a substitute for real rewards, high quality of service, or other qualities. However, it is possible that courtesy is a prerequisite of humane society. In a rehabilitation hospital where courteous communications were part of a specially designed hospital information system, employees were pleased with that feature and regarded it highly (8). It is difficult to evaluate the importance of this courtesy criterion precisely because experience with courtesy in automated systems has been so rare.

Criterion A5 has far-reaching implications for a system's cost and efficiency. One of the favorite methods for optimizing the efficiency and minimizing the cost of a bureaucratic system is to require the individuals being served to supply the necessary information at each procedural component with which they are involved. Further, in order to ensure an uninterrupted flow of work, recipients of service are required to stand in queues at each point. Yet very often the required information can be made available to each procedural component at relatively small cost. It may be particularly important to do this at times when participating individuals are under additional pressures. One pernicious example is the queuing of hospital patients before special treatment or diagnostic centers (such as physical therapy or radiology). Appointments for individual patients made through the hospital information system could eliminate the queues of sick people in drafty corridors so typical of hospital operations. Similarly, a good system could eliminate unnecessary queues and travel by job seekers. On the other side of the coin, we find that the repetitive and unrelieved need to supply a service to queues of recipients is often dehumanizing to service personnel, and the constant demands of the queue prevent trained personnel from applying their skills in a selective manner (8).

Criteria A6 and A7 may be related. Large-scale systems tend to be converted onto computers as cheaply as possible. In order to do this a global method of design is often used in which all subprocedures are rigidly defined into a single large structure. The more flexible, albeit much more expensive, way is to build a basic system of linkages to which different procedural modules can be attached. Whenever modifications are required it is then only necessary to reprogram the one affected module. One of the side effects of the global method of design is that it is difficult to modify the system to deal with errors that had not been anticipated. Yet errors of every sort, expecially those related to information input, are almost unavoidable in a system that handles a large number of transactions. There is a suspicion in the concerned data processing communities that many corporations leave some errors uncorrected because it is cheaper to lose an occasional customer than to correct for each mistake. The human interface would be a desirable component of a system, even when correction of error may not be the major need. Human contact may be needed for individuals in vulnerable positions, such as the unemployed or the sick, to answer questions about unavoidable delays in providing a service or replying to an application; or just to soften the impact of an impersonal bureaucracy.

The human interface is lacking in most systems we have examined so far, and it may well be that the interface will have to be provided from the outside. One extraorganizational scheme is to have a computer ombudsman serving a large community. Such an ombudsman service could be provided by a professional, consumer or governmental body, or by a combination of organizations, and would be the mediating link between the perplexed citizen and the perplexing system (13).

Related to A6 and A7 is A8, the criterion that management ought to be held responsible for the situation where faulty design causes discomfort and frustration to individuals unable to get relief or attention from a system. Poorly designed systems are often not corrected because no one is really responsible for their actions. As a consequence, Kafkaesque nightmares may be created for users and participants.

In many ways, procedures for dealing with exceptions may be the most necessary components of a humanized system. The human condition is never so homogeneous that a set of rules can be devised to cover all exigencies. Once bureaucratic procedures are structured, they tend to become rigid even though they may contain provisions to deal with human needs. Exceptions are always difficult to manage. To provide for such flexibility, it is absolutely necessary to provide access to focal points of information or control in order to accommodate a departure from the "norm" where the users' needs require it.

I do not believe that there are technical obstacles to incorporating in working systems the kind of criteria that would permit the consideration of exceptions. My main concern is that obstacles will be generated by unavoidable conflict among humanizing criteria and between such criteria and the use of the system. Consider criterion B1, for example. Some employers of manual job bank programs rely on the face-to-face system to weed out those whom they regard as undesirable applicants. Here is an unstated trade-off between flexibility and equity. Also unstated may be the need to specify whom the system serves. What defines a class of individuals depends, in each case, on the kind of services the system provides or the demands it makes on participants. It is easy to say that a system should at least be aware that affected individuals differ in many personal characteristics and needs and should be accorded correspondingly different types of treatment. However, to achieve that may require an explicit definition of the purposes of a system. For instance, does a job bank serve the job seeker or the employer? It obviously serves the needs of both, and when a conflict exists between these needs it may not be feasible to make that conflict explicit.

In a similar sense conflicts may be created by criterion B4. There is a large variety of situations in which individuals may not wish to avail themselves of services or to provide a system with information touching on their private lives. The whole idea of "choice" is foreign to most large-scale systems, whether automated or manual. The provision of choices may very well mark the border between the dehumanizing and the humanizing system. However, it will add greatly to the complexity of systems, because permitting individual choices may set up conflicts with other criteria or services, including some through which the system seeks to become less dehumanizing. For example, in Canada, Provincial Health Services send an account of services rendered to the head of household. This would seem to fulfill the requirement of keeping the user or recipient of a service informed. Other members of the family, however, might object to finding their health needs reported to the head of household (without necessarily detracting from the affection they might feel for their spouse, parent, or provider). While this problem could be alleviated by addressing the report to the concerned individual, other situations may arise that cannot be easily resolved without providing a wide variety of choices. The spouse of the head of household or the adult children may not wish to inform the head that they have sought medical services. In fact, reporting such information may be harmful to a course of therapy or may needlessly disrupt family life, as when members of a family are seeking treatment for venereal disease or drug addiction, for example.

Opinions are divided about the extent to which information about individuals ought to be withheld from them and from others. Yet there is general agreement that provisions are needed for making access to and evaluation and correction of that information possible.

Criteria concerning actions of the system with respect to information have been widely discussed, so no additional comments may be necessary except in one case - criterion C4. This would make it possible for individuals to add to the system information which they think bears importantly on their background or needs, even if the information is not important for processing their files. This might not add anything to the efficiency of a system, but would add a great deal to the psychological comfort of affected individuals.

Requirements for safeguarding the privacy of individual records may seriously conflict with requirements for humanizing an automated system. In general, the more information a system has about individuals who are affected by it, the more likely it is that it can be humanized, but also the easier it becomes to misuse that information and to violate individual needs or desires for privacy and confidentiality. The extent to which individuals are entitled to privacy or even wish privacy is a matter of political or social decision, as is the extent to which individuals ought not to be dehumanized by a system. Privacy versus humanization

is an issue that has not received sufficient attention, and our experience with
these concepts is too limited for it to be possible to compare requirements for
privacy with those for humanization or make judgements on which is more important.
However, it is clear that a very private system with no humane provisions may be
just as undesirable as a very humane system with no safeguards to protect the
privacy of its participants.

What makes procedural features desirable or undesirable with respect to privacy
or humanization can be determined only in the context of the purpose of the system and the safeguards possible. Some systems that list individuals and information about them are desirable and others are not. They may also be desirable
and undesirable to different people. For instance, a detailed file on handi-
capped children in the community would be useful for providing individual services, allocating community resources, and directing planning for schools and
recreational facilities. On the other hand, attempts have been made to keep on
file the names and records of minors who have been convicted of criminal offenses
and to merge such files with other record systems. This has met with opposition
from thoughtful members of the community, including members of the police department, and would be very objectionable, at least until adequate safeguards against
abuse of such systems have been firmly defined and can be implemented. In the
final analysis, it is not only a file's existence but its use which determines
its ethical value. Nevertheless, the social and political considerations underlying criterion D1 can be resolved within the context of a particular system.
What we are saying is that society can decide whether and how a file of handi-
capped children or of juvenile offenders should be assembled, maintained, and
used.

It may be much more difficult to deal with criterion D2. Central to the problem
of privacy is the very much enlarged information base available to government
agencies when it becomes possible to merge information from different files.
Merging of information may also make many systems more efficient and might make
their action more equitable or even more humane. But it may be more to the point
that under the guise of humanizing systems or making them more equitable (not
necessarily the same thing), the rights of individuals for privacy and freedom
from government surveillance in a democratic society may be seriously compromised.
For example, the new Insurance Corporation of British Columbia, which is regulated and run by the provincial government, provides compulsory insurance under
the name Autoplan for all drivers and car owners and bases its rate structure on
records of driver violations. It is disquieting to note the ease with which Autoplan has been able to merge court and police files with records of largely business activities of Canadians in British Columbia without a public examination of
this important step. Nor has there been public opposition to the extension of
Autoplan to other insurance areas. In a similar vein, Lauden (1) has shown for
four U.S. police and welfare systems how easily information from many sources may
be merged. These are perfect examples of the type of activities warned against
by Wiener (5), who predicted that the needs of large-scale government systems
would generate practices which would be discovered only after they were well
established.

It is thus clear that the extent to which a system can or will incorporate humanizing or dehumanizing features depends on economic, social and political decisions. There are limits to the power of managers, engineers, systems designers,
and scientists to provide for the inclusion of many desirable features in systems.
We suggest a set of ethical principles - criteria E1 to E5 - which, if followed,
will ensure that within any set of constraints a system will tend to be humane
rather than dehumanizing.

Largely because many transactions of an automated system are difficult to inspect
and by their very nature are less open to view than their manual predecessors,
the requirement that systems should not deceive or trick, criterion E1, becomes

of paramount importance. But even when a system is restrained from deception by
law, it may still try to violate the spirit if not the letter of the law. (Common
examples are billing practices whereby attempts are made to hide the amount
of interest that is being collected from customers or that would be collected
if the customer pays only part of what he owes.)

Computerized transactions make it possible for systems to assist participants
without needlessly exploiting their labor (criterion E2). The idea that users
must provide supportive services in order that a system may function is deeply
ingrained not only in the designers of systems but also in the individuals they
serve. Members of society are conditioned from birth to stand in line and fill
out forms in order to register, to pay, or to receive. They have been habituated
to supply information and contribute by their labor wherever they sought to receive a service, were ill, or provided a service for the government (such as
paying taxes). It is grotesque but true that when the Nazis led millions of
people into concentration camps and eventually into gas chambers, the victims had
to stand in lines and deliver their possessions, provide information, and perform all the necessary services required to part them from their goods, their
loved ones and finally their lives. Manual systems burden recipients of a service
with a great deal of effort to make the systems function smoothly. Computerized
systems do not need to do so, or not really to the same extent. However, the
temptation is always there to exploit the willing and conditioned cooperation of
members of society. A contrary attitude, that the system should be burdened
rather than the human components, needs to be fostered. Similarly, an attitude
should be cultivated by systems designers that all individuals, including employees, who come in contact with a system should be treated with the same consideration (criterion E5). It has been established that organizational structure produces characteristic patterns of alienation. For instance, Blauner (14) has
shown that workers may develop perceptions of "meaninglessness", "powerlessness",
and "work estrangement", depending on how they are fitted into an industry's
technology (15).

We have chosen to group criterion E3 with ethical rather than economic and social
or political considerations. Within the area of information systems and systems
control through computers, there are many types of employment that are relatively
pleasant and interesting, and offer opportunities to large numbers of individuals
which are difficult to find elsewhere. The overall cost of eliminating such jobs
may be high. This is true when computerization of technology affects jobs that
rely heavily on human skills and qualities of perception, attention, and intelligence. There are severe costs when sources of employment that provide interesting,
challenging, and above all human types of employment are eliminated. One example
of an endangered group, victims of the computerization of communication networks,
are telephone operators. It is questionable that replacement jobs for this large
number of eliminated positions which offer equally acceptable work for humans
are available. The cost of finding employment for the communication workers who
ordinarily would have worked for the telephone system has to be borne by society
and not by the telephone company, and there is not way to assess or repay the
costs to individuals who are forced into less satisfactory employment because opportunities for interesting and humane jobs are eliminated. From an economic
point of view, this example shows that a cost-benefit analysis of job elimination
through automation should not be based on the effects on a particular industry
alone, but should include society as a whole. While it is recognized that it may
be difficult for the systems designer to resist the temptation to eliminate such
desirable jobs, he should be the first to recognize when they are in danger of
being eliminated, and it behooves him as a human being to sound the alarm.

A FINAL WORD ABOUT ECONOMIES

Perhaps the most serious obstacle to the inclusion of humanizing modules is that
they reduce the efficiency of most information systems. Their inclusion will

increase overhead in terms of design effort, complexity of procedures, and execution time. It may even be necessary to add to the physical resources of central computers (to provide a larger memory, a greater ratio of input to output, and so on). Consequently, appreciable research along these lines is not expected to be initiated by systems designers and managers, whose primary commitment is to efficiency. While our discussion is not designed to come to grips with the concern of those who are highly cost-conscious, we are nevertheless suspicious of those who refer to humanistic features as negative externalities and who hope that some market mechanism will handle their underlying problem. There is also a "humanistic" side to the debate (12,16).

Lauden (1) makes a convincing case that the arrival of the third-generation computer offered new hope for administrative reformers, and indeed many administrative reformers attempted to fulfill this hope almost immediately. The new computer technology promised more closely integrated (which meant centralized) elements of federal, state, and local bureaucracies. It promised better decision-making, better government, better production, better distribution, and better allocation technology. Another important factor, Lauden stressed, is that the value to society of changes in (computerized) information systems does not have to be tested through the electoral process. Similarly, technological changes in industry rarely depend on decisions by stockholders. There are thus factors that shape computerized information systems and restructure means of producing and allocating goods and services or collecting information that are determined solely by political or industrial management and are neither controlled by nor responsive to social pressures. In the case of information systems, political ends are often achieved by management under the guise of instituting cost-saving efficiencies.

The utility of humanizing procedures will not be revealed in ordinary cost-benefit calculations but in the quality of life. Should we burden ourselves and future generations with dehumanizing practices designed and implemented today? Must not the wish to keep systems humane and dignified take its place with the desire to keep the air and the water palatable as a necessary countermotive to the drive of government and industry to be as efficient and cost-conscious as possible?

SUMMARY

Computerized management information systems increasingly determine all bureaucratic and management procedures that control the production and distribution of goods and services and the collection of information. Thus, they begin to dominate the economic, political, and social management of society. With this domination come procedural features that may dehumanize participants or users affected by the working of most public and private organizations. Yet, despite the overriding importance of a person's dignity and humanity, little is known in terms of scientific specifics about the operational meaning of these concepts or of the antecedent conditions that enhance or diminish them. It will be too late if we wait for knowledge to accumulate about procedures to be incorporated in information systems or information parts of systems to avoid dehumanizing or to add humanizing qualities to them. A set of guidelines has been developed in a series of workshops sponsored by the Canadian Information Processing Society, Canada Council, and Simon Fraser University. These guidelines may apply where organizational design needs may be met and management information systems implemented in such a way that they create a more humane setting.

References and Notes

1. The most recent analysis for computerized agencies is in K. Lauden: Computers and Bureaucratic Reform (Wiley, New York, 1974).

2. For an example of the impact of technology (but not computerization) on an organization see P. Blau, The Dynamics of Bureaucracy (Univ. of Chicago Press, Chicago, 1963).
3. Weizenbaum, J., Science 176.609 (1972).
4. Sterling, T., Humanists in Canada 25.2 (1973).
5. Weiner, N., The Human Use of Human Beings (Doubleday-Anchor, Garden City, N.Y., 1954); Science 131.1355 (1960).
6. Argyris, C, Integrating the Individual in the Organization (Irwin-Dorsey, Georgetown, Ontario, 1965); Public Admin. Rev. 33.253 (May-June 1973); Kling, R., in Proceedings of the Association for Computing Machinery, Computers in the Service of Man (Association for Computing Machinery, New York, 1973), pp. 387-391.
7. Bougeslaw, R., The New Utopians (Prentice-Hall, Englewood Cliffs, N.J., 1965).
8. Sterling, T., Pollack, S., Spencer, W., Int.J. Biomed. Comput. 15.51 (1974).
9. Galbraith, J., Organizational Design (Addison-Wesley, Reading, Mass, 1973); Whisler, T., The Impact of Computer Organizations (Pergamon, New York, 1970).
10. Gouldner, A, Patterns of Industrial Bureaucracy (Free Press, New York, 1954).
11. The guidelines were generated during a number of workshops held at Stanley House, a small estate in the Gaspe at which Canada Council schedules intensive seminars. Canada Council and the Canadian Information Processing Society sponsored one workshop each in 1973. Participating in various of these workshops and otherwise contributing to the formation of these guidelines were R. Ashenhurst, computer scientist (University of Chicago); M. Bockelman, police department (Kansas City); L. Brereton, editor, Humanists in Canada; C. Capstick, computer scientist (Guelph University); A. Close, barrister (Law Reform Commission); G. Cunningham, assistant commissioner (Royal Canadian Mounted Police); V. Douglas, psychologist (McGill University); C. Gotlieb, computer scientist (University of Toronto); H. Kalman, historian (University of British Columbia); R. Kling, computer scientist (University of California, Los Angeles); T. Kuch, philosopher (Department of Health, Education, and Welfare); P. Lykos, computer scientist (National Science Foundation); S. Pollack, computer scientist (Washington University); H . Schlaginweit, manager (British Columbia Telephone Co.); W. Rogers, provincial auditor (Alberta); D. Seely, computer scientist (Simon Fraser University); M. Shepherd, programmer (Toronto); T. Sterling, computer scientist (Simon Fraser University); and J. Weizenbaum, computer scientist (Massachusetts Institute of Technology). For a detailed description of the guidelines see Sterling (12).
12. Sterling, T., Commun ACM 17 (No. 11), 609 (1974).
13. The Canadian computer ombudsman scheme is developed around a joint effort of the Canadian Information Processing Society and the Consumer Association of Canada (see T. Sterling, J. CIPS, in press). The U.S. effort, spearheaded by the Association for Computing Machinery, has as its main concern eliminating an incorrect image of computerized systems and is thus different from the Canadian model.
14. Blauner, R., Alienation and Freedom (Univ. of Chicago Press, Chicago, 1964).
15. For confirming evidence of Blauner's findings, see F.C. Mann and L.R. Hoffman, Automation and the Worker (Holt, Reinhart & Winston, New York, 1960); C.R. Walker, Toward the Automatic Factory (Yale Univ. Press, New Haven, Conn., 1957); A.N. Turner and P.R. Lawrence, Industrial Jobs and the Worker (Harvard Univ. Press, Cambridge, Mass., 1965).
16. See, for instance, K.W.M. Kapp, the Social Costs of Private Enterprise, (Schocken, New York, 1950); E. Richardson, Work in America (MIT Press, Cambridge, Mass., 1973).

Reprinted from Science, 19 December 1975, Volume 190, pp. 1168-1172.

Conclusions

IFIP TC 9 – Working Group 1 "Computers and Work"
Conclusions and Recommendations from the Workshop on the Effects of Computerization on Employment

1. The Working Group considers the impact of computerization on the
   employment level and structures as a very serious threat to a
   sensible and continuous development in this technological field.
   The conflicts which became apparent so far seem to center more on
   "qualitative" impacts (like degradation of traditional skills).
   The employment effects of computer systems, nevertheless, are at
   least in the longrun overwhelmingly negative, in the short-run
   this is often concealed by "soft" measures of administering
   dismissals (e. g. not firing, but not recruiting, when someone
   leaves; or by transfers of workers within firms a.s.o.). The conflicts are probable to increase.

   Solutions are particularly difficult to be derived because computerization is a facet of the national investment. Particularly
   important, however, is computerization because it provides new
   and very complex means for new types of rationalization.

2. In view of this the state of the art in the discussion of computer effects on employment is considered by the Working Group as
   unsatisfactory.

   Major reasons for this are to be seen in a lack of methodology and
   in deficiencies of the statistical basis.

   The Working Group therefore recommends to furnish more detailed
   statistics on technological variables (computer systems, their
   "power", extension of "networks" a.s.o.) and the number of jobs
   affected on the plant, firm, industry and national level. It should
   be furthermore examined whether employment studies by applications
   or groups of applications could bring advances. With regard to
   methodology the Group recommends more interdisciplinary and multi-
   dimensional research.

   It likewise recommends to co-operate in this research more inten-
   sively with the "producers" (e. g. by asking systems designers and
   programmers on their evaluation of computer impacts on employment).
   The Working Group concludes that computer manufacturers should
   likewise assess and publish the short- and longterm employment
   effects of their products.

3. The discussion on employment effects of computerization should be
   enlarged to take into account the overall labour market situation,
   "structural changes" in the economy and on the labour market and
   the segmentation of the labour force into privileged groups (like
   computer experts) and e. g. deskilled groups (like workers in the
   printing industry).

4. The Working Group recommends that firms should furnish information on employment effects of computer systems to workers' representatives and this in due time and completely. The information
should cover plans for applications, the directives for systems
design and a thorough a priori evaluation of the consequences
for employment.

5. The systems design process should be examined in more detail. It
is a complex process which advances piecemeal but which nevertheless follows strategies. With regards to employment effects the
following intricacies of the design process should be taken into
account:

- The fact that it is in most cases a long-term process in which
  creeping employment effects may sum up considerably
- the fact that a substantive part of the planning may be done
  outside the firm (by computer and applications manufacturers,
  consulting firms a.s.o.)
- the fact that the design process permanently offers and selects
  alternatives and gives chances for a human choice.

6. The Working Group considers it as necessary, in order to control
employment effects of computerization to enlarge the discussion
on computer systems to the questions of for what purposes and
with which environmental effects computer systems are used and
designed.

IFIP TC 9 – Working Group 1 "Computers and Work"
Conclusions and Recommendations from the Workshop on the Effects of Computerization on Professional Skills

1. The Working Group considers the factual effects of computerization of professional skills as a very serious threat to a sound human development in work. On the other hand the Working Group maintains that computerization may bring new opportunities for enlarging and using human skills.

   The debate has produced evidence for a marked degradation of many traditional lines of work and the skills required in and for them due to the introduction of computerized systems and the re-organization of work as a consequence of the introduction of these systems. On the other hand there is also evidence for increasing skill requirements for small groups of workers.

   In spite of increasing skill requirements when the systems are designed and introduced the long-term effects of computerization have to be viewed more pessimistic at least for the masses of the workers affected.

2. Nevertheless this seems more to be due to the concrete forms in which computer systems are developed and used under the conditions given than to technological constraints inherent to computer technology, which as a very flexible technology allows for quite different patterns of development of skills.

3. Criticism was raised with regard

   - to research in this field: research in many cases is too limited with regard to the span of time considered and its methods of empirical research often are very superficial

   - the notion of skill: a new theoretical and anthropological idea of skill has to be developed in conformity with the development of productive forces, the changing role of human work and the demands for a human development of work

   - the statistical basis as well as the political mechanisms operating in the field of training and qualification were questioned.

4. Computerization apparently endangers not only the skills of many groups of workers but also of quite a few groups of specialists and of parts at least of the middle management.

5. For immediate practical measures the links between the labour market situation and the threats and opportunities given by computerization to skills have to be observed more closely. Some national examples may show that more public control and support of

training processes in information processing may give a better foothold also for a control of effects of computerization on human skills.

6. A thorough discussion of computer systems development with the workers affected and with the unions seems to be a necessary prerequisite to use the positive aspects of computerization for the shaping and extension of new skills and rewarding jobs.

7. A policy of support for the use of this potential should be looked for in three directions
   - to enable people to overtake other jobs
   - to influence the design of technological systems
   - to influence the decision-making processes.

8. Particular emphasis should be put on an permanent discussion on skill issues between the workers affected and those who promote the systems design and use.

Sources and Acknowledgements

The following articles, which are contained in this volume, are re-prints:

"Computers - a gift of fire" by C.C. Gotlieb, originally published in: S.H. Lavington (ed.), Information Processing 80, pp. 863-872 North-Holland, Amsterdam/New York/Oxford 1980

"Information technology and power in society" by Steinmüller, originally published in German in: WSI-Mitteilungen, August 1979, pp. 426-436

"Information technology - its impacts on skills" by H. Kubicek, originally published in German in: V.E. Frese, P. Schmitz and N. Szyperski (eds.), Organisation - Planung - Informationssysteme, Festschrift zum 60. Geburtstag von E. Grochla, Metzlersche Verlags-buchhandlung J.B. und Carl Ernst Poeschel Verlag GmbH, Stuttgart 1981

"How to design information technology" by H.W. Heibey, B. Lutter-beck, M. Töpel, originally published in German in: H.R. Hansen, K.T. Schröder and J.J. Weihe (eds.), Mensch und Computer, R. Oldenburg Verlag München/Wien 1979, pp. 261-274

"Humanizing Computerized Information Systems" by T.D. Sterling, originally published in: Science, vol. 190, pp. 1168-1172, 19 Dec. 1975; Copyright 1983 by the AAAS